Brasted Memories

A Chronicle in Time

A collection of personal stories and reflections on life in Brasted from the 1900s to the present day.

Collected by Karina Jackson
Edited by William Chopping and Karina Jackson

All stories have been kindly donated and approved by our story tellers

Corniche Brasted Publications

High Street

Brasted

Kent TN16 1HS

Tel: 01959 565245

Email: cornichebrastedpublications@gmail.com

ISBN 978-1-5272-2746-0

Printed July 2018

This book was printed and bound by:

Printdomain Ltd,

107, High St,

Thurnscoe,

Rotherham

S63 0QZ

www.printdomain.ltd/

Photographs

Photographs in this book are the copyright of the following:

Name	Page Number(s)
Joan Selden	18, 20
Hazel Shelley	37
James Barrington	41, 44, 79
Brasted Archives	48-50, 232, 256, 259
Gill Dunseath	51, 55, 56, 58
Rosemary Whittaker-Browne	61, 63, 68
Joy Edgar	97, 98, 100
Elizabeth Rich	105, 110
Harold Cuckow	132
John Bellingham	158, 166
April Williams	172, 176, 177
Jane Smithers	187, 192, 196-198
Pamela Day	203, 204, 207, 210, 213-215
Ian Brown	218, 219, 224, 225
Terry Everest	231
David Edgar	242, 244-247
Juliana Stewart	255, 257
Beryl Herpe	274, 281
Susan Wood	83, 286, 288, 289
Rob Peake	38, 87, 303, 307, 308, 311-313
Julie Taylor	316, 317
Michael Baker	147
Karina Jackson	17, 34, 40, 60, 77, 94, 104, 114, 131, 138, 153, 155, 165, 170, 186, 194, 202, 217, 229, 237, 251, 254, 267, 284, 300, 315, Front Cover, Back Cover

Cover Pictures

Front Cover - The Brasted Village Sign

The original Brasted Village Sign was unveiled by Lord Stanhope on June 12th 1951 as part of Brasted's contribution to the Festival Year. Mr G. A. McShane the artist, wrote the following description of the sign, for the Brasted Diary.

"One looks down on Brasted village, shown as a very decorative garden, complete with the church as we see it today, the River Darent, the old Bridge, the old Mill, flowers and doves, all surrounded by a low stone wall. This is in fact the 'Archbishop's Garden,' as ceded to the Archbishop of Canterbury in early times. In the distance are the North Downs with the chalk pit and the Pilgrims Way, complete with the early pilgrims on their way to Canterbury Cathedral. The Archbishop in 15th century regalia, dominates the whole scene as he gives his blessing. The story is brought to a close in our own Festival Year by including the Arms of Earl Stanhope, the present Lord of the Manor of Brasted."

The old faded sign was repainted by Paul Bowles of Ovenden Signs late in 2017. Dave Harman at Brasted Forge made and donated new hooks to rehang the aluminium sign. Durtnells offered their services free and working together they have presented our village with its new, refurbished and vibrant sign, now back on Brasted Green by Rectory Lane.

Back Cover – St Martin's Church

This splendid window is in St Martin's Church in St Martin's room. It was designed by John Hayward and fitted after the devastating fire that destroyed much of the church in 1989. Colin Waghorn leaded the glass and installed it.

The window portrays many historic and geographic features of our village. It depicts religious themes based around St Martin himself and reminders of the village's association with the Archbishop of Canterbury. The middle image is St Martin with our church on his lap.

It also illustrates the four boundaries that dominate Brasted all running diagonally across the window. The outer yellow image is the Pilgrims Way. The M25 is shown in white and the A25 in red. The River Darent runs through the parish in blue. On the left is the primary school that became our place of worship while the church was being rebuilt. Also shown below is Brasted Place with portraits and arms of some of the former owners.

Contents

Preface

This book started as a project for the Brasted Society and its purpose was to find out what the village was like in the past and how it has changed over the years. The sources for the project are the people who live in the village today and have either lived in Brasted all of their lives or those who had come to the village from elsewhere and become long term residents. For those who had lived in the village all their lives it was very important to find out what their experience of growing up in the village had been and to capture their personal stories. I asked everyone for their reflections on life in Brasted, from their earliest memories through to what they see now and how it has changed. Did the changes have a positive or negative effect on the village?

When looking for potential volunteers who would help me to tell the story of Brasted, I looked for people within a wide age range, so that I could gain as broad a picture of village life as possible. I also needed people who would be happy to tell me about their own lives and their recollections of the village over the years. Fortunately, I was able to find some wonderful people and their stories who would help me in my task.

What I found throughout all my discussions with the volunteers was a rich seam of life. I found that the village school and schooling was a large part of many people's experiences. Villagers undertook various jobs or tasks in Brasted, as they grew up and for employment after school. It soon became obvious that whole families worked together, to earn extra cash for the family purse. Children helped in the fields, or with hop picking or helped other families, in fact anything that would earn extra cash for the family was undertaken.

But it was not all a struggle for survival. The parish church and the Baptist church also played an active part in the lives of villagers. The village was full of shops that sold everything anyone could want. Pubs thrived on bringing friends together and giving working men a way of relaxing after a hard day's work. Everyone knew each other and the village was alive with social events for young and old. Many stories contain the names of family, friends and neighbours. I have recorded as many as possible so they will not be forgotten.

My story tellers were so kind with their time and sharing their lives through their memories. Most of our time together we laughed, but sometimes we cried as well. Occasionally stories were too personal to put into this book, but still my friends here were very honest about their experiences.

I hope you will be able to enjoy and compare the telling of events between stories such as the hurricane of 1987 and the Battle of Britain in 1940, both of which had a major impact on the village. There will never be another war like the Second World War so each experience recounted here is unique from a personal point of view.

In the book, each volunteer's story is recorded in full as told to me. Many stories have the same event and themes, but all of them are told from each individual's perspective and experience. I did not prompt any of the stories nor have I written anything that was not spoken about. Where possible, I have started each story with the earliest memories through to later life in order to create a chronological flow. However, all the discussions seemed to start with an, "Ooh, I must tell you this..." So, although much effort has been spent sequencing the events in each of my volunteer's lives, if stories jump about a little this is because it has not always been possible to gather them all together and create a smooth, flowing time line.

As mentioned, all these stories are written as they were remembered by my willing volunteers. However, memory sometimes makes mistakes, so if something is not in accord with historical fact or your own knowledge or recollection, please make allowances. We all see and remember things differently. Judge for yourself how life and times have changed through the decades.

Several of my friends here have sadly passed before the completion of this book, but I hope their contribution herein will keep their memories alive forever.

I would like to thank everyone that took part in this project and the making of this book. For being honest and so willing to share their stories. For giving their time freely and so generously and allowing me to use their photos as well as their stories. I hope we all enjoy sharing their fun and freedoms and feel sadness in their tragedies.

I'd also like to thank Tina Whiteley for her help and support with the original text and Rob Peake, Muriel Edgar, James Barrington and many others for their invaluable help.

Karina Jackson

December 2017

Introduction

The historic village and parish of Brasted is located in North West Kent, between the town of Sevenoaks to the east and the village of Westerham to the west. The village and parish are bounded to the north by the chalk hills of the North Downs and to the south, by the sand hills of the Greensand ridge. In between the hills lies the Holmesdale Valley through which flows the River Darent. It flows through a number of nearby villages as it meanders its way from nearby Westerham to join with the River Thames at Dartford.

There are three roads that cross the parish from east to west. These are the A25, the M25 motorway and the Pilgrims Way. A visitor passing through the district today, could be forgiven for thinking that the area has little history of interest and is just another sleepy Kentish village. An observant traveller passing through the village on the A25 (also known as Main Road, High Street and the Westerham Road), might see the village green, The White Hart pub, the village store and a number of antique shops, but little else other than houses, before the village quickly disappears in his rear view mirror. Travellers on the M25 motorway might not even be aware that they have passed Brasted at all, as the only significant feature that can be seen from that road is the tower of St Martin's Church. The third road that traverses the parish and lies at the foot of the North Downs is the ancient Pilgrims Way. Although the traveller using that road will not see much of the village, they will be passing farmland on either side of the road. Through the ages, farming has dominated the history of Brasted and its villagers almost to the present day and the link with the land is mentioned in many of the stories that follow.

But, scratch below the surface and the village and parish has seen much history, from pre-Roman times to World War Two. The community is one that even in recent times has witnessed much change as the economic and social changes that have affected Britain have also manifested themselves in Brasted.

This book covers memories from the early 1900s to the present day. The contributors have in some cases lived in Brasted for more than ninety years, whilst many of the others have lived in the village for forty years or more. Their stories tell of a vibrant, self-sufficient village where everyone knew everyone else and where many local people worked nearby, rather than further afield. London was a world away. As the twentieth century progressed, the influence of London and the modern world grew ever more powerful. By the turn of the last century the village had become more of a dormitory village and much of the energy that had characterised it earlier had been lost.

Almost all of the contributors to this book attended Brasted Village School where there were an array of different, sometimes eccentric, teachers. In the early days, the school taught children from their early years to school leaving age. After the Second World War, a new secondary school, the Churchill School, was opened at Westerham and the older children would attend there. The village school headmasters included the very stern Mr Warner and before and during the closure of the school, Mr Wilkins. As with all schoolchildren, their school years were characterised by outings, scrapes, much loved and hated school dinners, run-ins with the headmasters and threats of draconian punishment. The school also did much to foster a strong community feel for the village as children would join together to walk to and from school, playing endless games on the way there and back. For many contributors, much of this feeling disappeared when the school closed in 1988. Today children are driven to and from various schools in the district and the opportunities to forge lifelong friendships during the walk to and from school has at best been curtailed and in some cases lost.

A feature that characterised the village in many of the stories was the enormous number and variety of shops and businesses within Brasted. There were general stores, butchers, bakeries and café's, a chemist, cobblers, a fishmonger, a haberdasher, sweet shops and one or two antiques shops to name but a few. In addition, the village had a number of pubs and even within recent memory had six thriving pubs. Today there are just three pubs within the village boundary. Furthermore there were a number of builder's merchants and garages selling and repairing vehicles and supplying petrol. Today, many of these businesses have disappeared, to be replaced by visits to local out-of-town supermarkets and specialised retailers in Sevenoaks and beyond. In addition to removing the need to travel to purchase everyday items, the shops again reinforced the community feeling, as many of the shopkeepers and shop workers lived in the village and were known to many of the customers. The shops, notably the sweet shops, also provided lots of opportunities for the local schoolchildren to play tricks on the shopkeepers by ringing the shop bells and then running off before the shopkeeper came out to the shop counter!

Of all the village businesses, perhaps the influence of the local landed estates and farms were the greatest. The major village estate was, and is, the Chevening Estate, owned by Lord Stanhope until his death in 1967. A number of village farms, such as Park Farm, Mill Farm and Court Lodge Farm were rented from the Chevening Estate. The farms provided much needed work for the locals and the farmers also supplied milk and vegetables to Brasted and further afield. There are many stories about the farms in the book and how

12

for the local children, the farms provided a playground where there was fun to be had at all times of year. So long as respect was shown for the land and the wildlife, there were few boundaries.

The River Darent has always been of great importance to Brasted and its local farms. The river has been a friend to the village, providing water for the local farms, watercress beds, and swimming pool. The river today is much shallower than in earlier times, largely due to water extraction. In times past, it was used by the local children for both swimming and fishing. However, it has also proven to be a foe, periodically flooding, sweeping away farm bridges and inundating villager's homes, most recently only a few years ago.

Socially, the village contained a mix of classes, from a lord of the realm to village tramps. Lord Stanhope and other estate owners such as the Vestey family had an enormous impact on village life, providing work on their estates, but also funding for local projects such as the village swimming pool. Furthermore, they organised village parties and ensured that their workers' children had lovely Christmas presents. There were also local businessmen, such as George Alderson and professional people such as Dr Ward and the village policeman, who played an immense role in village life. All of them saw it almost as their duty to be actively involved in the wellbeing of the village and its villagers. Most important of all were and are the many characters who made up the community whose stories are told here. Although Brasted was a very close community, it opened its arms in welcome to people from near and far, taking them in as one of their own.

The Second World War had major effects on Brasted, as it lies directly under the flight path to RAF Biggin Hill. There are many stories of how villagers would watch dog-fights unfold in the skies above, and also of the great bravery of the pilots. Brasted also saw a number of army units billeted locally, which led in turn to any number of dances and lifelong romances. As with all wars there were tragedies, but also uplifting stories and these are recounted here. There are also tales of bravery, resourcefulness and humour thrown in for good measure.

In October 1987, southern England experienced the Great Storm. Of the many areas that took the full force of the storm, Brasted and the surrounding communities of Sevenoaks, Brasted Chart, Toys Hill and Ide Hill were amongst the areas worst affected. Swathes of trees were brought down, both in the surrounding hills and along the Darent valley.

The storm left the A25, the main road artery through the village, completely blocked by fallen trees. Some homeowners were unable to leave their houses for some days, whilst others struggled to work, only to be sent home again. Many villagers helped to clear the trees away from the roads to allow vehicles to pass. However, despite their valiant efforts, often carried out at great personal risk, the task proved too great and the army was subsequently called in to help clear the country roads. Many homes were left without electricity. The villagers had to rely on both their own resources and the help of others to eat and keep warm until power was restored. The landscape was changed completely by the storm, as new vistas suddenly opened up where once there had been countless trees. It is testimony to the healing power of Mother Nature, that many visitors to the area today would never know that only thirty years ago, much of what had been in place for centuries had been laid to waste.

The local church, dedicated to St Martin, together with its rectors, played a key role in the life of the village throughout much of the twentieth century. The rectors always, of course, officiated at baptisms, marriages and deaths, but they also looked after the wider secular and spiritual needs of the villagers as well, providing Sunday Schools and social events. The church itself witnessed damage in the Second World War and, with the exception of the bell tower, was all but destroyed in a catastrophic fire, in 1989. Many villagers joined in to help remove items from the church and rescue animals from the nearby fields. Just as after the Second World War and the Great Storm, the villagers came together again, this time to rebuild the church and recreate the fine building seen today.

Many visitors to the village, might also be surprised to learn that the village once had its own railway station, on the line which ran from Westerham, through Brasted and on to Dunton Green, where it joined the London main line. Opened in 1881, the line proved a vital lifeline to the villagers, village shops and local farms. The railway allowed locals working in London to easily commute to work. It was also used by local schoolchildren travelling to nearby Westerham, to reach their destination, often riding on the footplate. The line was closed in October 1961 when the last 'Westerham Flyer' ran.

Up until the 1950s, the A25 although always an important road, was not always busy and there was a time when the local children were able to use it as part of their playground. However, as the twentieth century wore on, the road along its entire length became increasingly busy as the southern route to circumvent London. As a result, the decision was taken to build the London Orbital Motorway, the M25. The late 1970s saw the building and completion of the new motorway which follows part of the course of the old Dunton Green to Westerham railway. The new road also went across some of the local farmland. The motorway had a marked impact on the village, instantly removing much of the A25 traffic, thereby making it safer to use for the local residents. However, the rapid increase of vehicle traffic since its opening has meant that once again the A25 is very busy and the road will never again be a part of the children's playground.

So, for our modern traveller passing through the village in his car, the sleepy appearance of the village is clearly deceptive. Behind the pretty village green, antique shops and ancient houses, lies a village that has witnessed many radical changes. The tragedies and heroism of war time, the building of major roads or the destructive and healing power of Mother Nature have all been experienced by the village. Great technical, social and economic changes have also impacted the village and transformed the community forever. Some things haven't changed; the beauty of the local environment remains, the river still flows through the village as it has always done and the farmers tend their fields and animals as they have through the centuries.

We hope you enjoy reading the stories in this book which provide a fascinating insight into Brasted, both now and then.

Karina Jackson and William Chopping

March 2018

Joan Selden

née Lawrence

Joan Sylvia Lawrence was born in June 1921 in Borough Green and was one hour older than her twin Jean Edna. Joan's father Harry George Lawrence (Tom as he later became known), was born on the 8th December 1901 in Wrotham, Kent. Her mother, Annie Elizabeth née Wells (Nan as she was always called), was born on the 12th January 1900 in Kemsing, Kent. The twins were completely different; with Joan having blonde hair and looking like her father and Jean with dark hair just like her mother. Joan says that no one believed they were twins. A perfect family all in one go and the family was complete. As Joan said, "having two together cooked mum and dad's goose!"

When Joan was aged four they moved to a council house in Station Road, Brasted. Harry had been out of work for a long time when George Alderson - a local businessman - offered him employment as a driver/mechanic and they moved to the village. Their house was among the first council houses to be built in the village. It was very 'modern' compared to older local properties, although they had gas lighting as electricity was not yet available. Downstairs there was a big living room with a fire powered range. The house had a bathroom and a separate small toilet which was accessed via a covered, outside porch. The outside walls were hung with fixed battens, however, the builder did not put mortar between the battens and the wind and rain blew in making messy, wet patches!

Harry 'Tom' Lawrence

Annie 'Nan' Wells

In her childhood days Joan reminisced that the winters produced 'proper snow'. She says she could hardly move when snow came up to her waist and Tom would have to go out and clear the passageway to the toilet.

Where Station Road becomes Hogtrough Hill and just above the railway bridge, the river had watercress beds that flourished in the beautiful clear water. Each weekend a lady from the local cottages would come round selling a huge bunch for ten pence (10d). Also, close to the railway bridge was a spring and water would stray onto the road. The area was known as 'wide waters' and Joan and her friends would lay on their tummies and drink the fresh water. She quickly added that as it flowed on to the church they would never dare drink the water there because cows were kept in the field it flowed through. She left the rest to my imagination!

Joan recalled that an elderly lady Mrs Caroline Forester and her son Norman lived in a little cottage, in Station Road, where she would sit for hours on end at her sewing machine. Caroline took quite a shine to Harry, but always called him Tom and somehow the name stuck. Everyone knew him as Tom after that. Caroline died on June 23rd, 1943 aged sixty-five, maybe not so very 'elderly' after all!

Joan's mum Nan did not like her real name 'Annie', though Joan never found out why she preferred to be known as Nan.

Tom was particularly talented with vehicles both maintaining and running them. He looked after the Alderson charabancs, cars and coaches and was the local taxi driver for many years. The charabancs predated the coaches and were an early form of motor coach. They were slate grey in colour and had rows of bench-style seats facing forward. Each was open-topped, but on wet days Tom would ask two other men to help heave on the waterproof roof. The charabancs most common function was to move parties of people to functions or take them on outings to the seaside. They were not built for comfort and George Alderson replaced them with coaches as soon as he could. If any broken vehicle part could not be found Tom would turn his hand to making a replacement, whatever it was. Often after work Tom would pop into The Stanhope Arms pub for a pint where Alf Pattenden was the landlord. Sometimes Tom would come home and start a sentence with, "Old Alf…" Nan heard no more, but turned around and said, "I know where you've been…"

Tom and Nan were both supporters of village life and Nan joined everything. She became a member of the Sundridge & Brasted Horticultural Society, British Legion, Baptist Sisters, Women's

Institute (WI), Mother's Union and was a staunch member of the church. She thought the world of the church and would volunteer her help with its upkeep. The hardest project was polishing the brass eagle lectern which is still used in St Martin's (the parish church) today.

During the Second World War three ladies marched up the High Street with sandwich boards hanging from their shoulders. This was Nan, Mrs Budgen and Mrs Barker advertising jams etc. for sale from the village Women's Institute. Nan along with Mrs Caplan were founder members of The Ever Greens, a club for folk of a certain age! They mostly met in Sundridge village hall, but would come to Brasted sometimes too. At Christmas time, Nan would cook the Christmas puddings on a three brick, gas stove. All the individual puddings were put into a huge aluminium bowl to steam away. Other

members would cook parts of a delicious Christmas lunch for all the Ever Green members. Nan also volunteered to sell poppies for the British Legion and did this until she was too old to stand about in all weathers.

The twins would go to Sunday school every week and later in the day Nan would take them to Evensong. Both girls found that very boring and they would jiggle and mess around until Nan put them one each side of her to keep them still. At Eastertime, Miss Bryan, the rector's daughter would take her Sunday school students out into the hedgerows to collect armfuls of primroses. There were so many flowers that they filled every window sill in the church. During the Easter service, a screen was

20

dropped down from the ceiling and a magic lantern show[1] projected on to it. It contained the Easter story and Joan and Jean were transfixed.

One day Mrs Barker organised a Women's Institute play to compete against other WI groups. Joan remembers the lead player had to dance. This was Mrs Barker who was a big woman and her dancing was not so very elegant. They did not win any competitions that day!

In 1935 Joan and Jean took part in a play entertaining the annual gathering of the Brasted Guide Company. It was held at the village hall and various entertainments were performed. Their play was called The Obstruction, and was produced by the girls themselves. Joan took a star turn along with her sister Jean, Freda Seale, Violet Water and Peggy Wells. Freda Seale also sang a solo and the evening finished with games and thank you speeches.

Joan also remembered performing a French play with Jean and Alice Evans. Alice did the dancing and Joan remembers the play was about an aristocrat (played by Alice) who was taken in by a dance troupe who agreed to hide her. The aristocrat had to borrow dancing shoes, but they were too big. As a result, her identity was discovered, but it all turned out well in the end.

As Joan commented, "there was no television and you had to make your own entertainment. It was fun! We were glad of these things to do." They would wrap their hoops in crepe paper and dance with them, swirl scarves around and busily flap fans all in the name of

---

[1] A magic lantern show is an early type of projector using pictures such as photographs or paintings mounted on a transparent plate and projected on to a screen such as a wall or ceiling.

entertaining friends and visitors to the village hall.

Joan loved her life growing up in Brasted. She would wander over the fields with her friends and when their mothers called them in, they could hear them shouting from anywhere. The village was so quiet then. At night she would lie in bed and listen to the steam engine shunting up and down. On Tuesday evenings the bell ringers would practise in the church tower. Some years ago Joan heard the Brasted bells again on a Radio 4 programme called Bells on Sunday. What a delight and what happy memories. Joan and Jean would play in the road with hoops, tops and skipping ropes with no fear of traffic. They could whip their hoops way down the road without a second thought.

The streams and rivers running through Brasted always provided a happy playground. Mind you, Nan would not let her girls come back wet or muddy. As twins, they were dressed alike and very smartly. Did that stop them? Of course not! They could wade in and out of the river and then brush themselves down. If their socks got wet they would hang them on a tree branch to dry before going home. "We didn't dare tell mum!"

Mr Palmer of Park Farm, would let them make shelters in his fields in the summer. They were expected to take them down again at the end of the day and they did. He never batted an eyelid at the children, although his cows were not always so kind and were very curious by nature. They took a great interest in what was happening and would come over and investigate. Joan says that she is still afraid of cows to this day! Mr Palmer also had sheep, but they never bothered the children or vice versa. They were all taught not to disrupt or vandalise the countryside and they didn't! You had to take care of your family, friends, clothes and the village - it was just under

-stood that you would.

The boys taught Joan how to play cricket in the fields. There was no fancy equipment, just a jumper at each end, with wood for wickets and sticks for bats. They had no proper cricket balls, just a simple ball that someone brought along. Joan absolutely loved it and has the same passion for the game today. She listens to ball by ball commentary on the radio Test Match Special and has a better collection of cricket books than most libraries!

Out playing one day Jean broke her arm. She was on a plank of wood, balanced over a fence playing see-saw. The other person suddenly jumped off and Jean tumbled to the ground, breaking her arm in the process. A short while after, Nan needed to take Jean to see Dr Ward and Joan went along too. Nan forgot to pack a fresh vest for Jean and left the girls waiting while she rushed home. One of the village boys was around on his bicycle and Nan's fading voice warned Joan to stay off it. So, what did she do? Why, she got on it, of course! Almost in the same breath, she fell off and felt a terrible pain in her arm. Her hand just went floppy and looked like a piece of hanging string. So, as Nan returned she hid it behind her back. Jean stepped forward and immediately informed her mother that Joan had ridden the bike, but worst of all she had fallen off! "That's it", Joan thought, "I'm in for the biggest telling off now." So unexpectedly, Nan sat on the bank and burst out laughing. Dr Ward sent her straight to Sevenoaks Hospital, on the bus and there were the twins both with a 'wing' out of action and in slings.

Fun was innocent and Joan remembered that the Alderson family had an orchard and one apple tree, partially hung over the road. The children waited and waited for a lovely big red apple to drop, but it never seemed to. One day, Don Williams offered to take off his boot and throw it at the apple. Well, what a shock it was when said boot missed the juicy prize and got stuck up in the branches! They simply had to own up and all went to find Mr Wiggins, the Alderson's foreman. He gave them a good telling off, but came to help retrieve the boot. There were no apples for them that day or any other. Even when the apples did fall, they dropped behind the hedge and no matter how hard they pushed their arms through they never could reach a single one!

Mr Spinks, the farmer at Mill Farm, had a walnut tree that the children also found very tempting. Trouble was, his dog always seemed to know they were coming and kept them clear of the tree. They never had a walnut either! Mr Spinks also ran the village dairy at his farm, from where the Day brothers[2] who worked for him would collect milk and ride around the village delivering it from their horse and cart. Nan would put out her empty jug with a saucer or mug over the top and the brothers would fill it up. The family had a black Labrador dog called Ben who was let out each morning to have a walk. He had a terrible habit of raiding other people's milk jugs, where he would drink as far down as his nose would reach. Then he would pick up the jug and take it home. Poor Nan was forever trying to return the jugs and then paying for replacement milk. Ben was so infamous for his behaviour that the local paper ran an article on his antics.

With Joan laughing, she told me how she and Jean would walk around the churchyard. They would look for graves with bunches of flowers on them. Using empty jam jars - they would split the flowers

---

[2] Sometime later the Day brothers took over the tenancy of Mill Farm from Mr Spinks. See also Archibald Day's chapter.

and put some on the graves that had none. "We just felt sorry for them. See, innocent amusement that hurt no one", she said.

A lovely clear stream flowed through Mill Farm and meandered down to the swimming pool in the recreation ground. The swimming pool was wonderful and Nan would pack the girls some sandwiches and they would spend the whole day there. It was always green from algae, with dead frogs and fish floating around it, but Joan says they never caught any illnesses from it. It simply didn't matter.

The school headmaster Mr Warner taught Joan to swim in the pool. He asked who wanted to go and would march the volunteers up there. As they went through the gate the girls changing cabin was on one side and the boys on the other. The cubicles were covered by a curtain of tarpaulin. Joan remembered clearly how cold it was changing into her swimming costume. In her words she said, "It was so cold I thought I was going to die!"

The water in the pool was equally cold, as it was filled by fresh river water. They slipped in and Mr Warner put a rope noose over their heads and under their arms. Then, they walked out about twelve to fifteen feet and Mr Warner pulled on the rope and hauled them back to the side. "You either thrashed about trying to swim or you drowned", said Joan. Once they could swim about ten strokes, the children were given a free pass to use at the pool at any time except Sundays. It lasted until they left school. That was a huge benefit and one of the only good things Mr Warner did. Joan was later taught to use the diving board and loved her days spent at the pool. They also had a wooden chute where the boys would spray water across the top to make it slippery. What fun it was to glide down and fly into the pool. The bottom was cemented around the rim, but it was agony to step into the middle on the stony bottom. One had to be prepared for painful feet.

School was fun except for Mr Warner who appears in so many of these stories! One day, he had been "beastly" in Joan's words. She was in class Standard 4 or 5 and close to leaving school. The class decided to take revenge and at a given signal they would throw their ink wells at him and set about him. As the moment arrived, they lost their nerve and Mr Warner never experienced their wrath. One day, Jean had the cane for an ink blot in her book. It was hard for Joan to watch her sister being punished.

Mr Warner did appear a little more kindly when his wife had to spend time in hospital. Each day near lunchtime he would tap on the classroom window to summon Joan. She was sent to Fuggles Bakery in the High Street to collect his lunch for him. When she left school he presented her with a book.

Joan's first teacher was Miss Cartwright, an 'ancient' lady. On Friday afternoons she would have the children file out into the playground for a treat. They each had water poured into an empty potted meat jar to drink. Then she would come round to each child with a sweet on a pair of scissors. She did not want to touch the children, so used the scissors to drop a sweet straight into their mouths. It really didn't matter how it arrived: the sweet was delicious!

School dinners were cooked by Mrs Day on a wonderful little range. She would get to the school at 7 a.m. to light the range, in time to cook the lunches. She made all the meals single-handed and served such dishes as meat pies, stews, treacle tarts and roly-poly suet pudding which was cut off in slices. The treacle was kept in a separate jug which they all looked forward to even though it was well watered down. There were never any snacks between meals, so everyone was hungry by dinnertime.

School lessons included cookery classes once a week. The girls went to Sundridge village hall where the lessons included practical help on looking after the kitchen and cooking utensils. They were taught what ingredients to buy and use for cleaning pans. There were certainly no Brillo pads available then! To this day Joan's family all agree that she makes the best pastry of any of them. They also had needlework classes and learnt to knit. Nan had to buy two stool frames and the twins used twine to weave the tops. Joan enjoyed the basket weaving class and made a tray with a glass bottom. The stool and tray are both treasured keepsakes in her family.

Joan remembered two school outings in her time. The first trip they had, leaving from Brasted Station, was a wonderful visit to the Cadbury's chocolate factory. Near Birmingham Joan got smut in her eye from the steam engine and for much of the day she could hardly see anything. Still, you don't need to see to enjoy the taste of chocolate. They were given so much that the trip home left them feeling a little queasy. It probably did ensure that the box of assorted chocolates handed to them to take home did actually make it!

The second trip was to the annual Military Tattoo at Aldershot in Hampshire. The event drew large crowds and was organised to raise money for military charities. All Joan could remember was being bored stiff and wondering why Mr Warner chose the Tattoo for a school outing!

While at school Joan remembers a visit from Mrs Mary Barker of Mount House. She had a grass verge at the front of her property where she planned to put waste baskets, one at each end. She told the children that if the verge stayed clear of all rubbish she would give each child a chocolate egg at Easter and crackers and an orange at Christmas. True to her word, as the verge stayed rubbish free the children had their rewards. There was a report in the Sevenoaks Chronicle in December 1941 stating that the school children sat down to Christmas dinner with no crackers or oranges after seventeen years. The reason given was the departure of Mrs Barker. By moving away she must have been a sad loss to village life. The Barker family were always supportive of the village and had opened their grounds for the first school sports day in 1934 and also hosted the annual Young Farmer's Club show. Mary's husband Claude ran the successful and busy Brasted Choral Society.

Sometimes on the way home from school Mr Greenaway, the coal merchant, would trot past with his coal horse and cart. Joan says she and her friends would climb on the back of the wagon and hitch a ride home. However, if he suspected they were clinging on at the back he would lash his whip past them, calling, "you varmints", but they clung on unseen anyway. Joan laughed out loud at the memory and said it was grand fun. The village blacksmith had his forge by the village green and the children would sometimes watch him shoeing the horses.

The Oxford and Cambridge Boat Race day was always fun. The twins would save their money up and then buy brooches from Rosie Rice's shop, in the High Street. Jean supported Oxford and had her dark blue badge and Joan bought her light blue Cambridge badge. They would join the boys at the river and find tree bark to model into boats. They dammed the river at a chosen spot and enjoyed boat races of their own.

Sometimes Tom would drive the Alderson coaches on outings to the seaside and would joyfully announce he had a couple of seats free. They would pack themselves up and have a day out. The Alderson's were fond of Tom and the relationship was one of great respect.

Tom was called on for many trips including driving the darts teams or the boy's football team from Westerham. He would drive the school bus from Ide Hill and Toys Hill dropping the children at Brasted School. At the end of the school day he would take the children back home again. He also drove the taxi for many years and was often late home as he waited for the arrival of the last steam engine of the day so that he could take the late workers back to their homes.

Joan and Jean were encouraged to be each other's company and Nan did not want the twins visiting friends uninvited. However, they did enjoy the company of Joan Firmager the next door neighbour's daughter. Joan married a Canadian soldier and later emigrated to Canada. On several occasions the family shared holidays in Hastings with their friend Peggy Wells and her family.

In 1938 Joan started her three year training course as a nursery nurse in association with Guy's Hospital. It was a wonderful career for her kind, caring self. The first year went well, but war was declared and London was considered too dangerous for the nursery. Matron, a staff nurse, seven trainees and forty children were evacuated to Wittersham in Kent. It took two big London buses to move everyone along with all their equipment. They went to Wittersham House, owned by Captain Oliver Lyttelton. He was the President of the Board of Trade for Winston Churchill's coalition government at the time. His house was more like a mansion built on four sides with the nursery having one entire wing. Luckily it was well-appointed, as a chicken pox epidemic hit the children soon after arriving. So the Newcomen Day Nursery continued in its new home and Joan took her second year exams there. However, Wittersham was soon deemed to be too near the coast and in the line of German bombers. Again the nursery was moved and this time to Tunbridge Wells. Joan remembers one occasion when she was off duty, but dog fights were going on overhead, as the Battle of Britain raged. Matron forbade her to leave the shelter and she spent her entire precious day off inside it.

It was in Tunbridge Wells that Joan met a young sailor who needed help with directions. She helped him out and was asked out for a date in return. This was Francis Wilfred Peter Selden, born and bred in Penshurst. Well, Penshurst was only six miles from Tunbridge Wells - this was his stomping ground! It was a ruse that paid off handsomely, as soon Joan and Frank entered into a very happy marriage. Frank applied for special leave and they married by licence in St Martin's Church, Brasted in October 1941. Joan wore a beautiful white satin dress and carried a bouquet of pink carnations. Jean, already Mrs Clark, attended her sister. The wedding cake had no icing and neighbours and friends contributed the fruit in the cake from their rations. They had no money for an elaborate reception so a small gathering in her parent's home sufficed.

Joan remembered the first time she visited Frank's family at Killick's Bank in Penshurst. She had not been there long when the air raid siren howled and they all went to a shelter at the bottom of a field. From there they watched and listened to the rat-a-tat-tat of the machine guns as they fired at each other.

Joan's father, Tom, refused to enter a shelter at all. He would take to his bed saying, "If I'm going, I'm going in my bed." On one sad occasion, Joan watched one of our Hurricanes, flown by a Polish pilot, fighting six German Messerschmitts. Our pilot finally lost his battle and Joan remembered seeing the burning plane as it spun through the air and crashed by Hogtrough Hill, by Pilgrims Way. Another time she wanted to go outside and watch the planes, but

Nan refused to let her. Nan was a local fire watcher and Joan pleaded to take her mother's hard hat out to protect herself. "Oh no, you won't", said Nan, so Joan's last plea was, "I'll wear it back to front." The helmet stayed where it was and so did Joan. Joan captured the meaning of the war spirit as she told me, "we were never scared."

Frank spent twelve years in the Navy and was away for much of the war and Joan never knew where he was during that time. Meanwhile, Joan lived in Biggin Hill for part of the war by which time the couple had had the first two of their five daughters. One day the siren went and she put her daughters safely into a cupboard under the stairs. She could hear the action was very close and looked out of the window. The whole valley seemed to be ablaze from multiple incendiary bombs. Biggin Hill was a major German target and was hit by many bombs particularly during the Battle of Britain. They never heard what went on that day or any other, as the news was always secretive and only positive events were ever reported in the papers. Later in the war, doodlebugs[3] were frightening as they thundered overhead on their way to London.

Tom and Nan moved to 6 Rectory Lane, Brasted after the war and twice Joan remembers them being flooded. They lost a lot of furniture and the water left an awful mess. It rained so hard that the water poured down Chart Lane and flowed along the High Street. Brasted Green and Rectory Lane are the lowest points in the village and nothing could be done to stop the water gathering there, either then or now as it still floods in the same areas.

---

[3] Doodlebugs - Flying rockets developed by Germany in the Second World War and armed with an explosive warhead. They were also known as V1s and V2s.

Nan met a very sad death in 1985. She was waiting for a bus outside The White Hart when a Sevenoaks District Council lorry started to reverse. The driver didn't see Nan and she was run over and died from her injuries. She was cremated in Tunbridge Wells and her ashes spread in the beautiful gardens there. Each year Joan and Jean would take a bunch of flowers to the St Martin's Church in her memory. Joan retired after the shock of her mother's dreadful accident. She had been a warden in old people's flats. From that time onwards she has never had a television in her house and instead listens to her radio and is also an avid reader. She is surrounded by the love of her five daughters who constantly make sure she is fine. She has such a wonderfully cheerful demeanour and our time together was full of fun and laughter.

Jean died on Christmas Day 2016. Joan always sent her a Christmas card with a robin on it and she was relieved to know that Jean saw her card before she died. Jean's wake was held in The Stanhope Arms. "What a change," was Joan's remark. When her father used the pub it had wooden floors and a little counter. There was a small room on the left with a tiny fire. The landlord was mean with his coal so it was never very warm. You could go in with your jug or pint glass and buy beer to take home. Somehow it was much smaller and darker than the modern pub she went in this year.

What does Joan most regret about seeing Brasted village now? She and Jean would often play in the river in Rectory Lane. They would have hours of fun walking down the steps into the water. She says there is now a gate firmly padlocked and covered in barbed wire. That really upset her and she didn't want to see it. Children don't have the freedom to make their own innocent fun without fear of health and safety accidents! She also regrets the loss of the High Street shops. They were all useful and every shopkeeper made a living. None went bust even though there were three baker's shops, two butchers and four different grocery shops.

March 2017

Postscript - 27th July 2017

Today I went to Joan's funeral in St Mary's Church, Westerham. Far from being sad, it was a wonderful celebration of the life of a beautiful mother, grandmother, great grandmother and friend. She had fallen and hit her head as she went down. Although appearing to recover she faded a few weeks later. Bless her for leaving her aura of sparkle and kindliness behind her and passing it on to her five daughters.

Hazel Shelley
née Wood

Hazel Evelyn Wood was born in July 1920 in the Greenwich district of London. Her parents were John Bernard Wood and Amelia Evelyn Smith. Amelia was usually called Evelyn by her family and friends. John and Evelyn had three children, with Hazel being the youngest. They lived happily in Belvedere until their house was bombed early in the Second World War.

The family moved to Toys Hill Farm House in Ide Hill and settled into the community. Hazel remembers having regular deliveries of paraffin for her mother's cooker. It sounded a rather dangerous practice and Hazel confirmed it certainly was! Hazel and her friends Muriel and Monica Anthony became land girls working for Toys Hill Nursery. They tended tomatoes, soft fruit, potatoes and seasonal vegetables, but heavier work was done by the men. The nursery had several greenhouses including a couple that were heated to extend the growing season.

The girls had a van and were responsible for three rounds of deliveries per week. They shared many giggles driving to Edenbridge, Brasted and Brasted Chart. On one occasion, when driving back from Edenbridge, they looked up to see a plane with a clear swastika symbol coming towards them. They could see the pilot's face as he flew by so low. The girls fell out of the van and had to climb a high bank to hide in the woods. He wasn't interested in them though and carried on to another target. This was probably the same pilot that flew over the Foxwold estate and waved to the land girls working there. On the Brasted route, the land girls would stop at Mrs Stott's tearoom for a morning tea break. Although they had regular customers, anyone could walk up to the van and purchase their wares. Hazel did not drive and earned herself eleven pence(11d) per hour, but the girls that could drive were given an extra penny (1d) and earned a whole one shilling (12d) an hour for their work.

One of the greatest highlights was a trip in the van to the cinema in Sevenoaks. Without seats in the back, the land girls would sit on upturned apple baskets excitedly looking forward to the film. Once there the evening would start with–powdered eggs scrambled on toast; it was all such a delicious treat.

Hazel married Eric Williams (her first husband) when she was nineteen and her only son Neil was born in 1944. While Hazel was pregnant the bombing was very heavy, with doodlebugs flying through the air. Her family insisted she went to stay with her mother-in-law in Dorset. She left her own mother in Kent and Neil was born in Dorset, although after six months they returned to Toys Hill.

During the war the army tried to bivouac in the woods of Brasted Chart, but they found themselves covered in wood ants and gave up. Hazel told me that the word Emmet means ant and that the nearby property, Emmetts Garden, earned its name from the local ants and anthills they built all over the area.

Part of Hazel's wartime volunteer work was to take on the duty of calling at each house in the area to ask how many evacuees they could each take. Her parents billeted an airman from RAF Biggin Hill. Italian prisoners of war were housed at Toys Hill and worked on the land. Her father would buy cords of wood from them.

After the war, housing was very short and our troops were being demobbed exacerbating the housing shortages. Hazel's father and her brother Lionel set about building three family homes in Brasted Chart. They bought several acres of land from Sir Archibald Hurd, an editor of both naval magazines and The Daily Telegraph. He lived in The Shaw on Brasted Chart. Lionel used his skill as a surveyor and also did the architectural work for the new houses. John acted as the clerk of works, a job he already did for a living. John worked for the civil service and had been responsible for many large projects including cinemas, hotels and large stores. To clear the land they were faced with felling about five hundred trees before they could start any building!

First they designed April Cottage, but built the garage first to store all the building materials, before building the rest of the house. Initially all the families lived there, John and Evelyn, Lionel and his wife Margaret and Hazel and her little family; all seven together. Next came Quidington a family name and when completed her parents lived there. Lastly, Pinehurst was built for Lionel and Margaret.

Hazel settled into Brasted Chart and enjoyed a neighbourhood group called The Chart Fellowship. Up to thirty ladies would meet in each other's houses where they would listen to a booked speaker. With no television, Hazel looked forward to these Thursday evening meetings. As she thought of the numbers she commented, "about thirty, how I managed, I don't know!" She and others with children formed nursery groups in their homes to be sure the children could enjoy company. Brasted Chart was a quiet place with nothing like the pre-school classes children can attend today. She also ran a Sunday school in Toys Hill village hall for groups of up to ten children. In fact, Neil was christened there by the Four Elms vicar who brought a mobile font to the hall. All the local children were christened there. Everyone would help each other and try to be involved with the neighbourhood.

April Cottage

Brasted was full of shops, which supplied all they needed. Giles Day from Markwicks would visit her parent's house and take their grocery order and it would be delivered two days later. Hazel would walk into the village for her shopping and think nothing of the miles she had to cover. Walking back uphill was a little more challenging with her heavy pram! Clothes could be bought from Swans as well as any haberdashery needs. All chemist needs and plenty of good advice could be found at Hebbs, the village chemist. Markwicks welcomed a Father Christmas every year and all the local children were very excited at the prospect of visiting him. The village also had a regular 'Court Leet' fair (a medieval fair), Hazel remembered watching the parade and it was so cold she had to visit Mr Hebb to buy Neil some socks to warm his feet.

As Neil grew and started school he would catch the bus outside their house. It ran every two hours and stopped when hailed. Hazel's husband, father and brother all had jobs in London, so they all travelled together by car to Brasted train station.

Hurricane damage at Toys Hill

Brasted Chart was very badly hit and cut off after the hurricane of the 16th October 1987. Hazel was living by herself and remembers that her trees mostly fell towards her neighbour's properties and they took care of the huge clearance project with chain saws. The whole area was devastated, with trees solidly blocking Chart Lane and all footpaths. Soon after the storm, Hazel remembered clambering up and over or underneath trees in an attempt to reach Neil who lived about a mile away down Chart Lane. As it turned out, he did the same and they met in the middle. With no power for more than a week, Hazel used her open fire to cook meals and using that they could heat water and soup or any canned goods from their cupboards. The meat in the freezer lasted for a week or so as it slowly defrosted. That was also cooked on the fire. She smiled at the memory, "it was great fun", and obviously quite an adventure. The fallen trees in Chart Lane finally became such a problem that the army was drafted in to help with the work of removing them.

Over the years Hazel loved her pet 'pussy cats'. Poppet was her first cat, followed later by Tigger and Jim. They often had a habit of bringing in live mice that had to be chased out again. Now she enjoys a neighbour's cat who settles on her patio to enjoy the sunny position.

Her comment on the changes between her early life and now is sadness that no one simply pops in to visit any more. Everyone phones for an appointment and life is much quieter. She knew all her neighbours and now she doesn't. In fact, the house next door is a second home and used as a part-time country retreat. Brasted Chart is more isolated than ever for her with no car and no longer a bus service running through it!

August 2016

Barbara Barrington

née Cox

Barbara Cox was born in May 1921 in London. She married David Barrington in 1941. He was born in Tenterden, but at that time worked in an antique shop in Park Lane, London. Barbara worked close by in Selfridges in Oxford Street, London. An early memory for Barbara was during the war when the air raid siren went off in Selfridges. The hairdressing staff would move all the customers to the basement and continue their work until the all clear was sounded. No one panicked as it was part of wartime life. Selfridges was bombed in the blitz when wave after wave of Luftwaffe bombers attacked London on the night of the 17th – 18th September 1940. Barbara remembers the top floor being well alight with flames shooting from the windows. The fireman worked frantically pumping water into the building to halt the destruction.

After their marriage, Barbara and David started their life together in Lenham Heath, near Maidstone, Kent. David had always wanted a shop of his own, ideally with passing trade, so when a shop in Brasted High Street came up for sale he considered it the perfect location. They moved there in 1948 with their two small sons. As Barbara said, "make a move and a baby comes along!" Her third son,

James was born two years later in the upstairs bedroom.

In those days the shop, David Barrington Antiques, was much smaller, with W. Jones the Bootmaker next door. He would turn his gas light on promptly at 4 p.m. and Barbara remembers the tap, tap as he worked away making and mending shoes. On a less uplifting topic, cockroaches would eat away at the leather in the shop!

After the bootmaker left, David extended his shop to the size it is today. The pretty bay window was installed by Durtnells, the village building company. Later they put a large display window into the old bootmaker's shop, which replaced much smaller windows.

David Barrington Antiques

Before David bought his shop it was part of a small complex with a bakery on the right-hand side known originally as Hall House and currently as Tilings. A courtyard between the houses was used as a holding pen for pigs and cattle awaiting slaughter for the village butchers. Single rows of blue brickwork in the drive indicated where the individual pens were positioned. There was a path through to the river for animals to use as a right of way. The courtyard also had its own supply of water from a well. The cobblestones now seen at the front of Tilings were evident in a 1900 postcard of the area and are probably from a much earlier age.

At the back of the courtyard was the Brasted Men's Working Club. It was a crude corrugated iron building where army and airmen used to drink and play darts. They could drive straight into the courtyard and fall out and fall back into their vehicles! During the war it also housed people bombed out of London. They had left by the time David bought his shop, but the dartboard was still sitting there from the days of the Working Men's Club. The shed came down to make way for the current new house.

David's first vehicle was an Austin Devon pickup truck. To move his family Barbara would sit in the front and the boys would climb into the open pickup. Barbara would wind down the window and tell the boys to "sit down or you will get a bee in your eye!" One day they took the family and Mrs Carter, a friend and a neighbour, to the beach at New Romney. She arrived with her deckchair to sit in the open back and the three boys sat around her. There were no drink drive laws then so sometimes very unsteady vehicles would pass by with happy drivers trying to keep their vehicles in a straight line.

When the family went to Sevenoaks for business they would stop at Mr and Mrs Harrison's antique shop. Mrs Harrison delighted the family by throwing sweets and bananas into the pickup. They never needed to lock the vehicles doors and nothing was ever stolen.

Markwicks was the village grocery store that supplied everything. It even had the old post office inside and sold stamps from a machine outside. Barbara would give them her shopping list in the morning and later young Neil Taylor would deliver her goods by bicycle. He would still be wearing his short trousers straight from school.

Markwicks also had a Morris delivery van which was driven by Cyril Towner. Mr Giles worked on the bacon slicer while Mr Luxford was the manager.

Mr and Mrs Kimber had a wet fish shop where the fish was displayed on a large marble slab. Mrs Kimber was known to be strict and quite a task master. Mr Kimber would set off on his bike to cycle to the train station to pick up their fresh supplies of fish. One wonders how he managed, but he would cycle only as far as The Stanhope Arms where he would take his liquid refreshment. The station would unload the fish and send one of the station boys down to the pub to meet Mr Kimber. Rumour has it that he was known to occasionally fall off his bike as he cycled home in his drunken state. Goodness knows how Mrs Kimber reacted when he arrived home, something that is probably best left to the imagination!

In 1880 Tilings, then called Hall House, had a terrible fire and the fire pump was called from Sundridge. It was stationed at what is now Combe Bank School. The current house still has charred black timbers in the attic from its unwelcome adventure.

In the 1980s a car pulled urgently into the lay-by outside the antique shop. Having started its journey near Valence School, it had a petrol leak and was severely on fire. The Barrington family could hear their windows cracking from the heat and the outside of the shop was badly damaged. They desperately pulled furniture away from the exploding glass. Both the Westerham and Sevenoaks fire engines were called with the Westerham crew most delighted to be on the scene first. The damage was quite a nuisance to put right.

The car fire outside the Barrington's antique shop in the 1980s

A funny story was told about The Bull Inn where the landlord could not understand why his electricity bill was so high. One Sunday he went into the cellar to see the meter spinning round even though the pub was closed and no lights were on. It turned out that the Baptist Chapel opposite had somehow taken its feed of power from the pub and was quietly running on free electricity!

The traffic in Brasted used to be regularly jammed solid before the M25 motorway opened in 1979, as the A25 was the best gateway to Surrey and beyond. With the new motorway the villagers revelled in the peace and quiet. It all seems hard to believe today as we take our lives in our own hands when negotiating the road at any time of day or night.

April 2016

Postscript

Dear Barbara passed away on 30th January 2018. A service was held at St Martin's Church where many friends and villagers filled the church to pay their respects. This much respected lady will be sadly missed by the village community.

Archibald Day

My daughter, Kiri interviewed Arch Day, our neighbour, for a school project about the village she lived in. He was so gracious and willing to help and told her about his life, both at school and work.

Arch was born on the 14th July 1912, in Brasted. He married Annie Ealden on the 20th November 1937 in St Dunstan's Church, Cranbrook, Kent. They moved to Brasted, where they had two sons. Arch's father, Harry, was also born in Brasted in 1873. Harry was a stockman and worked at Mill Farm where Arch, and two of his brothers later took over the dairy business. Arch and Annie moved from West End to Pym Orchard retirement housing to make their last years a little easier. Arch died in 2000, aged eighty-seven.

Over to Kiri.

Memories from Arch Day...

Mr Day was born in 1912. He went to school in the local Brasted School. Each class had about forty pupils, and around one hundred and thirty children went to the school. The school had three lady teachers and a Headmaster, Mr A C Warner. In class, girls sat on one side and boys on the other. The school day mainly consisted of prayers, arithmetic and drill (now called Physical Education). School was very strict and the headmaster would cane anyone who was naughty. You would get one whack on each hand, and one on the bottom, as well, if you were really naughty. Mr Day had the cane three times, and one of those was for nothing. He fell over and washed his knee and he was then accused of making the towel dirty, but he hadn't used it. One day, while playing football in the playground, the ball was kicked into a garden and broke windows in a greenhouse, after that football was banned. It was the cane for everyone when they forgot. There was no school uniform, in fact, no change of clothes - they had to last all week.

On the way to school, Mr Day would play marbles. Some of the children had spinning tops which they spun in the middle of the road with a whip. Another toy was iron hoops which involved rolling an iron hoop along the road without it falling over. When the iron hoops broke they were taken to the local blacksmith, Mr Chalcraft for repair. When the hoops were fixed, Mr Chalcraft would say, "And don't come back!", but they always did.

Fuggles, one of the three bakers in the village, had a parrot. When the door opened and the bell rang, the parrot said, "Shop." As a boy, Mr Day opened the door on his way to school, and when the parrot shouted, Mr Day disappeared off to school, leaving the shop empty. One of the village sweet shops sold mouth organs and Jews harps. Four boys at a time were allowed into the shop, and they all tried them, but nobody had the money to buy one. Mr Day left school, at the age of fourteen and became a dairyman, working for Mr Spink. When Mr Spink retired, he and his brothers rented Mill Farm from Lord Stanhope. Arch was a dairyman and milkman for forty years.

At fourteen he would walk his rounds with milk and measuring cans. The small can held about one pint and large can six to eight pints. Customers would come out with their jugs and he would give them the required amount, plus, "a drop for the cat". The milk was taken round while it was still warm. Milk cost a penny ha'penny (1½d) for half a pint, threepence (3d) for a pint, and sixpence (6d) for a quart, during the summer. In winter it cost threepence (3d) for half a pint, threepence ha'penny (3½d) for a pint, and seven pence (7d) for a quart. The milk cost more in winter because it was more expensive to keep the cows.

Mill Farm in the 1940s

Arch Day harvesting the hay with his father in the 1940s

Arch Day with the hay wagon at Mill Farm

Arch Day, then graduated to a bicycle, with a large basket on the front for his deliveries. He wore a large navy blue apron tied round his waist.

After the bike came horse and cart deliveries. His first horse was called Dolly, and his second horse, Bonny. Both were chestnut with white blazes. Bonny worked for fifteen years before going blind and she was then sent for slaughter in Basildon, it was the saddest parting Mr Day ever had on the farm.

During the war the brothers changed to motorised vehicles for milk deliveries because the bombs frightened the horses. One of these was an electric float guided by a handle at the front, but with many batteries hanging underneath powering it. It was the most modern delivery vehicle that the villagers had ever seen.

Brother Henry Day with the milk float

Kiri Jackson (aged 10)
1995

Paddy O'Donoghue

How could I write about our wonderful Brasted characters and not include posthumously, Paddy O'Donoghue, who made such an impact on this village?

He was born in 1919, in Kilgarven, County Kerry, in Eire. His parents scraped a living on a hillside farm, with a family of six to support. The land was challenging and everyone helped with the burden of farming it. There was no electricity, running water or toilet. Tragically, in 1933, Paddy's mother died in childbirth. Life became intolerable and a year later at the age of fifteen, Paddy left for Liverpool. He soon went home however, as Liverpool was not for him. However, when he was eighteen he left again, this time to stay with his uncle, Jeremiah Lynch, known as Jerry, in Ide Hill. Jerry ran the Wheatsheaf pub with his wife, Mary Ann née Kirby, a native of Ide Hill.

Jerry, born in January 1878, had come to Ide Hill at a prosperous time and set up a taxi business, coal merchants and building company. He and his wife ran the post office for a while too. There was plenty for Paddy to help with, although he needed a career and chose to learn hairdressing. At the time, Paddy, had saved all his money to buy his poor, old Irish grandfather a cow. However, his grandfather died before a cow was purchased and Paddy bought himself a pair of hairdressing clippers instead. Initially, and *'fleecingly'*, he practised cutting wool on sheep, but soon graduated to the pub customers, in the back room. He had an accordion and could play the spoons. He could make music on his comb, covered with Izal[4] toilet paper. The *'betting is on'*, that he entertained the pub clients, for a penny or two!

During the war, Paddy, being Irish was not allowed into the military. Instead, he chose to join the Westerham Fire Service. It was a harrowing time and Paddy faced situations none of us could imagine, the worst being his attendance at an evacuee home for children which had been hit by a flying bomb. The home, Weald House (now Hoplands) on the edge of Crockham Hill Common, was hit on the 30th June, 1944 when a doodlebug hit a tree and was deflected on to the home. Twenty one children and eight female staff were killed in the tragedy, Kent's largest single civilian loss of life during the war. All the victims were buried in Edenbridge Churchyard[5]. Some experiences were more fortunate and Paddy would tell of a house in Scords Lane, Toys Hill which took a hit as the lady of the house was having a baby; half the house was destroyed whilst the mother safely bore her child in the other half!

One day, at a local dance, Paddy met Joyce Beryl Langdon and that was it for him. He was well and truly smitten and in his words she

---

[4] Izal was the brand name of a very 'unforgiving' toilet paper. The paper was quite hard, but when wrapped around a comb could be blown through as a cheap and cheerful mouth organ. Izal also found a use as tracing paper.
[5] Oliver Fielding-Clark who was Vicar of Crockham Hill at the time and one of the first on the scene, gives more details of this tragedy in his autobiography, Unfinished Conflict.

was, "an absolute cracker." Head over heels in love, they married in December 1947, at the Roman Catholic Church, in Sevenoaks.

Soon after, the old barber in Brasted chose to retire and asked Paddy if he would take over his business. It was a golden opportunity for cash-strapped Paddy and Beryl and they moved to Brasted. The place was in a terrible state, but they worked together like Trojans to get it straight. Once they settled into their new home, Paddy started to display his huge community spirit. He soon knew everyone and they adored him back.

He and Beryl lived a few houses away from the tiny shop, which had no toilet facilities or running water of its own. If nature called, Paddy had to pop home leaving his shop, for as long as it took.

His passion was racing and despite his many activities he still managed Wednesdays in Brighton, for horse racing and Catford Stadium, on Thursday evenings, for greyhound racing. Such was his passion for the races that he was well known by many clients, for leaving them with half a haircut, if an important horse race was on the television. Off he would rush home, still in his white jacket, waving at everyone. Customers could wait for up to thirty minutes or more, before Paddy returned, either in the money or not! As a result, some customers would only visit in the morning! When a television was installed in the shop, his customers would wait while he threw his arms around and yelled encouragement at his chosen horse. They all loved him for his playful spirit and infectious excitement. Each day, he would enthusiastically study the racing pages and place his bets on his fancied horses. Young Billy Rich, the village chimney sweep's son, would visit and together they would have their eyes glued to the form of each horse! Paddy called everyone by a nickname, so Billy was 'Brough', after Brough Scott, the horse racing commentator. When the telephonists in Brasted exchange saw the doll's eye board come up with Paddy's number they always rushed to answer it. They had to be quick, as it flashed up and down in urgency to be answered. They knew a bet had to be placed right away and Paddy needed a connection!

Paddy was a well-known character and one day, Winston Churchill asked his chauffeur if he knew of a barber. Of course he did, Mr Jenner, knew Paddy. It was arranged for Paddy to visit him at Chartwell. What did they talk about? Horses and horse racing, what else!

Another time, he cut the hair and shaped the beard, of actor, Jack Sutherland. He had a photo taken with him which he kept in his shop. Jack was appearing in 'Anne of a Thousand Days', a film being shot, at nearby Hever Castle. Paddy had a handsome horse that well-matched another, belonging to a lady at Vinesgate, on the Chart. Both horses were hired at seventeen pounds (£17) per day, to appear in the film. On the first day, Paddy's horse was loaded with two bales of hay hanging at his sides. The horse did no more than take off, damaging a Rolls Royce and a big van, before he could be stopped. Paddy was paid his seventeen pounds (£17) and the horse was sacked, they did not want it back again!

While Paddy looked after the men's grooming, Beryl decided she would become a hairdresser too. She attended the Morris School of Hairdressing in London and went on to open her shop, Beryl of Brasted, for the ladies.

From the start of his Brasted days, he involved himself in village life and his charming character attracted everyone around him and to his various enterprises, one of which was the village carnival. A committee was formed and it was agreed they would hold village carnivals every year. On carnival day there was Paddy, up the front on his favourite horse, dressed up as his chosen character, his lovely Irish voice urging everyone on. Who could not love this charismatic man?

Paddy at a Brasted Carnival dressed as Prince Monolulu

To help fund the carnival, Paddy would arrange bingo sessions at the village hall. Several dances were also arranged, including one to find the carnival queen. All these fund-raising events assured the success of the carnival or other village entertainments. Paddy supported willingly anything for charity in his larger than life manner.

Paddy was not your typical Irishman, as he barely touched alcohol! He would have been perfectly happy going into a pub and ordering a pint of milk! He may have ordered a shandy, after a hot day of haymaking and at Christmas a cup of tea would arrive, with a drop of whiskey in it. Mostly, he could be the life and soul of the party and be perfectly sober!

Paddy at another of the Brasted Carnivals he helped to organise

Paddy had developed a strong love of animals during his farming days, which never wavered. He would ride when he could and kept horses and ponies. He rented fields from the Foxwold Estate and was in his element making hay and keeping his horses. The green fields reminded him, of his homeland. Sometimes the local children would help him and earn sixpence (6d.) for their labours. His daughter, Jill, had her first pony called Prince, when she was ten. Paddy taught her to ride and greeted all the farmers, as they rode through the lanes.

One day, Paddy was told of a horse being kept by gypsies, at Dryhill Park, Sundridge. She was starving, so Paddy stepped in saying that she was a fine mare and offered a tenner for her. She was a big, white horse called Dolly and Paddy brought her back to Brasted. He had her for many years and lots of riders had fun on her. She would calmly let children ride her, try to jump her, or simply sit on her while she kindly stood still.

During one adventurous holiday, Paddy was sitting on a plane waiting to fly to America. He heard a familiar voice saying, "Hello Paddy, can you do my hair for me?" and there was one of his many friends. He would always pick up hitchhikers, with never a fear for himself. In Anglesey, returning from a trip to Ireland, he spotted O'Callaghan from Dunton Green and drove him all the way home. Another time a little lad ran away from his home in Sidcup, Paddy took him in and counselled him into going back. The second time he ran away he simply went straight to Paddy!

Paddy had fabulous Irish friends and when Pat O'Keefe moved into Sundridge Place Farm the two of them were inseparable. These two Kerrymen were in their element trudging through mud and muck! They decided to visit Ireland together and while there, they bought a beautiful, Connemara pony. She was like a sofa on legs. They bought six carriages, ranging from a governess cart to an old landau from the Chevening Estate. The landau cost the same as a new Ford Fiesta car at the time and then, they had to repair and restore it. This done they hitched up the ponies and hired out their services. To complete the look, they dressed in black trousers, a white shirt and a cravat.

To their great pleasure, Gloria Hunniford, the television and radio presenter, hired them for the wedding of her daughter, Caron Keating. So, as a trial run they set off one day, with Gloria, Caron and his two grandsons in the landau. Jill, his daughter, followed behind in her car holding back the traffic. As they clip-clopped through Brasted, they waved at a friend, Marion and tried to discreetly point at their grand passengers. Marion was so pleased to see them, she eagerly waved back, looking nowhere else except at Paddy and Pat. They simply could not show off their celebrity clients. What a disappointment! The practice went well and they did the honours on Caron's wedding day, driving her to the St Peter's Church, in Hever. Later, during her radio show, Gloria publically thanked them for their lovely day.

Paddy O'Donoghue's Landau and guests

When Paddy's granddaughter married, she arrived at the church in Ide Hill and Paddy sat rooted to his horses and landau. "Are you coming in, Paddy?" he was asked. "I'll stay with the hurses," (use an Irish accent) was his reply. He was persuaded to leave them though and eventually attended the wedding.

In 1971, Paddy and Beryl opened a grocers shop in the village. Markwick's grocery shop was closing and they filled the gap. The then local MP, Mark Wolfson came to help celebrate the opening. Some years later it was a sad day, when Paddy and Beryl finally closed up shop for the last time. Paddy and Beryl had reached retirement, but they didn't abandon the village. Instead they passed the business on to new owners David and Diana Davies without missing a day. In his retirement, Paddy looked forward to more leisure time and still visiting local racecourses. He continued to visit his old customers at home, to cut their hair and share some laughs. Paddy's daughters told me three things that, for them, epitomised their father.

1. Paddy would stand outside his shop and the vehicles going by would all be hooting. Paddy greeted them with his thumbs up and, "whaaay," as they drove by.
2. His great shared community spirit.
3. Everyone was given a nickname which he never forgot to use. No one was called by their given name.

Paddy died in 2008 aged eighty-nine. The church, capable of holding four hundred and fifty people was completely packed, as so many came to say their farewells. Every age, every class and all sending their love. The village is the poorer for losing such a convivial and big-hearted character.

October 2017

Rosemary Whittaker-Browne

Rosemary Whittaker-Browne was born in Balham in June 1923. Her parents were William Whittaker-Browne and Blanche Evelyn Lewis. Poor Blanche had a bad time with the birth and decided that Rosemary would have to be an only child. However, her parents did all they could to have her mix and play with other children.

They involved her in the local church, where the vicar recommended that Rosemary went to Sunday afternoon 'entertainment', run by his daughter. She had to sit in the vicar's study, on a drab brown, leather sofa and listen to bible stories with all the other young children. She remembers how cold and sticky the sofa was on her little bare legs. Rosemary took the stories to heart and, one day so much so, she was inconsolable with sadness. The vicar had to take her home to her parents, still sobbing. "Sunday school may not be for you dear. Come to church with us," said her mother. Her delight in this new venture was to find the hymn numbers in her parents' hymn books for them. It's funny what you remember!

At the age of about six, Rosemary went to the local infant's school. She was excited to hear that a party was planned in a local field and Rosemary was told that she was to present the lady that planned the party, with a bouquet. She was thrilled, as she learned she had to curtsy prettily, as she handed over the bunch of flowers. The curtsy was easy because Rosemary was taking dancing lessons and knew exactly how to do it properly. She and her mother chose a suitably pretty dress which was specially washed and prepared. So off she walked across the field, but suddenly, oh no, she tripped up and went flat down on the ground. The flowers survived, but the dress had to be brushed down and cleaned up as much as possible. That turned out to be the first and last time she was ever asked to present flowers!

Rosemary has a lifelong passion for dancing and aged about ten she went to the John Tiller Academy for dancing and musical theatre. Based in Cambridge Square, London she loved her lessons. She remembers the rectangular hall had mirrors, down both sides of the long walls. She would practise her steps all the way down and then turn and come back. Her teacher was Miss Jessie, who was strict and exacting and the lessons could be exhausting! One of the most famous products of the school was the  Tiller Girls, a ladies dance group that appeared in theatres and on television for many years.

Her parents moved around a bit and at another small school she met a spiteful, spoilt little boy. He sat two seats away, on a long table. He wore expensive clothes, not at all like the drab school clothes most of the children were dressed in. Rosemary had long hair and this naughty boy kept reaching around and pulling it hard. The more

Rosemary was annoyed, the more it pleased him and he carried on. Finally young Rosemary had had enough and she stood up and slapped him as hard as she could. He screamed and the teacher did no more than tell him he deserved it. He was moved away from her, but later that term he was expelled, and as far as Rosemary knows, he was expelled again, from his next school. She told me, "It gave me much pleasure to sock the nasty little brat!"

Rosemary loved school and did very well. Her grandmother, Blanche's mother, had helped her to read, and spelling was her strong point. Grandmother, Alice Grace Lewis, was a gentle soul who told her interesting stories and taught her how to appreciate music. She was a big influence during Rosemary's childhood.

Grandfather, Edwin Alaric Lewis and grandmother Alice lived in Ash, near Canterbury, in a magnificent property, called Great Weddington House. It still is a magnificent Regency country house, built in the 1830s and is now a grade II listed building. Rosemary described it as a huge place, with beautiful large grounds. Grandfather was much older than his wife, as it was a second marriage for him. He was a qualified doctor and kept a pony and carriage in a small barn. The house had an attached farm, but her grandparents had no interest in it, so it was leased to a local farmer.

Blanche, Rosemary's mother, was the youngest child of Edwin and Alice and she and her siblings were born and grew up in Great Weddington House. Rosemary remembered one story grandmother told her about her mother. The family had a dog and cat and, one day when the cat walked into the house, the dog saw its opportunity for a bit of fun. He chased the cat outside and it flew up a tree nearby. Blanche tried to rescue the cat, but the dog was leaping up at the tree at the same time. It knocked Blanche flying and she banged her head hard which left her bleeding. Her father led her to his surgery to repair the damage. She went back outside, still sobbing and told the dog what she thought of him. How dare he be so mean to the cat who had equal access to both the house and garden. Then, she remonstrated with him about her poor, bloodied head. The more she accused the little dog, the lower his ears sank, and the more sullen his eyes became. He was truly remorseful, well at least for that moment!

Blanche Whittaker-Browne

Blanche's sister, Java Grace, lived in Deal with her husband Frederick Spicer. They had four children, Frederick born in 1914, Reginald in 1916, Percy Lionel in 1919 and Marjorie in 1921. Percy was a fine boy and Rosemary enjoyed playing with him. One day, the children all went out to play in the farm close by, but had to climb a five bar gate to get there. Rosemary could not make it so Percy kindly lifted her over. Grandmother Alice, encouraged Percy to play instruments and make music. During the Second World War he joined the Marines as a musician. He lost his life on the 29th May 1941, aged twenty-one, during the evacuation of Crete. His ship, the HMS Orion, took a direct hit from a bomb, whilst carrying nineteen hundred troops. Hundreds of lives were lost that day. The family were beyond sadness in grieving for him.

Back in Balham, Rosemary and her parents started to move around, finding places that suited her father's need to work in London. He was based in Africa House, in Holborn, and one of the moves took them into London itself. They disliked it horribly and called it the 'big smoke', so they soon decided to move back to the countryside. This took them to Beckenham, and a large house in Kent House Road. Rosemary was signed up for a school in nearby Sydenham, but was too young to attend, by one term. The local school was Alexandra Infants School, so she took a place there, at the age of ten. Here she had an Irish teacher, who turned out to be perfectly brutal with his students. One day he rolled out a map of the county of Kent and Rosemary was thrilled as she knew it well. He had a habit of standing up and throwing out questions. He suddenly pointed at Rosemary, in his intimidating manner and asked her to spell a place name. There were two places that sounded the same and, to her dismay, she spelt the wrong one. He called her up to the front of the class and took out his cane. She was horrified, as this was a completely new experience for her. She quickly figured out that her left hand was best to offer up, as she was right-handed. He walloped her hand three times and sent her back to her place. However, she refused to shed a tear, even though it hurt very much. Rosemary is and has always been a strong-minded person and she determined he would never do that to her again. He must have seen something in her eyes, as he never asked her another question for the rest of that term and then she left the school. She never told her parents, as she resolutely planned never to be walloped again, and never was!

Senior school years were more settled, as Rosemary moved to Strathmore College in Sydenham. Miss Muriel Tuck was the headmistress and a very kindly lady. Rosemary and Blanche were invited to tea and shown around the school. Miss Tuck sent out a welcoming letter and everything felt easy and civilised. Miss Tuck took the English class and Rosemary says she was a good, responsive pupil. She found herself behind in history, but no worries, she was given extra lessons to help her catch up. When exam time arrived,

Rosemary came first. She did have to work hard at her French lessons though. The walk to school each day was very long and she was grateful when her parents bought her a bike. It eased the pain of lugging her heavy bag to and fro each day. The school motto was 'nil sine labore' as Rosemary says, "nothing without labour, how true!" These were happy years, but as Rosemary was entering the sixth form, war was declared. Many houses in the area were requisitioned by soldiers and the school suddenly closed. Miss Tuck was elderly, so maybe she was ill or retired, or perhaps lost the premises to the mounting military presence. Whatever the reason, that was that and Rosemary left school.

Before war was declared and Rosemary had left school, her father died. She may have visited his hospital bed once or twice, but mostly Blanche went by herself. As Rosemary said, "people were much less open then and such things were not talked about. Nowadays people talk more openly and that is much healthier."

Rosemary was a girl guide for many years and in 1940, her unit were set a task by their captain, Gwen Williams. They were tasked with keeping their girl-guide diaries daily, in Morse code[6].

After she left school, Rosemary and her mother, moved to Slough, where there were plenty of jobs on offer. She had an interview with the Weston Biscuit Company, and was hired to 'learn the ropes'. This meant time spent in all the administrative departments, where she learnt many skills, including typing and shorthand. She worked there for a while, but the draw of the 'country air' was too strong and

---

[6] Editor's Note: Rosemary showed me the diary and it was clear she had done a splendid job. I couldn't understand it of course, but then, nor could Rosemary anymore!

Rosemary moved again, away from the town.

It was duly arranged that she would work at Hurst Farm, in Crockham Hill near Westerham. She and her parents had visited the farm previously, to stay in the guest accommodation, so the owners knew her well. To Rosemary, they were Uncle Tommy Steven, Aunty Connie and their daughter Ann. The farm was originally a medieval hall house, built around the turn of the 1500s. It was beautiful, set in rolling countryside and full of interesting features. However, Blanche brusquely refused to move from Slough, as she was happy driving and delivering for a large bakery. "I'm not sitting on a farm getting fat," she insisted.

Meanwhile, when Rosemary arrived at the farm, she was happy to start helping the Steven family. She cared deeply for the animals and loved the countryside. Daffodil, the cow, was everyone's favourite. She knew the animals and "they were my friends." She would feed them all and help move the cattle, but milking was not for her! She did deliver the milk locally though. The only temperamental beast was Billy the bull and Rosemary would not go within an arm's length of him!

She became involved with village life and twice a week she volunteered at Crockham Hill village hall. They had an emergency canteen, run by Mrs Lancaster, where servicemen would visit, for a little bit of relaxation and freedom from duty. Soon, she was asked if she would consider teaching dancing to the many East London children evacuated from their homes to the area. She did and was helped by a gentleman (whose name she has forgotten) who was a talented and keen ballroom dancer. So classes started and, although she wondered if the children would come, the classes proved very popular. The lovely thing about learning such a skill as a child was

66

that it could be taken into adult life. One day, a small gang of children were looking down from the top of the steps. Asked why they were there, the reply came, "We want to see what you're doing mate!" So the class was explained and away they went. At the next lesson, there they were, each queuing up at the door. One shy little evacuee girl, called Frances, was particularly talented and Rosemary enjoyed teaching her very much. When she first arrived, she asked, "Would you teach me?" "Of course, I will dear", replied Rosemary and so she started. One day, Frances came and told Rosemary her mum was coming and she had to go home. She wanted to see her dad and the family dog, but she wished Rosemary could go with her. That little girl left and Rosemary never heard from her again. She often worried about what became of little Frances.

Back at the farm with the war raging, when the siren went, they all gathered in the middle of the house, in a strongly built passageway. Sometimes, guests would be visiting and they all gathered there too, like Noah's Ark, two by two, waiting for the all clear.

Aunty Connie was a trained nurse and if anyone was hurt, she was called out to them. On one occasion, she went to a German plane that had crashed on the Downs. One boy asked why she was going to help a German. "It matters to me if anyone is hurt; I am a nurse, so I go," was her retort. A local man, Nobby Clark, who manned a search light in the field next to the farm also rushed to the crashed plane and helped to arrest the downed pilot. Sadly, a man, barely more than a boy, lost his life in the crash. Aunt Connie went to the young man and sat with him, until an ambulance took him away, but his injuries were too severe to survive. Nobby was a small man, dwarfed by the airman. He insisted the swearing German remove his wonderful, fur-lined, leather boots and Rosemary remembers them marching into the farm courtyard, with little Nobby holding up those huge boots, like a trophy. "Ouch, ouch," were part of the utterings from the bootless man, as he stepped on the stony ground. If the other words had not been in German, they would have been unprintable here anyway! The British army were already in the yard and took away the grumbling, furious prisoner.

After the war, Blanche came back to Kent. Once more, Aunty Connie stepped in and they returned to a rented cottage, owned by Hurst Farm. Blanche worked in the guest house on the farm and Uncle Tommy took Rosemary to see Mr Brill, an eminent solicitor in Westerham about a work position. He had offices in London, but Rosemary found the staff very 'hoity-toity,' and the journey from Crockham Hill was almost impossible so the job came to nothing. Subsequently, at the labour exchange in Sevenoaks, she was told to interview with Durtnell the building company, in Brasted.

They urgently needed a new secretary, as the last girl had just run off with a man from the local timber company! Well, who better than Rosemary? She turned up and was shown into the 'governor's' office. There was grandfather, Richard Durtnell, on the left, still wearing his homburg hat. On the right was Geoffrey Durtnell, his son. Richard seemed to take a shine to her straightaway, but Geoffrey was more cautious. No matter, Rosemary was hired to start the follow -ing Monday, with the instruction to clear up the mess the last girl had left.

Rosemary's hand stitched design celebrates the major events of her life.

68

A good place to start was the stationary cupboard, full of mourning stationery. Durtnells had run a funeral business, employing their carpenters to make coffins. She went to Geoffrey to ask if they were likely to do anymore funerals. "I hope not," was his reply, so the stationery had to go. It really wasn't good to write to clients on black-edged paper! Rosemary had a contact through playing tennis in Westerham. She knew the Hooker brothers who had a stationery business. They found her a ream of plain paper and envelopes to match. Her career was launched and it lasted the rest of her working life.

Geoffrey would call her in for dictation and she would use skills she had learnt in Slough. He was kinder than he seemed in her interview and as he began to understand her abilities and unwavering character, she was given a free hand to do as she wanted. She admired the company and supported their reputation for being, "the best building firm you will ever find, they are unique." She watched the company pass from father to son and then on to the next generation and fiercely upheld the firm's standing in the community. She worked long and hard at Durtnells and that is how she came to spend so many years living in Brasted village.

In the early days, she gallantly cycled to work each day, up and down Hornshill, Westerham. Finally, in 1969, she enquired of Durtnells if there was any accommodation available in Brasted. She and her mother were offered a property at 1 Vines Cottages, High Street. An old couple had lived there and the cottage was completely neglected and condemned. Durtnells gained permission to repair and upgrade it, especially for them. The whole place was gutted and restored by the best craftsman Durtnells had to offer. Cecil Wood, the master bricklayer knocked out the old fireplace and built a beautiful new one. Rosemary chose good quality bricks and Cecil expertly put them in, arranging the bricks in perfect courses. Since then, Rosemary has always gently cleaned them and proudly kept them in their original, perfect condition. The bathroom was replaced and the kitchen upgraded. Things actually worked, and the cottage had electric lighting. At the same time, it was impossible to put a spade into the garden, so Tom Hollands came in with his rotavator. An old bath was found buried near the gate, but first they had to be sure it was not a bomb. This area had been quite a target in the war, with RAF Biggin Hill located just a few miles north of Brasted. It was gently excavated until the rim was visible and a large hole found in the middle of it. It certainly could be dug up and removed safely! After four months of hard work in May 1970, Rosemary and Blanche moved into their lifelong home. The cottage and garden were a dream for both of them.

Rosemary worked for Durtnells from 1947 to 1983, but in truth, she never really retired. She was always called in for special projects and was simply classed as one of the family.

Meanwhile the Whittaker-Browne household had to have a cat to love. A little tabby cat came from Westerham and a local stray soon took up residence too. However, the feline that really completed their household was a wonderful black cat with huge white whiskers. How could she be called anything but Whiskers! She ruled the roost, and Rosemary found her a cosy jumper to sleep on. When the fire was burning brightly, Whiskers would move closer and closer, until her head rested on the fender. The smell of singeing alerted them to this cosy cat's dilemma! Whiskers was vocal and would make her needs known by miaows and purring. One day, there were cats on the television and Whiskers looked up at her family and gave a loud, indignant miaow, as if to say how dare there be extra cats in the house – something must be done to remove them! When nothing happened, she took her paw to the screen and even went under the television to find the interlopers! With that the television went off to save her anguish – job done! (Who was in charge of this household?)

There were some old apple trees growing in the garden, and one had a hole right down the middle of its trunk. Poor Whiskers lost her dignity, when she accidentally fell down into it. After she was fished out, the hole was filled with bricks and clutter, so this could never happen again. Sometimes, Blanche would buy fish from Mrs Kimber, in the village and cook it just for her beloved pet. Sadly, Whiskers met her fate on the main road, when she was discovered in the corner of the Recreation Ground. Her little paws were neatly crossed as though she was simply sleeping, but alas she wasn't! Rosemary and Blanche were so distraught, they simply couldn't face having their hearts broken again and agreed never to have another cat.

Blanche and Rosemary were 'home birds', but they did enjoy walking and would do so all around the Brasted lanes. They would marvel at the flowers in the hedgerows, and watch the birds and wildlife. Blanche always insisted on feeding the creatures around their cottage. Rosemary remembers one Christmas when the meal was completely cooked and ready. So it was only half a surprise, when Blanche chimed in, "No, no, the birds first," and could not be persuaded that having dinner first was a better idea. It was freezing cold, but out they had to go to the back of the cottage, where the birds would be waiting on the fence. In no time at all there was a clip clop and over the fence appeared the ponies from the field. What could Blanche do? She fed the ponies as well before enjoying her own Christmas dinner. The ponies belonged to Paddy

O'Donoghue, the village hairdresser and were always ready for treats from Blanche and Rosemary.

Blanche took after her doctor father in character and was always looking to help others. On Monday mornings she would go to Westerham and inevitably met someone she could treat to coffee, at The Kings Arms. One day she heard of an old couple in West End who had very little. She never wanted anyone to feel difficult about being helped, so she arranged with Mrs Day, the milkman's wife to help these people out. She bought a chicken and Mrs Day cooked and delivered it, as the couple knew her very well. No one ever knew that Blanche was behind the whole thing. For Rosemary, this caring act was typical of her mother and epitomised her generosity and kindness to others.

Rosemary and Blanche would attend services together at St Martin's Church, although they did not go every week. They supported the church and Rosemary particularly liked the Rector, Tony Curry. She hand-designed and cross-stitched, a beautiful picture of St Martin's which she wanted to will to Tony, after her death. Well Rosemary is amazing and still going strong at ninety three. She has outlived Tony and so the picture will go directly to the church instead.

The garden has always been an important part of Rosemary's life and she loves growing her plants and sharing them. Her huge, red poppies are magnificent and she hands out their seeds every year. The snowdrops are gorgeous, but how they arrived at her cottage is an interesting story. Tom Steven of Heath Farm, had a sister Mary Gilmoor Robertson Steven. She never married, but ran a local poultry business, at a property she called Gilrobess; so called from a compilation of her own names. Her parents were Scottish and she was particularly proud of her Scottish snowdrops. Mary's brother dug up a patch and delivered them to Blanche and Rosemary. They have since spread to large areas around the apple trees and will always be fondly known as the 'Scottish snowdrops'.

On Monday, the 16th July, 1973, a school coach crashed off the A25 into Rosemary's garden. It was mid-morning and had been raining heavily, when a forty-one seater coach, careered off the slippery road. The road surface had recently been tarred and scattered with granite chippings. However, the chippings were mostly in the gutter, leaving the water soaked surface like a skating rink. So the coach slithered around the road before toppling over and falling down the bank into the garden. As it fell, it took trees and shrubs with it. Thirty-one children were on board, together with three teachers and the driver. They were mostly evacuated through the sunroof as the coach was wedged, upside down. Amazingly, no one was seriously hurt although many were battered and bruised. Blanche had been in Westerham and was greeted with the chaotic scene, as she left her bus. She walked to her front door where a chief police officer was guarding the entrance. "I'm sorry madam, this is a private house." Her reply is lost in time, but he quickly let her through! Blanche immediately put the kettle on, for tea all round.

The coach party were taken into various cottages, before a fleet of ambulances took them to Orpington Hospital. That evening the sunshine came out and as Rosemary put it, "everyone came to gawp." Heavy lifting gear had to be brought in to remove the coach and take it away.

That left Rosemary and Blanche with the task of clearing up the glass from all the windows of the shattered, written-off coach. A stake and wire fence was quickly erected, so no one could fall on the mess. Each day they took out their garden kneeling pads and collected glass placing it into any container they could find. It was everywhere, but together they made their garden safe again.

That night the Parish Council met and a decision was taken to move the thirty mile an hour sign further away from the houses to slow the traffic before it entered the village. It was, and today it still sits in its new position, beside the Recreation Ground. Do cars take any notice? Many of us think not as we try to cross the road!

Like mother, like daughter, Rosemary is a very determined and optimistic lady. She always looks on the positive side, but is mindful that sometimes one has to deal with sad, yet inevitable situations, such as her mother's funeral arrangements. What sort of final farewell did her mother want? It was something she needed to know, as after all, it was only the two of them that could plan these things. Finally, Blanche decided on cremation and when she was seventy-seven, in 1976, those wishes were fulfilled by Rosemary. Her ashes were spread in the beautiful gardens of Tunbridge Wells Crematorium, as St Martin's Church did not yet have a cremation plot established in its grounds. However, as a testament to Rosemary's dedication and devotion to her mother, with great pleasure, she was able to add Blanche to the Book of Remembrance in the church. When the day comes, Rosemary has chosen to be cremated and laid to rest in her beloved St Martins. Let's hope that day is a long way off!

In her retirement, Rosemary has joined a great group of Brasted ladies and enjoys weekly outings to the Ide Hill Village Market. They buy fresh vegetables, cakes, prepared meals, flowers and Rosemary's favourite, homemade marmalade. They sit and have coffee and cake, while they all catch up on their week's activities. What a pity it is that so many of these village markets have closed now, as they provide an important community asset that isn't only about products!

In 2016, Rosemary suffered a stroke. Her friend, Rita, tried to contact her one evening, but had no reply to her phone call. She walked round to the cottage, but the curtains were pulled and it looked as though Rosemary had gone to bed early. The next morning, she went round again and still the curtains were pulled; a cup and saucer sat on the draining board unwashed. Alarm bells rang, and Rita rushed back to inform Durtnells. Not only did they rent the cottage to Rosemary, but she was a Durtnell in all but name. The police were called and a window broken, to give them access to the property. Rosemary had collapsed in her bedroom and was found on the floor. All her friends rallied round, and she spent eight weeks in hospital. She applied her usual willpower to exercise and returned herself to health, not needing any walking aids in her house.

She hardly goes out now, but all her friends have mobilised to help her. They take her shopping, book her medical appointments and offer her transportation. This is the spirit of Brasted that shines forth in a way that Blanche and Rosemary always admired. This was what they loved most about living here.

What does Rosemary miss and how has Brasted changed? It was the loss of all the shops. They were terrific and there was no need to leave the village. May King, at Cowlards, sold the freshest bread and there was a greengrocer and a butcher. The village even had its own chimney sweep and petrol garage. All needs were catered for by cheerful, happy people who knew you and looked after you.

February 2017

Postscript

Rosemary has an amazing memory and this story is told in her own words. Therefore Brasted was not mentioned until later in her life story as recounted here.

Joyce Furst
née Cole

Joyce Helen Cole was born in September 1927 in the tiny house her parents occupied at 1 Alms Row, Brasted. She was born into generations of the Cole family who have long lived and worked in Brasted. Her line can be traced back to Thomas Cole, born circa 1781 in Brasted and before him the family came from Edenbridge and Westerham. So this good Kentish girl was the daughter of Henry Elvey Cole born on the 13th September 1891. He lived all his life in 1 Alms Row until his death in 1978. He married Naomi Hazelden in 1924 in the Sevenoaks area and they had two daughters, Joyce and Margaret.

Joyce remembers Alms Row when it had no electricity supply and the sitting room had a gas mantle with a globe over the flame. When the mantle needed changing it was a frustrating task for Naomi. The fabric element was so fragile that if it was touched it could easily be damaged and rendered useless immediately. The scullery was lit by an oil lamp secured to the wall and upstairs was lit by candles. The toilet was at the end of the garden and a bucket of water, for flushing, had to be carried down from the house.

The Cole Family Tree

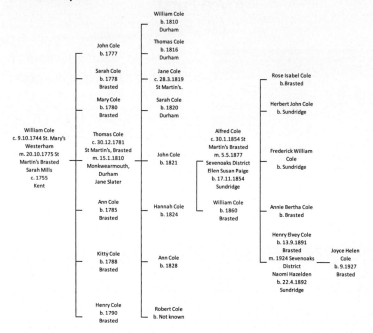

Joyce would periodically get sent to Smith's Garage, opposite The White Hart pubic house, at the end of the village. She had to carry a large, wet accumulator (an early form of rechargeable battery) which was used in the only radio in the house. The garage recharged it and once again the family could listen to their radio broadcasts. The second garage in the village was on the corner of Chart Lane. Mr Bond sold petrol and had a spare parts shop behind the pumps. Mrs Bond ran the post office which was beside the parts shop. Until Joyce was eight, her grandfather Alfred Cole lived with them. He was a fun loving man and sang and bounced the girls on his knee.

Alfred had been part of the Combe Bank part-time fire brigade. They had moved to Sundridge Main Road in about 1900 when the horses

78

pulling the fire tender were mostly supplied by the Alderson family in Brasted. The brigade entered many competitions sometimes travelling to places like Brighton and Leytonstone. At one of these events Alfred was presented with a beautiful silver fireman's helmet for his prize. Subscriptions to this private service slowly dropped off and finally the station closed. The premises are currently the village shop and post office at 144 Main Road, Sundridge. Alfred died on the 16th July 1935 and was buried in Brasted Church.

Combe Bank Fire Brigade with Alfred Cole (centre standing)
wearing the silver fireman's helmet

Joyce's father Henry, known as Harry, worked for the Vestey family on the Valence estate. They were beef barons owning large farms in South America and very wealthy. Their land in the village stretched south from opposite the Brasted Recreation Ground to Quebec Square in Westerham and way back into the countryside. Occasionally, the Cole family would walk over to meet Harry as he worked and take him a flask of tea and something to eat. Harry worked long hours particularly during harvest time. He would leave home at 6 a.m. and return around 9 p.m. The period of daylight dictated the length of his working hours. Harry tanned in the sunshine and, "looked as brown as a berry in the summer," said Joyce.

Joyce enjoyed the Christmas parties the estate arranged each year for the workers' children. They played games like Pass the Parcel and had lovely sandwiches, cake and jelly. The Vestey children would make an impressive entrance by walking down a large, wooden staircase in their beautiful party clothes. At the end of the party the fathers walked up the drive to collect the children and lit the way home with lanterns.

The Cole family would also receive a generous box full of Christmas foods from the Vestey family. There was always a Christmas cake and an iced cake for the children. It also had a small pheasant in it and traditional mincemeat. Each year the children had a gift, which their own families could not possibly afford. One year it was a party dress (not that Joyce attended many parties!). Then she had a dressing gown and on another occasion a gym slip to wear to school.

The Vestey Company became very successful and acquired many companies here and abroad. They owned Oxo and opened the successful Dewhurst Butchers business. Their shops were some of the first to have glass windows instead of exposing meat to the open street. They started the Blue Star Shipping Line, registered in London and Liverpool, to import and export their products. During the First World War they were credited with supplying the country with much of the badly needed protein in eggs and meat.

Other village Christmas parties were held at St Martin's Church, the Baptist Chapel and Joyce Alderson always gave a party in Church End

House. Joyce says she had a lovely childhood and belonged to all the clubs, groups and gatherings that she possibly could.

Joyce went to Brasted School at the age of five. She hated the headmaster Mr Warner who was a severe disciplinarian. The cane came out every day for the boys. The girls were not caned, but had to look on in horror. No one went home and told their parents of the beatings, as their fathers would take off their belts and whack them again. Mr Warner ruled by fear, so on her last day Joyce was relieved and pleased to walk out of the gate, never to return.

As a child she was free to wander all around the village. She went into the hills, up the Chart and all around Colinette Farm. She and her friends would collect arms full of wild flowers and grasses. In season they found wild strawberries and blackberries and, if they simply could not manage another mouthful, they took some home for the family. They could sit and make daisy chains and laugh and play together. School would encourage them to bring in flowers or berries to help teach the pupils about the hedgerows. At Eastertime they found bunches of primroses and wild violets to take home, which smelled heavenly in their houses. They would walk for miles and think nothing of it.

The only thing that worried their parents were the tramps that wandered about the neighbourhood. They were drawn by the offer of beds to sleep in at Sundridge Hospital. The tramps were usually quite harmless, but rather scary. Naomi would give them a pinch of tea and fill their billycans with hot water in the hope they would move on quickly.

Joyce didn't need an appointment to visit anyone in the village and she was made welcome anywhere she went. That lasted into adulthood where everyone knew nearly everyone else in the village.

You could always stop for a chat and a cuppa. Things are so different now and Joyce finds she hardly knows anyone anymore. Many of her old buddies have moved on or passed away and new neighbours disappear behind closed doors.

During snowy winters the children would take a metal tray and slide down the hillside behind what is now Jewson Builders Merchants in Rectory Lane. It was private land, but no one chased them off. The boys could not be in snow without throwing snowballs and the girls had to get them back. Making a snowman was a must! They stayed out all day until hunger drove them home. Joyce remembers being hot and sweaty inside, yet her feet, hands and face were freezing cold. Winters were more severe and snow more plentiful in those days, unlike the milder winters we have experienced since the later 1990s and so far in this millennium.

Her mother, Naomi, had accounts with the local shops. Everything was put on the tab through the week and when Harry was paid on Friday the tab had to be settled on Saturday. Naomi taught her girls that if the tab was not cleared straightaway the family could not buy supplies the following week. It operated on trust with none of the borrowing benefits credit cards might offer today. Joyce learned her lessons well and never allowed herself to fall into debt. Brasted shops could supply all the family needs except for good shoes. Naomi's sister-in-law Janet Hazelden lived in nearby Riverhead and they visited each other every fortnight. Janet would take some money from Naomi and on her next visit to Sevenoaks would invest it on her behalf in a shoe club. The shoe shop was on St John's Hill. That way the money built up and a bus ride to Sevenoaks was a family outing to buy shoes when necessary. They had perhaps a pair of summer shoes and another pair for winter and Naomi was careful that they fitted properly and did not damage her daughter's feet.

Naomi was an excellent housekeeper and she passed on her skills by example.

At the age of ten Joyce, her friend Joyce Day and fourteen year olds Dennis Homewood and Charles Bailey, were asked to plant an oak tree on the village green. They were chosen as they had been born and raised in the village. The occasion was the coronation of King George VI. An English oak sapling was chosen from Lord Stanhope's estate with the expectation that the tree would stand for at least three hundred and fifty years. Queen Elizabeth I was on the throne three hundred and fifty years previously and it was hoped the tree might witness the same amazing unfolding of history. The event was supported by the school and many villagers watched the proceedings. The occasion was finished with the singing of the National Anthem.

George V Silver Jubilee Celebrations
(Left to right - Faith Murkett, Freda Seale and Joyce Cole)

Rumour has it that the oak would have grown too big for the area and a horse chestnut tree now stands on the village green in place of the oak tree. If only they could now see the horse chestnut now and know that it is currently planned to reduce its crown to make it a little smaller! What a pity they could not have done that with the old oak tree.

Joyce joined the brownies at Brasted along with her buddy Iris Medhurst. Miss Pym, the daughter of Sir Charles Pym who lived at the Foxwold Estate in Brasted Chart, was their Brown Owl. They worked for badges such as cooking and sewing. Sometimes they went on forays to Brasted Chart to wander in the woods. Joyce cannot remember any camps, fires or cooking though. The following is a quote from the Sevenoaks Chronicle dated the 12th May 1939:

'Through the kindness of Mrs Frank Williams, the Brasted guides and brownies held an enrolment meeting in Brasted Hall gardens on Wednesday evening 10th May. An interesting feature was the 'flying up' ceremony at which Iris Medhurst and Joyce Cole received their wings, while Cynthia Seal was enrolled in the brownies.'

Once the Second World War started a lot of these groups seemed to fizzle out.

The Brasted Baptist Chapel offered an excuse to get out especially during the winter. Her parents could not object since she took part in the Christian Endeavour and Band of Hope groups. They gave magic lantern shows and Joyce remembers watching missions in Africa. The services were much livelier than the St Martin's Church of England service. She was sent to St Martin's on Sunday morning with a penny (1d) for the collection, but would beg her mother to be allowed to attend the Chapel on Sunday afternoon. Naomi could hardly argue and sent her off with a ha'penny (½d) for their

84

collection. The service took place with the Pastor standing at a lectern on the stage. He preached about hell fire and brimstone as the fate of the unfaithful. There were prayers and lots of jolly choruses. The singing could surely be heard from here to Westerham! Once she saw a baptism where the stage was pulled back and a huge tub underneath filled with water. Everyone taking part in the service was dressed in white robes, a symbol of purity for entering the church. Each person was dunked completely and welcomed into the Christian community. Joyce couldn't get over it and rushed home to tell her parents all about the ceremony.

The Brasted Baptist Chapel

Once a year Harry treated his family to a holiday in Brighton. They stayed in a fine boarding house for a week and not just bed and breakfast! Breakfast, dinner and tea was the format for every single day. They went to the cinema and theatre and on the way back the girls had a milkshake. The family did almost nothing for the rest of the year and none of Joyce's friends enjoyed such a lavish holiday.

Her mother explained that Harry had been injured during the First World War and was awarded a generous pension. His war papers record that on the 19th of April 1916 Harry suffered a severe head injury. He was hit by flying shrapnel and had a long, deep scar on his head. He was discharged as no longer physically fit for service in September 1916, with a disability pension.

For the first year of the Second World War it was hard to know there was a war on at all except for rationing. However, the Battle of Britain was terrible and brought the fighting directly overhead. The planes were zooming through the sky and their guns could clearly be heard crack, cracking urgently. Of this battle, Winston Churchill said on 20th August 1940, "Never in the field of human conflict was so much owed by so many to so few. All hearts go out to the fighter pilots, whose brilliant actions we see with our own eyes day after day."

Joyce remembers watching the skies and hearing the sirens every night at the height of the raids on London. Her father erected an igloo-style air raid shelter in the garden, dug into the vegetable patch. Joyce never went into it without a shovel and always sat at the door. She felt it triggered her lifelong claustrophobia by being shut in the small, damp, smelly hole in the ground.

One day, as she watched from The Bull Inn, a plane dropped out of the sky and crashed at Hogtrough Hill beside the Pilgrims Way. That fateful sighting was on the 11th September 1940 when a Hurricane piloted by Sgt Stefan Wojtowicz fell out of the sky burning fiercely. He had found himself in a dog fight with six ME109's and managed to destroy one and probably a second one before they downed him. Sgt Wojtowicz's bravery is commemorated in a plaque erected on Hogtrough Hill.

Sgt Stefan Wójtowicz

"One of the Few"
He bravely fought 6 Me 109s
destroying 1 and 1 probable
before he was shot down nearby
on 11.9.1940. Aged 21.

"On our wings
sing the wind of liberty"

Za naszą i waszą wolność
(For Our Freedom and Yours)

Aged just twenty-one he was flying with 303 Squadron (Polish) from RAF Northolt. Sgt Wojtowicz was also remembered in a bible presented to St Martin's Church. The dedication in the front reads:

Presented to Brasted Parish Church by the Brasted Air Raid Wardens Service in grateful memory of the airmen who gave their lives during the Battle of Britain during 1940, P/O C E English of Jesmond, Newcastle upon Tyne and Sergeant Pilot S Wojtowicz of Poland who fell in Brasted. To replace the Bible of 1852, damaged by a flying bomb July 4th 1944'.

The village was lively, with the military taking over most of the large houses throughout the area. Dances and concerts were often held in the village hall. A man would arrive with a gramophone, or a band might turn up and sometimes the military musicians played in the evening. These times became especially animated when the Irish troops arrived. Aged about sixteen Joyce loved to go to the dances, but only if she could find the money. There was one kind soldier who danced with all the women. He danced wonderfully and taught Joyce the steps. She did have to leave before the end as her father would be furious and clip her around her ears if she was late.

Joyce left school two months before her fourteenth birthday and started work the next day at 8 a.m. She was employed by Mr and Mrs Turville - Stubbs, the licensees of The Bull Inn. She had already worked there during school as a part-time helper. Her task was to look after their three little girls and a baby for seven shillings and sixpence (7s 6d) a week. All her food was provided and as these were the war years and rationing left everyone hungry, this was a prized reward. She worked six days a week with Thursdays off. This job lasted from July until the following April when their other employed girl, in charge of cooking and cleaning, left. Joyce was offered an extra half-crown (2s 6d) to do everything and was insulted at the prospect. She decided there and then to walk out with nothing else lined up and no security in contributing money into her parents' household.

Soon after, at a village concert, Naomi sat beside Mrs Waters, a neighbour, and related the unhappy story of Joyce walking out of her job with nowhere else to go. She was told that the Co-op had been taking on staff in Westerham and suggested Joyce try there. The advertised jobs in the shop had already been filled, but the Co-op butchers next door needed a cashier. So, knowing nothing of book-keeping she was offered and accepted the job. She had four days of training in accounting and rationing. One shilling's worth of meat a week and two pence (2d) worth of corned beef per person! She worked at her little cash desk for eight years. Two boys worked for the Co-op and both died in action in the Second World War. The first played accordion at some of the concerts. He joined the air force and was a rear gunner when he was killed. The other was in the Navy when he lost his life. They were both just boys and the sadness was numbing.

Children were very much seen and not heard in Joyce's childhood. Nothing of an intimate nature was discussed or explained. So it was most confusing when she watched two ladies from the munitions factory in Westerham holding hands and having a kiss and a cuddle. This was new and what was it all about? She asked the butcher why and he quietly explained they were lesbians.   Truth is when he finished she really knew no more than before he started!

The Cole family were not interested in the cinema, but Joyce was taken there by a neighbour Mrs Wells and her daughter Madge. When she could, she watched Shirley Temple films and the actor Wallace Beery, but it was not a comfortable place to be. It was known as 'the fleapit' and certainly lived up to its name. On one occasion she was bitten so badly on her leg that the wound kept weeping and sticking her sheer stockings to her skin – ouch!

Working in the shop meant Joyce always knew when bands were playing and dances were planned in Westerham. Her social life took off and along came John, a good looking man with a light Scottish accent. She told her friend how lovely the fair haired, Scotsman was. "He's not Scottish", her friend said, "but Polish from the camp in Tandridge." This was Czeslaw Furst, although he introduced himself as John. He had served in the Polish army in Scotland and learned to speak English there. In 1947 Britain suffered a particularly severe winter and with the war finally over the Poles were relocated throughout Britain from their Scottish base. Czeslaw and his buddies were sent to Nissen huts erected in the Tandridge woods. From there they were expected to make their future in this immediate post war period.

Back to the dance and why did Joyce only know him as John? All the Polish boys tended to be called Jonny and the name John stuck with him all his life. As he searched for work, Westerham offered him a social life and of course, there was Joyce. This liaison brought Joyce into conflict with her family, as prejudice coloured her father's view of John. It all came down to an ultimatum of whether John was welcome into the family home or not. Sense prevailed and Joyce and John were married in 1952, destined to be lifelong soul mates.

John started work for Locomotors, a garage in Brasted, but then moved on to house building. He had to chase work and they started life together in Grove Park near Lewisham while John took work in the building trade. They searched for accommodation and found a top floor attic room. The property was a rooming house awaiting demolition after bomb damage in the war. They had to carry water up to their room and share a bathroom and toilet. They didn't care, they were in love and together. As Joyce says, "as happy as Larry." They moved back to Brasted as John found more building projects in Westerham. Each time a project was completed, John looked for another chance of employment. He returned to Locomotors where all went well until Joyce had their second child. With no other help, John had to care for his wife, new born baby and young child, forcing him to take an unscheduled week off work. He was sacked on the spot for his actions! No contracts or Government rulings helped at that time with the protection of workers.

John made his life in Brasted, but would visit his family in Poland when possible. Towards the end of the war the Soviet Union had advanced through Poland and in 1945 the Iron Curtain came into being. It divided Europe into two areas, with Poland segregated in the east behind the Curtain. The Soviet Union isolated itself and its satellite states away from any contact with the West. Families were separated and this caused much heartache. Joyce was lucky three or four times to gain permission to travel behind the Iron Curtain and visit John's family. She had to register with the Polish police when she arrived and they made sure she left on the right day. The police were scary with visible guns in their belts. In England Joyce had never had a holiday longer than one week, so two or three weeks in Poland made her homesick. To help herself she would make a proper, strong cup of tea (not the weak Polish variety) and a slice of bread and jam so it felt like England. The border control restrictions eased with the ending of the Cold War in 1991.

The housing estate in West End was built by Sevenoaks Council in 1935. It took land that was once a beautiful field. Those moving in used hand carts to transport their household belongings to the houses. The windows were larger than those in the small cottages that people had moved from and the occupants had to afford and make new curtains. There were no lights in the toilet until a local man was employed to install lighting in all the houses. Joyce's parents Harry and Naomi would not budge for any promises of 'modern' living. However, in 1961 Joyce and John moved there and Joyce remembers the inconvenience that the bath only had a cold water tap. There was a copper in the corner that boiled all the hot water for the property. Son, Robert played football for Redland Tiles as a goalkeeper so when he came home covered in mud he had to slosh around in cold water first before using the precious hot water.

When Joyce's children started school she became a school governor. She would attend meetings to deal with any matters arising from the school. If a new teacher was needed she would attend the interviews and help to choose the most suitable applicant. Then, there was the paperwork, which became ever more complicated and finally Joyce felt it was time to resign. Mr Wilkins, the headmaster was a lovely man and understood her decision and why she had made it. However, she was present at the meetings that oversaw the closing of the school. Pupil numbers had dwindled and Sundridge School had their own kitchen for cooking food which Brasted did not. Thirdly, Sundridge School was not on a main road with all the hazards of increasing numbers of vehicles. Those points swung the decision away from Brasted School and it closed in favour of Sundridge. When the school closed, Joyce felt it was a terrible shame. She currently sees all the new children in West End being taken to school by car. They cannot meet their friends and laugh together as they walk to and from the school as Joyce had done.

For years Joyce and her friend Freda Wood ran the village library. They opened the village hall once a week from 2.30 p.m. to 4.30 p.m. for villagers to select and change books. These were delivered from Maidstone and could be ordered by request or chosen from a random assortment of titles and subjects. As interest in the service waned, both Joyce and Freda would cart piles of books around the village to try to keep it going. Arch Day, a near neighbour, would have lots to read and Joyce would struggle along to keep him supplied. Ultimately, the library had to close, due to lack of interest.

Joyce and John had three children who all grew up in Brasted. She lost John in 2006, but muses on how he would have loved their nine great grandchildren. In a final act of selfless love Joyce took John's ashes back to Poland for burial. Permission was granted easily from Poland, but here in England the documentation was challenging. It was a terrible battle to persuade the authorities to grant permission. Finally it was agreed and his casket had to be lead-lined and it was wrapped in red and white tape before being allowed on the plane.

Ten of the English family went and Czeslaw Furst was laid to rest with his parents in Bydgoszcz with the blessings of both sides of his family.

Joyce feels Brasted has changed hugely and has lost its village atmosphere and camaraderie. The sociability has dwindled and it is easy to become isolated. She doesn't know many people, all the useful shops have slowly closed and people drive out of the village instead of walking around. The cottages are now so expensive they are out of reach of so many young people and their little families. She mused that perhaps we should have used the old shops more, but sadly the rise of out-of-town supermarkets was unstoppable.

Joyce's bug bear about the village today is the road, the A25. It is no longer easy to see the beautiful countryside behind it. It is so full of traffic and dangerous at any time of the day for pedestrians. The east of the village has two zebra crossings, but there is nothing on the west side, as cars roar in from Westerham. Thirty mile an hour signs are ignored by drivers who are only forced to slow down when they reach the bend at Church Road. Days out to Sevenoaks often start for Joyce by catching the bus on the corner of West End and traveling the wrong way to Westerham. There she waits for the bus to turn around and return to Sevenoaks where she wanted to go in the first place. It saves crossing the A25!

Joyce feels that in her lifetime things have changed more dramatically than in any other period in history. From no electricity, no mains water and horse drawn milk carts delivering scoops of milk from churns. Since then it has become a computer age to which she says, "It's all double Dutch to me. To think man has even landed on the moon."

February 2017

Joy Edgar
née Herbert

Pamela Joy Herbert, always known as Joy, was born in February 1927, in Lingfield, Surrey. When she was seven, her father moved the family to Westerham, where she grew up and lived until she married.

As a young girl, she and her brothers would cycle over to the Darent Valley Swimming Baths in Brasted. They would pay their threepence (3d) and spend many happy afternoons, in and out of the water. Being river fed, it was bitterly cold and rather primitive, with a pebble bottom and grass banks. Much later, when she lived at Park Farm in Brasted, she became aware that the raw sewage from the farm, plus the same from Westerham, all drained into the River Darent! The swimming pool rapidly lost its appeal.

One snowy winter in Westerham, she and her brother, Owen, went sledging on a lovely big hill. Owen sat her on the sledge and off they flew down the hill, up a bank and before they knew it they'd landed straight in the icy trout lake! That certainly was a chilling experience in more ways than one! They would take their fishing nets to the river Darent near the spring on the Squerryes Estate and scoop up tiny fish to fill their jam jars. Sadly, despite their best intentions their treasures always died.

Before marriage, Joy, with a twinkle in her eye, described courting as, "very exciting". Her marriage proposal was a slight surprise though, as it came about when Gordon Edgar, her beau, wanted to rent Park Farm in Brasted. The farm was part of the Chevening Estate and he applied to Lord Stanhope for the privilege of renting it. He supplied two backers who were his father, Reginald and a close friend, Jack Steven from Force Green Farm, Westerham. All went well until Lord Stanhope asked Gordon if he was married, as he didn't like to rent property to single men. Gordon said, "No, but he would see what he could do!" So he asked Joy to marry him and, in saying yes, she got both a new husband and a farm to look after in one foul swoop. Her parents were not best pleased, as she was only eighteen and on the same day as the proposal, she was accepted for training as a nurse.

Gordon was just twenty-two, when they married in 1946. He had met all of Lord Stanhope's requirements and they moved into Park Farm. The farm has a plaque on the front, saying it was built in 1703, but Joy said parts were older than that. Behind the house is a passage with rooms beside it. These rooms were originally used to house cattle, with a hay store overhead. It was an old-fashioned method of protecting and insulating the cattle from severe weather. The house is beautiful and has a particularly magnificent oak staircase that came from Chevening House when it was renovated. It has three landings and a beautifully carved bannister.

As a boy, Gordon had lived at Court Lodge Farm, which his parents, Reginald and Ellen, had rented from Mr Dark. Joy remembered that Mr Dark was rather fond of The Bull Inn and after his imbibing, he would climb into his pony and cart to ride home. The pony knew exactly where to go, which was just as well, as by then Mr Dark didn't! The Dark family had many farms through the valley and Joy says the area from Westerham to Chipstead was known as 'Dark Valley', rather than by its proper name, of the Holmesdale Valley.

During the war, some of the Dark family lived at Park Farm. The air raid sirens for attacks were frequent and the Dark family would pop down to sleep in the cellar, on its damp, stone floor. It must have been miserable. The farm took several strikes from German bombers. One bomb fell very close, landing just behind the house where there were fruit trees and a horse in the garden. Sadly, the poor horse took the full force of the bomb, which also damaged the back of the farm house. Another fell in the fields and scattered thousands of small pieces of metal. Later, Gordon's cattle would pick up the metal shards, in the grass and the vet would be urgently summoned to operate. It was rarely successful and the unfortunate animals usually had to be put down.

At Court Lodge Farm, Gordon's father, Reginald, was focusing on building a herd of Shorthorn cattle. Each calf had to conform to an exact type, including four white feet. Any that failed this standard, were packed off for slaughter! Court Lodge Farm, finally went to Bob Steven, (Jack Steven's son) and he changed again to Friesian cattle, famed for good quality, dairy production.

Park Farm occupies a long narrow tract of land, stretching southwards from the chalk hills of the North Downs, through the Darent riverbed and up to the sand and gravel soil, south of the A25 road. It was dissected by the Westerham to Dunton Green railway track and later by the M25 motorway. While the M25 was being constructed, the heavy motorway machinery often cut through the power lines to the farm. Gordon, finally got so fed up with the outages that he drove all the way to Hertfordshire to buy a generator. After that they always had power to milk the cows regularly and enjoy uninterrupted electricity in the house.

Harvest time at Court Lodge Farm

When Joy and Gordon married, Joy was new to farming and had to learn fast. It was hard work, with none of the modern machinery that farmers take for granted these days. She had to learn to scrub floors and blacken the range. Washing was manual and all clothes had to be scrubbed hard, including hats, coats and farm overalls straight off the farmyard. "They were dirty," she sighed. There was no running water and everything had to be pumped up from the well. This included all the water needed in the house and water for the cattle to drink. The bedroom had a string hanging through the ceiling, attached to a tank with a ballcock. As the tank level dropped the string climbed higher up the wall, indicating the need for more pumping! By 1947, the Edgar children started to arrive and Joy complained that the water had bits in it and was no good for babies. The farmhouse had to be connected to the water main.

Before they rented the farm, it had often been used for hop growing, like most of the fertile land throughout the valley and even now, hops still grow in the hedgerows every year. Gordon wanted a dairy farm, following in his father's footsteps, except he farmed black and white Friesian dairy cattle, as they produced more milk than his father's Shorthorns. Joy was not allowed to deal with the herd, as Gordon firmly felt it was not woman's work and for that she was grateful. Her job was to fill in the accounts and farm ledgers. She enjoyed doing this, as she was already trained in ledger work from her previous job, in Westminster Bank. Book-keeping was perfect for her.

Hay making at Dunsdale Farm

Both children, Helen and David Edgar were born at Park Farm. When the birth of Helen was imminent, Miss Maylam the district nurse, summoned Dr Ward from the village and out he came. When he arrived at the house, he did no more than plonk himself on the settee with a book, calmly waiting for nature to take its course. Joy was in no mood to wait and told him, "never mind that book, let's get on with it," and they did. Sister Soap (sic), worked with the doctor and they frequently had arguments about how things should be done, but Dr Ward always won!

The doctor was a lovely man and quite a character. He would drive around, rather badly, in his little car. The windows were always wound down and the roof was open. This was the case even on the frostiest of mornings when he would simply put a jumper on for extra warmth!

One day Helen was nursing in Edenbridge and had a shocking fall. She had the family car with her and was unable to drive. The kindly, Dr Ward took Joy at 6 a.m., on a freezing cold morning, down to Edenbridge, where she was able to collect both her daughter and the car. We hope Joy remembered to wear a thick coat and very warm gloves, for the journey down in the good doctor's car!

At the farm, Dr Ward, would be most entertained by the farm cats. He would laugh out loud, when Joy called them and a trail of tabby cat tails wound their way across the yard. Each cat had its own special name.

The Edgars always kept dogs, usually spaniels. The river gave the dogs much pleasure and one favourite spaniel named Gemma would always jump into the deepest part with a huge splash. Once in, she would thrash around enjoying herself and come out shaking her soaking fur everywhere. On one occasion, they were walking in the woods and a cuckoo kept calling. The poor dog mistook the sound and thought she was constantly being called back by Joy or Gordon!

The family also had a terrier called Astor. Gordon had gone down to the forge in Brasted one day, for a repair job. Astor, rolled out into the yard and Gordon said, "I'll have her," and he did. Astor was a master at catching mice and rats and taught the other dogs how to hunt.

Brasted had many shops and between them, they supplied everything anyone could want. Folk would come in from Westerham for their shopping, as Brasted in those days, had such a good

Gemma

selection, with wonderfully friendly proprietors. Joy recalled how sad it is now, as Westerham has developed into a thriving community shopping centre, whilst Brasted has lost almost all of its shops. At that time, Joy would pack the children into her pram and walk into the village, for all her needs. The chemist shop was owned by Mr Hebb and, if Joy had any requirements for her children, Mrs Hebb would advise and help her.

Miss Swan had a superb haberdashery shop and Joy would take the children there, for any clothing needs. Miss Swan would sit them on the counter and tell them to hold their arms out straight. She would measure their wrists by wrapping socks around them. When the sock fitted, it was the right size for their feet, she never used a tape measure.

David could be a bit of a tinker as a boy, and liked to feed his sister berries that he found around the farm. One day, Joy was particularly worried and called in Dr Ward urgently. Again his calm advice was

100

to let nature take its course, which it safely did without any medical intervention.

On one occasion, Joy was busy ironing when out of the blue, a lady walked into her house. "Hello," she said, "I was born here!" It transpired that her father had lived in Park Farm for three years. Her father was an artist who had exhibited at the Royal Academy in London and, although Joy could not remember any names, the surprise meeting had left its impression on her.

Another time, a scout troop arrived on the farm. They had to practise marching and camping to gain their Duke of Edinburgh Awards. Joy had been in the brownies and guides and was most sympathetic to their request to stay overnight on the farmland. Somehow, it became obvious that in their antics, every single boy-scout had managed to fall into the river. Luckily Joy was prepared! She lit all the fires in the house and put fire guards around them, on which she laid out all their socks to let them dry. The next morning, their scout master had to further apologize, after some of the boys had lost their penknives in the hay. You could say they were dib-dib-dobbed in. The hay pile had to be laboriously taken apart to find the penknives, as they could not risk the cows accidentally eating them.

Joy talked of the day St Martin's Church burnt down in 1989. She was close by, in Mill Farm, quietly washing up, when she saw flames and smoke rising high into the sky. She heard the crack of the stain glass windows exploding. Gordon was at Park Farm and seeing the same smoke, rushed to Joy worrying that the fire was at Mill Farm. Joy was deeply upset and Gordon told her to stay away from the turmoil. She rang her daughter Helen, then living in the Channel Islands, who advised her to sit down and have a cup of coffee! As Gordon was rushing across the fields to Joy, Tony Curry, the rector, was also rushing across the fields from his home, in the rectory. Gordon, Tony and many other locals bravely dashed into the church to save whatever they could. The young man who had caused the fire was standing outside, watching the flames and the commotion and the police easily 'collared' him. However, he was a simple young man from Valence School and was deemed to have a mental disability. He could not be held responsible for his actions. Afterwards, Tony helped to rehabilitate the man and Joy felt that was a marvellous thing to have done and in that sense some good came out of a bad incident.

Joy now lives in Orchard Cottage, on the former Dunsdale farmland, close to Westerham Golf Club. She explained how the cottage came to the family. During the war, Grandpa Harry Edgar (Gordon's grandfather), his wife, Uncle Dudley and Aunt Phyllis Collier (née Edgar), all lived in Wimbledon. They hated being in the suburbs during the bombing and decided to move into Court Lodge Farm, with Reginald, their son. They asked grandson, Gordon to look for a suitable local property and Gordon found Stone House, part of Dunsdale farm. This farm was part of the Valence School complex. Harry managed to buy the house and subsequently built the bungalow, Orchard Cottage close by. Tragically, he died before he could move in. It is a lovely bungalow with pretty views across the fields and is far enough away from the A25, not to hear it rumbling. Just an idyllic spot and a serene happy place.

June 2016

Postscript – August 2017

Sadly, this lovely lady passed away on the 24th August 2017, after a short illness. Her service at St Martin's Church, was mostly the same as she had chosen for her dear Gordon. They are now buried together in a happy reunion.

Elizabeth Rich
née Sells

Elizabeth May Sells was born in December 1929 in the East End of London to her parents Charles Ernest Sells and Elizabeth Eveline Treadgold née Hanson. The family soon moved from London to Tatsfield, Surrey and then to nearby Biggin Hill, Kent. In 1937 her step-brother, Bob Treadgold took a job at The White Hart pub in Brasted and the family moved with him to the village. They rented a cottage in Coles Lane from Mr Palmer of Park Farm, Brasted. By 1939 Bob had become a boot repairer and used a hut at the end of their garden for his work. He also sold Wall's Ice Cream from his tricycle as he rode through the village. He would always carry a knife and if his clients could not afford the penny (1d) or two pence (2d) he would take his knife and cut the ice cream in half. Bob suffered from ill health so was not called up for military service during the war. Instead he worked for Mrs Hinton in Biggin Hill, cycling up each day to repair shoes. That still left him in the thick of danger from wartime action.

So life started in Brasted and Elizabeth, always known as Lizzie, went to Brasted School where the headmaster was Mr Warner. The two teachers were Miss Amy Cronk and Miss Jane Flora McDonald who taught the infants class. Miss Cronk wore glasses and would amuse the children by casually lifting the hem of her skirt to clean these glasses before placing them back on her nose. Mr Warner was strict and took the cane to the boys. One day he shook Lizzie and tore the seam of her jumper. She went home and her mother was furious. She did no more than go down to the school and have a terrible row with Mr Warner, he never did it again! He would also tell Lizzie's older sister Marjorie, "I wish you were more like your sister and stop talking so much!" The school children would be asked to collect rose hips which were made into rose hip syrup. It provided a rich source of vitamin C in times of food rationing when more regular sources were in short supply.

Lizzie with her grandparents and elder sister Marjorie Sell about 1934/5.

Just before the war, two of the school children were chosen to plant a cherry tree on Brasted Green almost opposite The White Hart pub. Charlie Bailey and Joyce Day from Barton Cottages were given the task and lifted the tree into a pre-dug hole. Sadly, the cherry tree later died and the horse chestnut that is still on the green was planted in its place.

Each Monday at school the children were given spellings to learn and the following Monday they were tested. Bob, her step-brother was sixteen years older than Lizzie and helped her each week to learn them. During the war the girls were urged to knit scarves for the soldiers and had to take their needles and yarn home. Lizzie produced a lot and was asked, "Does your mother help you?" "No", she replied, "my step-brother does!"

Lizzie would meet up with her buddies so they could walk to school together. They were Mary Sanders of Glebe Cottage, Church Road, Cathy Avery and Pam Still from Station Road. When they reached the Darent bridge in Church Road some of the boys would tease them and put a chain link barrier across the road to block their way. Ernie Swift, Roy Still and their friends found it very funny to hold them back until the school bell rang. The children would then have five minutes to get into school and the boys were older and ran much faster. Ernie earned the nicknamed 'Narna' a short version of banana and he kept that name for life. He must have had something special going for him as Mary Sanders fell for his charms and they married in 1956.

Many years later, Lizzie was in St Martin's Churchyard when a lady walked up to her. "You're Lizzie Sells aren't you? I'm Pam Still." Her brother Roy Still had emigrated to Australia. Lizzie smiled as she told this story as she'd always been threatened with being sent to Australia when she was naughty as a child. Now it is a place of choice for a new life.

Brownies was a thriving institution for the girls of the village until it was abandoned when the Second World War started. They would

106

meet in the 'Annexe' which was on the corner of Church Road and the A25. Today it is a private residence.

Sunday school took place in buildings behind the Baptist Church on the main road. Mr Oakley ran the school during the war, but he could hardly cope with the numbers. Marjorie Sells, Lizzie's sister, stepped in to help and took a class for younger children. They mostly studied the New Testament. Sometimes all the children sat together and were entertained with a magic lantern show.

On their birthdays they were sent up to Mrs Cramp who lived in a bungalow in Church Road. She would hand over a card with a verse to celebrate the occasion.

> 'Fear not: for I have redeemed thee
>
> ISA, 43:1

> May you know His wondrous peace,
>   And His love which cannot cease.
> So may the Lord your birthday bless
> With His own peace and happiness.'

The card would be signed, 'With all best wishes from The Sisterhood Members'

For naughty fun Lizzie and her friends would knock on doors and run away before they were answered, a fun game called 'knock down ginger'. Mr Eberlie of Brasted House was a good target as the door was always opened by the house keeper.

Lizzie never fancied swimming in the Brasted swimming pool as it was much too cold. It was two pence (2d) to swim and a penny (1d) to watch so she paid her penny (1d) and just watched. At the time

Mr Strickland ran the pool. He lived at Combe Bank Lodge almost opposite The White Hart pub. The children called it the spider house as it had boarded up windows and they were covered in spider webs.

During the war Lizzie remembered a barrage balloon floating above the field near the bridge in Church Road. Later it was moved closer to the train station. Lizzie and her friends would count the planes as they went out from RAF Biggin Hill and later count them back again. One day they were busy counting when someone shouted, "They're not ours," and they rushed inside their bungalow to the shelter. As the house did not have a cellar the family used a Morrison Shelter. This had a thick wooden top like a table and a cage-like construction underneath. In 1944, during a bombing attack, there was a terrific bang and when they came out all the hall mats were in a heap. A bomb had fallen in the field by the church and it had sadly killed a favourite horse of the local children. He was a large, white cart horse called Colonel and everyone was upset. The church was badly damaged too with broken windows, lost roof tiles and cracked walls, but the Sells household suffered no more than a few tiles off the roof and of course rucked up carpets!

Lizzie's mother Elizabeth, took in many evacuees who were allocated to Brasted households by Mrs Page of Village House. Her mother already had two or three children when she was asked to take three more. One little boy did not stay long as his mother quickly came and took him home. Two little girls aged three and a half and four and a half, both from London stayed much longer. One day, after she was married Lizzie answered a knock at her door. The two ladies announced they were Audrey and Helen Wilson, the two little evacuees. They had gone to the old bungalow and the next door neighbour, Ian Brown told them how to find Lizzie. To this day Lizzie is still in touch with one evacuee who had come to them from

Camberwell.

During the war Lizzie and her mother would go to Brasted Station and take the steam engine to London Bridge. Frances Treadgold, her step-sister, had married John Martin locally and then moved to Bow. Lizzie remembered the fare they paid was eleven pence (11d) and the ride as quite an adventure. She and her friends knew Mr Sidney Seal, the station master and he would let them ride for free to Westerham. Daphne Seal, his daughter, was a little older than Lizzie and also went to Brasted School.

Lizzie told me about the Day brothers delivering milk from Mill Farm. Arch would take off on his bicycle and Henry and Fred would drive a horse and cart. Lizzie told me the horse would bolt on hearing any loud sounds and all the children thought it was scary and were afraid of it. It could be spooked by anything, but especially passing army lorries and even tanks driving through the village. Mr Herbert Day lived at Barton Cottages and although not related he would regularly give Henry a cup of tea during his milk round.

Mr and Mrs Shorey lived in the High Street in a house called Streatfield. Lizzie said she loved the house as it was totally detached with no close neighbours and no noise! Mr Shorey had a field with some cows in Rectory Lane. He was often seen with a wooden yolk across his shoulders and milk churns hanging from each side. If a boy offered to do the carrying he was rewarded with two pence (2d). Along with her friends, Lizzie would gather up a jam jar on a piece of string and go fishing for tiddlers in Tanner's pond. "Ooh, it was as green as anything," she said smiling at the thought. The pond was filled in when Durtnells built a car park over it for their work vehicles.

When Lizzie was seventeen she learnt to drive in her father's Austin 7. Later, her father bought another Austin 7 which he had converted into 'van' style coachwork. Many Austin 7s were easily converted for different purposes including very successful racing car versions and for use as military vehicles. However, Mr Sells was delighted with his and let Lizzie take herself out in it. One day Lizzie borrowed the car and took it to Westerham. Driving up Madan Road a small boy rode into her path on his three wheeled trike. She swerved to miss him and hit a telegraph pole damaging both the front and back of this precious car. However, her father repaired and restored the coachwork and off they went again.

In 1951, Elizabeth Sells married William (Bill) Rich and set up home at 2 Elliotts Lane, Brasted. Bill was born in Brasted and had been brought up mostly by his gran while his mother worked in the fields. He was a chimney sweep whose partner was Mr Stan Seale from Sundridge. They would go about their business on a motorcycle with a box sidecar. Below is a 1947 advertisement for the sale of one of Bill's motorcycles.

William (Bill) Rich

1934 B.S.A. Three-wheeler, good condition; nearest £145.—Rich, 2, West End, Brasted.

After their respective marriages, the two chimney sweeps separated and each carried on successfully supporting their own families. Sometimes Lizzie would go out with Bill and once went to Chartwell. Hoping to see the house she was most disappointed as everywhere they went the rooms were covered in dust sheets. However, Lizzie worked in a house for a while on Hosey Hill and would often see Winston Churchill as he was driven by his chauffeur Joe Jenner who owned a taxi firm in Westerham.

Bill swept the chimneys in many of the local large houses and Lizzie also went to Squerryes Court with him. There they were ushered up to the top of the house and Bill needed help carrying his tools up so many staircases. Lizzie remembered the surprise of being confronted by a stuffed fox as they walked in through the main door.

Sometimes one or both of their sons would go out with their father. On a trip to Knole House, Sevenoaks young William went along and a man from the household walked in and said, "Do you want a look round, son?" It was no more than Lord Sackville himself and off they went together. Bill had a contract to sweep the chimneys of Walthamstow Hall School in Sevenoaks, an exclusive fee paying girls' school. He would come home saying, "That school is supposed to be posh, but you should see what the girls write on the walls!"

Bill had two allotments in the village and would spread his collected soot all over them. As in all good traditions he would often arrive home as black as the ace of spades and lucky it was too as superstition has it! In the winter when chimneys were in use, Bill would do some logging to stoke the fires ready for chimney sweeping in the summer period.

After their marriage and while in living in Elliotts Lane they had a handsome black cat called Monty. One day Monty arrived home with a fine plaice in his mouth which he must have stolen from Mr Kimber, the fishmonger. Lizzie laughed and said, "I couldn't take it back could I?"

Before having her family, Lizzie took a job in Bessels Green working in a typewriter factory, H M Rose at 47 Westerham Road. She showed me her plastic wages pot that her cash was put into each week. It was a typewriter ribbon case and still in good condition despite being nearly sixty years old!

On the 31st October 1961 they moved to 2 White Hart Cottages and in September, 1968 the cottage suffered severe flooding. It has flooded a number of times since, but on this occasion the water was about three feet deep and flowed straight through the front and back doors. Bill and Lizzie put their two sons upstairs and put a board barrier across the top of the stairs to keep them safe. Little voices kept asking, "Can we come down yet?" It ruined all their furniture. Mrs Bird from next door called out for help as she couldn't find her gas meter. Bill went next door only to find it was under the water and rather useless. Cars were always a problem during the floods and many people seemed to drive past just to look at the flood water. That was all very well, but they created waves that washed straight into the cottages.

As time went on Lizzie slowly watched the once thriving Brasted shops close. As the shop owners retired, moved on or died many of the premises became antique shops, others were converted into houses. For a while coaches would stop to allow tourists to walk around so many antique shops in such a short distance. As the village filled with cars and the High Street ran out of parking spaces even that tradition faded. As Westerham thrived Brasted diminished as inevitably life and times always move on.

July 2016

Postscript

Sadly, Bill died twenty years ago and Lizzie has finally been persuaded to move closer to her son in St Leonards, Sussex. After all these years she is leaving Brasted, but takes these wonderful memories with her. I have never met anyone that could remember the names of people from her past like Lizzie. What a privilege it was to hear such accurate stories.

John Blake

 In the meantime what was happening in the nearby village of Sundridge? John Charles Blake was born in April 1932. His parents were John Charles Blake senior, known as Jack, born in 1904 in Riverhead, Kent and mother, Florence Elizabeth Ayres, always called Cissy by her family and friends. She was another local girl born in 1907 in Sevenoaks, Kent. However, Florence's mother, Mary Alice Beard had a closer link to Brasted having been born in the village in 1881. At the time, her father was employed in the area as a shepherd.

John had a sister Betty, who was five years his junior. As none of the family used their given names, John is known to us all as either 'Blakey' or 'Jono' and his sister Betty was known as 'Bessie'. He and his sister were born in Rose Cottage in The Square, Sundridge. It was a small cottage partitioned into two dwellings. Mr Page lived next door, but currently the cottage has been renovated into one single property.

Where Jono grew up has changed quite a bit. The local village shops have gone and The Square is not obvious as the area around the traffic lights and close to The White Horse pub. There was once

Dove's the butchers, a post office, and a bakery in the village together with the old village hall. All have now gone, replaced by an office block, built into part of the area. Two cottages known as White Horse Cottages, were positioned right by the road in what is now the car park of The White Horse pub. The two Miss Browns shared one and Mr Wybourne lived with his family in the other. They were later pulled down to widen the main road. The pub was made larger and "messed up", as Jono put it.

Jono had many jobs as a boy, mostly designed to help his mother cope while his father was away on war duty with the Royal Army Service Corp. Before her marriage, Cissy worked in service and starched her cap and 'pinny' to perfection. Should any marks appear, they would have to be changed and washed completely again. After her marriage, she went out every day to clean houses to support her young family. This left Jono with the task of looking after his sister. Bessie went to Sundridge School and Jono went to Chevening School. Every lunchtime, Jono would run across the fields to collect Bessie and take her home for lunch. He would return her to school and rush back in time for his afternoon lessons. Some of his school buddies were Derek Pucknell and Des Hall. For entertainment they would roam across the local fields and the farmers would let them go anywhere they wanted. No one chased them out claiming they were on private property.

As a boy, one of Jono's Saturday jobs was delivering meat for Frederick Dove, the butcher. He wasn't allowed to use the bicycle and had to walk with his filled basket as far as Sundridge Hospital, about one and a half miles all uphill. For this he earned a shilling, which he promptly had to give to his mother.

The village baker, Percy Jeffrey was from Cowlard's Bakery, in

Brasted. He was known locally as 'the midnight baker', as most of his days were spent drinking in the pub so he had to deliver his bread at night!

The old milkman, Alfred Moody would call each day. He had a three-wheeled cart with a big milk churn in the middle and smaller ones around it. Cissy would leave a jug at the door, with muslin over it held in place by weighted beads. Mr Moody would stir the milk well, so no one had too much cream and then ladle it into the jug and cover it up again. Cissy worked for him for a while, washing out milk bottles, as the dairy was a short walk past The White Horse. She would then fill the bottles and Jono would put cardboard caps on top, as sealed caps were not yet available. The dairy was up a steep path behind houses and Jono often wondered how Mr Moody could push his fully laden cart, down the slope without it running away with itself and him. Talking of running away with itself, he also remembers seeing the Day brothers' milk cart and horse bolting through Sundridge, having run from Brasted. Their milk churn had tipped over and the milk spilled out in big blobs all the way down the road.

The family regularly picked hops and strawberries for Herbert Wood at Penn Lane, Ide Hill. Jono's Aunty Ayres was the forewoman and supervised the proceedings. Hops were picked into hop pockets. A few extra leaves were permissible, but not too much foliage or stems. Aunty Ayres would check the pockets and crossly empty out any that were not perfect. The hops were weighed by the bushel and paid by volume. Jono was just a nipper and he was nominated as the kettle boy. He would build a wood fire and boil up a billy can. He said, the trick was to put a little wood into the can to stop smoke contaminating the water. Everyone took something along to eat during the long working days.

Charlie Akhurst of Warren Farm, Sundridge would let Jono and his mates catch rabbits in the fields. They would take two ferrets and set up a net, one hundred yards long. The ferrets would spook the rabbits out of their burrows and they would hurtle themselves into the nets. There, the boys would 'clout' them over the head to finish them off. Next, they had to be gutted before they could be taken to Dove's Butchers. Mr Dove would give them sixpence (6d) a rabbit and the next day the boys would go back to collect the skins. When the rag and bone man came round shouting for business, he would give a penny (1d) for each rabbit pelt. All in all, theirs was quite a lucrative business. Occasionally the ferrets would stay down the rabbit holes and the boys would go back the following day and dig them out.

It was quite acceptable to take the odd cabbage or swede from the fields. No one took advantage and the farmers said nothing. If more were taken to be sold on, the farmers would certainly have taken action and the privilege removed.

Charlie sometimes asked Jono's dad, Jack to break in horses for his daughter. Jono told of one farm horse that he was very fond of. He was a Belgian draft horse called Nobby. He had the typical look of a strong, well-built, but compact horse. His legs were short, but as a breed they are renowned for their strength and stamina. Nobby would pull the hoe up and down the fields day after day, up and down, up and down. Mind you, at lunchtime his internal clock was perfect and he would simply stop and wait for his nose bag to be fitted. One day, Jono took him to Jack Stevens, the local blacksmith, "a lovely bloke." It was a very pleasant visit. However, Jono decided to ride Nobby bareback down the hill and across the fields to home. As the horse thundered on, Jono found himself bouncing uncontrollably forward and ended up sitting right behind Nobby's ears. Billy the Kid, he was not!

Frank Kimber was the farm carter and in charge of the horses. If things were not right, like dirty harnesses, he would certainly tell you in very plain English! He had a beautiful pair of grey horses that would pull the Westerham carnival wagon each year.

Scrumping was a good way to spend some hours, so the boys would go into an orchard near Sundridge Church. If someone came along they would have to scale a huge brick wall and drop eight feet down the other side to the road. Surprisingly, no one broke any bones, but they were apt to limp all the way home!

The local farms had chickens wandering free and the boys would follow them and watch carefully. If they went under a hedge and squawked loudly they knew the chicken was laying an egg and, if they were lucky, they might find half a dozen under there. These were welcome additions to the larder. When Jono and his mates turned their hand to collecting swans' eggs, that was an altogether more dangerous experience. Jono tried to take one from a nest on the pond at Combe Bank. The swan spread her wings and attacked wildly. Jono ran like hell to save himself and never tried it again!

In winter, Jono and his father would go to the pond by Combe Bank to ice skate. Jack had a pair of wooden clogs with horseshoes nailed to the bottom, to form a blade. This helped him glide across the ice. In more destructive mood, the boys would go with hobnail boots and stamp on the frozen lake. If it squeaked and cracked they high-tailed it off the ice, before they fell through. In better weather they would go fishing in the pond for bream and chub. One day, Jono took the catch home. It stank horribly and his mother would not allow it in the house. So Jono left it outside that evening, in the hope that it would mellow overnight. It had certainly done something, and that was to disappear - probably taken by a purring cat!

Sometimes the boys would walk into Brasted and pay their money to swim in the pool. Mr Strickland was the pool attendant and when their time was up he would yell at them to get out. "Blooming freezing it was too," said Jono.

Fairy cycles were a good mode of transport and were kept together by any means. One time, Jono had a frame and rear wheel and with good fortune, he found a pram wheel in the hedge. It became his front wheel and that bike did a good turn around the area. The bikes were basic and brakes were very manual! Jono would stand on the pedals and put his foot back onto the rear tyre to stop it. On another occasion he had a ladies' cycle and riding down Worships Hill, the welding broke and the front wheel shot off. He splattered into the road, but recovered unhurt.

A fun mode of transport for the children were homemade go-carts. Ideally, they had two sets of pram wheels with axles that could be fixed to a central board. The board pivoted in the centre and two pieces of rope were attached to each side of the board to enable the driver to tug on either side and steer the cart. A favourite downhill section was from Sundridge Church to the A25 crossroads. Unfortunately, Jono had gathered such speed by then, the only way to stop was to crash into The White Horse wall! "You had to be careful as they could take the backside out of your pants and mother would go mad," he said. "You dare not put your feet down either, as you would ruin the bottom of your shoes!"

The local bobby was Sergeant Reginald Giles, known as Gy-lo. He knew everyone and certainly the true villains. "He was a good old boy", said Jono. "If you did something wrong you could expect a box round the earhole! It was no good crying, because you knew it was wrong." In 1931 PC Giles was called to an East Surrey bus that had caught alight near a petrol tank. He borrowed a fire extinguisher from a car, and at considerable risk to himself managed to subdue the flames. By the time the fire brigade arrived the blaze was mostly under control. He was also presented with a bronze medal by the RSPCA, for bravely rescuing a snarling, injured dog in Sevenoaks. Sadly, PC Giles died prematurely at the age of forty seven, after a long illness. He had served Sundridge for nearly fifteen years.

Jack Blake was in the Royal Veterinary Corps when he first started his army career and animals featured in Jono's home life. They had a wonderful Heinz 57 variety dog called Peggy. She was much loved by the family. Jack worked at the Dryhill Quarry, digging stone until its closure in the 1950s. An owl had a nest close by, but the female was killed, so Jack took on the care of the two babies. They became devoted to him and would travel everywhere on his shoulders. They even went to work each day, sitting tight while Jack cycled up the lane to work. Sadly, it was finally decided that they had to go, as the neighbours were complaining about the night time, "hooty, hooting!"

During the war, there was much fighter plane activity over Sundridge and several of them crashed close by. On the 7th September 1940, Jono remembered a hearsay story of heroism, although he did not witness the incident itself. Spitfire X4009 was thought to have run out of ammunition and as it spiralled down it collided with a German Dornier 17 plane and brought it down. The Dornier crashed behind West Kent Laundry in Sundridge. The German crew died and were buried in Sundridge Churchyard. Jono and his friends, Mike Morris and Jonny Hartshorn, made a sign for them that read, "Here lies someone's daddy." However, Mr Brealey, the Parish Councillor was furious and made them take it down again. The boys were upset, because if it had been one of their fathers, they would have liked someone to do the same for them!

Still, on the devastating side of war and that particular event, the Spitfire pilot was Flt. Lt. (Pat) Paterson Clarence Hughes, an Australian native born in Cooma, New South Wales. He was leading the men of Squadron 234 stationed in Middle Wallop, Hampshire. His plane was damaged in his attack and was spinning downwards. As it fell it collided with the Dornier, probably more by luck than judgement. He did eject from his crippled plane, but his parachute candlesticked (never opened) and he fell into the garden of what is now 16 Main Road, Sundridge. On the 7th September 2005, a service took place in the garden to honour Pat and a brass plaque was presented for his gallantry. It is on the wall, by the front door of the bungalow, for anyone to see. The service was taken by the Reverend David Attwood of Sundridge Parish Church. It concluded with a one-minute silence and then a fly past by two Spitfires from Biggin Hill Airfield. In 2008, the Shoreham Aircraft Museum installed a memorial beside Main Road, close to where he fell, for everyone to see. Pat was presented with the DFC (Distinguished Flying Cross) for his bravery, in his successful and celebrated short time flying with the RAF.

As a small point of interest, the laundry site where the Dornier crashed had been converted from a paper mill. The mill had been responsible for making the paper used for the old, large, white five pound (£5) notes which were legal tender until 1961.

Another Spitfire came down and crash-landed at old Chipstead corner, planting its nose into a bank. The visual damage was no more than a broken propeller, although the engine may have failed, to cause the crash. The pilot was spotted running across the field, up a bank and back to the road. There he found a lift to take him straight back to RAF Biggin Hill and into another Spitfire. A bomb dropped in the marsh area opposite the old Lamb pub in Sundridge, blowing out its windows. The crater is still there, to be seen today.

On another occasion a Heinkel 111 crash-landed on Moxson's Farm in Church Road, Sundridge. Jono and his mates watched it come down and started to rush across the fields, hoping to be first on the scene. They had plans to arrest the crew themselves! However, rather luckily, the Canadian army had also seen the landing and beat them to it. The boys stopped in their tracks when an army officer emerged from his vehicle, carrying a huge gun. The German flight crew survived and were arrested by the Canadians.

In Sundridge, during the Second World War all the planes that crashed in the south of England were collected and stored ready for recycling back into the war effort. Some even came out of the sea and still had crabs in them! They were dumped on top of each other in a meadow, on the right hand side of Combe Bank Drive. The area had formally been a small aerodrome and landing strip, built around 1910. The hangars were later converted to a bus station. Jono would watch the guards in the field and, at any opportune moment, he and his mates would make their way to any planes with Perspex in them. Having cut it out, they would make jewellery, like rings and hearts, with stones in for their girlfriends. It was a laborious job, as all the melting and shaping had to be done over a candle. At night when it was pitch black, the crabs made a scary scratching noise that sounded quite ghostly. He noted that you could always tell the German planes. They 'smelled' different to the British planes! After the war this site had to be returned to its original condition and all signs of the planes disappeared. The barracks were demolished and the site is now a housing development as a spur of Combe Bank

Drive. The RAF vehicle repair hangar, opposite the barracks was also dismantled.

Jono would watch Mr Dove go out in his uniform as a Home Guard officer. He smiled, as he remembered they would sleep overnight in an old car, up Chevening Road. The fields were covered in poles with wire running between and a barrage balloon flew close by. The Home Guard were stationed there for any downed planes or German parachutists. The idea was to catch any enemy running through the barriers. One day, Bob Hall spotted a doodlebug overhead and took the only rifle they had and fired at it. For such boldness, or should that be foolhardiness, he was put on a charge for wasting ammunition. Sometimes things just ain't fair!

Another barrage balloon was flown on Pilgrims Way, close to Westerham Hill. There was an army rifle range close by. A sign hung at the entrance to the balloon field, which read:

Happy band of Pilgrims
If onwards you would tread
Come and get a cup of tea
Before you go to bed

The Observer Corp was stationed on Brasted Hill. It would watch and identify planes as they flew near them. If they were enemy planes, they would ring RAF Biggin Hill so the aircraft could be intercepted.

Combe Bank was used as a military convalescence home during the war. The officers could often be seen walking around the village. Rose Cottage was well named, as the garden was full of roses. Jono would sell them a bunch to take home to their wives or girlfriends at the weekends. Cissy would go to Combe Bank to collect ENSA (Entertainments National Service Association) tickets and then attend concerts in the hall there. These were available to both military personnel and civilians.

It was in the River Darent that some of the best watercress grew. On Sundays, Jono would climb into the water and scoop it out. He was tasked with dividing it into bundles and Jack would sell it at The Lamb. Jono mused that he didn't get anything for his work and, on complaining, his father would start with, "I have kept you for……" and there was no arguing with a sentence starting like that!

Rose Cottage had a Morrison shelter for protection from masonry and debris, should a bomb explode near the house. During the day it served as a table and at night it became a cage for the family to sleep under. However, Jono could be found more often than not, outside watching the skies. The search lights would pick up flying aircraft and off went the ack-ack guns from somewhere close by. In the morning, pieces of debris and shrapnel littered the ground. On one occasion, Jono passed a bungalow as usual, on Chevening Road, walking home from school. The next morning it was a pile of rubble having taken a direct hit from a bomb. The family inside were all killed in this tragedy.

Mr Hutty had a paper shop (now the medical centre) in Sundridge and was often seen driving around in his Austin 7 Tourer with his two Dalmatian dogs eagerly enjoying a ride. This car had a canvas roof which was mostly removed so Mr Hutty and the dogs could feel the wind in their hair. One day he was returning from his wholesaler with the dogs as usual and his stock needs. Coming around Chipstead Corner he managed to turn the car over and Mr Hutty and the dogs were thrown out along with hundreds of cigarettes rolling across the road. The dogs caused havoc running out of control while the cigarettes were spread all over. As luck would have it, an army lorry was just passing and the soldiers jumped out to help. They put the car back on its wheels, caught the dogs and picked up the cigarettes. All safely reinstalled Mr Hutty took off again to complete his journey. This car must have been a little battered as another story also has Mr Hutty going **** over tip and being hauled back onto his wheels again!

Jono left school just before his fourteenth birthday. He took an apprenticeship with Stanhaye, later taken over by Sennocke Company Engineering in Sevenoaks and Stormont Company Engineering in Tunbridge Wells. Jono learnt to drive in a Morris 8 service van, which belonged to the Sennocke Company. He stayed with the company until he was eighteen and left in 1948 to join the army. As his father had done before him, so he too joined the Service Corps and was sent to peace-keep in Trieste, Italy. It was a free state and he had a great time in what he described as, "a lovely posting". His service career lasted two and a half years, as the extra six months guaranteed him only three years registered as a reservist, instead of the usual five years, if he had left after two years.

Back home, his next job was with Bowser, the Sundridge coal merchants. The company shared a yard at Brasted Station, with George Alderson, who also ran a coal merchants business. It was somewhat embarrassing that Cissy used George Alderson's coal. One day, she ordered a bag of nutty slack and Jono undertook to deliver it in his Bowser truck. Unfortunately, Mr Bowser was drinking in The White Horse and spotted him removing the sack and tipping it into the coal bin. "You owe me money for that sack," he said. "No, I don't," was the reply, but it was difficult to explain that the coal had come from Aldersons! "You should use my coal," was Bowser's parting shot.

On Sundays, Jono would shovel fourteen tons of coal out of the bins, in the train yard and two days later had to shovel whatever wasn't sold back again. The vans were hired from the railway and if they were not returned on time, empty and clean, Bowsers risked being fined. This system was called demurrage. For that task Jono earned ten shillings (10s) and, "it was hard work."

Sometimes, they would load up the coal and stop in Brasted for a cuppa (tea), or the gaffer might buy breakfast. Jimmy Well's Transport Café in the village offered a welcome stop and the High Street could just about take a row of parked lorries and vehicles. Tom Maudsley, had a high class café and newsagents opposite and he was furious that so much transport took up all the parking. Goodness, it was a welcome stop though, at any time of the day.

Another Bowser job for the summer season, was delivering strawberries to London. Tommy Walton from Halstead had fruit and flower stalls in all the London Underground stations and the strawberries were destined for each stall. Two men went and one always stayed with the lorry when it was parked, "because of the local children. We wouldn't have none left," recalled Jono, smiling at the memory. The Walton family had long been victuallers and, in the 1881 census, The Rose and Crown pub in Halstead was run by Charles Walton, Tommy's father. It is a grade II listed, flint-built pub and still celebrates Tommy today with pictures of him across its walls. Trams ran in London at the time and many of them lost wing mirrors to Jono as he tried to manoeuvre the strawberry lorry between the pavement and tramlines. The old tram drivers would ring their bells, but Jono was away and travelling.

Occasionally, Jono would be asked to drive the Bowser school coaches if the normal driver was off sick. "I wasn't a proper coach driver though, like Tom Lawrence who drove the Alderson coaches." Still he was tasked with picking up school children, in Ide Hill and Toys Hill and taking them to Westerham School.

Jono worked for Westerham Brewery three times, on and off; first as a driver and later as a drayman. It was thanks to the brewery, that Jono met his future wife. Her father worked for the firm and took a small team of people out with him one day. There was not enough room on top, so Jono found himself crawling under the canvas. There beside him, he found Ted Boake's daughter Mary, and as they say, the rest is history. "Beer has always got me into trouble," he said, smiling broadly, but not elaborating!

Jono also had dealings with the blue buses at the Sundridge garage. He remembered as a boy that they looked so big, but he was tasked with driving the last George Alderson coach to Stanley Berwick Ltd. The coach, a twelve seater Bedford vehicle, was very narrow and known affectionately as the bean can. The driver was seated centrally and in order to make hand signals he would balance on the left cheek of his bottom so that he could put his arm out of the window to signal. At Berwicks, it was used to take the local workforce back and forth, while building new houses, on the old West Malling airfield. At the time, Jono was working for City Timbers in Brasted, but he was given time off to move the coach. While the bus station was still located in Sundridge, the last bus had a special duty. It would collect the local farmers and customers from The Red Lion pub, in Ide Hill. The driver would individually deliver each drunken, merry person to his or her own front door before finishing for the night. How sad that this type of service barely exists today!

After his marriage, Jono moved to Westerham to live with his in-laws and worked for two years for Westerham Brewery. Then Jono and

Mary moved to Charcot where they were allocated a brand new 'pre-fab'[7]. He said it was the most up to date building there was with a built in fridge and washing machine. The heating came through a hole in the skirting board and if the dog was covering it up, the place was freezing. A shoe or two thrown in the direction of the dog soon moved it on! From Charcot it was impossible to get to Westerham for work, so instead Jono changed his employment to the Kent County Council depot at Penshurst Station. You could leave a job on Friday and pick up a new job by Monday back then! There he would go out to mow council grounds sometimes with manual machines, but if the normal driver was away he would drive the Ferguson tractor with the attached mower. It had a peg sticking out on the side and if he got too close to the edges it would break. Far better to break the peg than the mower! Inside the tractor was a whole box of the hazel wood pegs ready to replace the broken ones. One task was to wash and repaint road signs. The first day the white post was painted and the next day the black lettering was painted.

However, missing their family, Jono and Mary soon moved back to Westerham. Jono had many jobs some full time and some odd jobs that were often given out over a pub bar. "You either earned a couple of pints of beer or perhaps ten bob (ten shillings) for these jobs." When Timmy Wells moved into the transport café in Brasted High Street the place was a terrible mess. He asked Jono to get him a couple of bundles of battens from Morewoods, near Tubs Hill. He did and Timmy provided him with free breakfasts for weeks.

---

[7] A prefab was a pre-fabricated house built in post war Britain to address the acute housing shortage brought about by war time destruction. Although originally built as temporary homes, many prefabs are still in use today.

One day with no transport, Jono was walking down Westerham High Street at 4 a.m., with his tool bag. The local bobby spotted him and immediately wanted to know what he was up to. "I'm going to do a job," was his surprising answer. "What job would that be?" asked the policeman suspiciously, but it was a repair to a car that was needed for that working day. So Jono walked to the yard and the policeman accompanied him. Seeing everything was fine he left Jono to it. Later he came back and Jono cheekily said, "You are just the kiddy, can you help me?" So he handed him a rope and together they manoeuvred the gearbox back into position. This time the officer left saying, "They will never believe this back at the police station!"

On a more long term basis, Jono went to work for English China Clays based in St Austell, Cornwall. The clay was used in many manufacturing businesses and Jono was part of the delivery service. He was sent all over the country, from Cumbria to Kent and could book a night's stay away, when necessary. He would take his load to Watford for the Basildon Bond Paper Co. Milk of Magnesia was a major use of china clay and was a popular product for all sorts of stomach disorders. Many pills and potions have china clay in them, so most of us have used it, one way or another. At weekends Jono could park his trailer in the layby near Redland Tile Co., in Dunton Green. He would then drive his cab back home to Westerham. Monday he was off again for the week, until the following Saturday. After fifteen years, Jono decided to leave and asked that China Clay give his job to a young man with a family and mortgage to support.

During the 1987 hurricane Jono heard nothing, not a whisper! He left Westerham in the morning and picked up his mate Harry Sanders, to take them both off to work. At the traffic lights in Sundridge the road towards Combe Bank was closed, so they blithely went on down the main road. It really wasn't until Dunton Green that everything was blocked and they could get no further. Harry left the lorry to walk back to the yard, to find a JCB, or something to clear the fallen trees. He failed to get help, but the road was finally cleared by lunchtime. The owner of their company, Mr Lavers senior, lived in French Street. He sued his neighbour, as he had been complaining that a big tree in his neighbour's garden was dangerous. In the storm it came down on his tennis court; ouch!

The yard was at the bottom of Star Hill, under Fort Halstead. "Old Harry, my mate, used to patrol the boundary. If he was bored, he would walk up to the top of the quarry and run a stick across the fence with the fort. The alarm would go off and the guards jumped to attention. Old Harry, he would quickly scarper down again."

Jono retired in 1997 and has been enjoying himself ever since. On reflection, what did he miss and what had changed in his lifetime?

"Pub life has changed so much and no one makes conversation anymore." With China Clay, Jono could go to any pub and in no time the locals would be chatting to him. They would take an interest in what he did and talking was easy. Not only that, they would remember him the next time. That was Jono's sadness and like many people as they retire and get older, the local village pub is one of the only places people gather, for company and friendship.

November 2016

Harold Cuckow

Harold's father Leslie Frank Cuckow was born in August 1903, at 2 Algernon Terrace, High Street, Brasted and lived in the village most his life. He grew up with his parents with his parents George and Kate and his sister Kathleen. After their deaths, George and Kate were buried together in St Martin's Church, Brasted. His sister, Kathleen lived at number 2 all her life, and Leslie moved from Brasted to Westerham.

Leslie Cuckow married Bertha Yeomans and their son Harold in 1935 was born while the family were living in Westerham. Harold was educated at Hosey Hill School. He says that during the war the word education was not strictly true, lifting his eyebrows to express the lack of teaching. He said, the children spent most of their time down 'holes', sheltering from German bombing attacks. He recalls that when the children were at school at the end of play breaks the headmaster would give two blasts on his whistle to summon the pupils back. The first whistle signalled that everyone should stand still with no talking. Well, the playground had no fencing and in the quiet you could hear all the 'nibbos'[8] who had strayed into the woods, careering back to the playground. With a crash, bang wallop

---

[8] Children

out flowed the heroes from their cowboys and Indian games. Harold said, "they were knackered when they got back". If anyone spoke after the first whistle it was one hundred lines detention.

Out of school, they would happily and safely play in the streets. Westerham had many terraced houses which presented an opportunity for mischief as they could thread string through maybe five door knockers; then, at the given moment they would pull each end and 'leg it' like mad as each resident came to answer the 'knock' on their doors.

Harold's Aunt Kathleen helped to run the Brasted Red Cross through the war years. He remembered her wearing a very smart tunic for her duties. He, like many local children, collected war souvenirs, such as spent cartridges and shrapnel. On one occasion, one of our planes, flown by a Polish pilot, was shot down near Hogtrough Hill at the crossroads with the Pilgrims Way and that was a major target for the young collectors. They would then swap items and perhaps get a marble or some other small prize in return. Adults particularly would rush to collect

Aunt Kathleen and
father Leslie

Perspex from the downed planes. Harold remembers listening to Lord Haw Haw and would shout back, "Oh, shut up," to his propaganda spiel.[9]

---

[9] Lord Haw Haw was an Irish American who broadcast German propaganda to Britain in the Second World War in a programme called *Germany Calling*.

In the early days of German bombing, some families dug trenches in their garden to protect themselves from shrapnel. Many families simply hid under the stairs or under tables. Later on, Anderson and Morrison shelters became generally available for better protection. He remembers that the Spitfires at RAF Biggin Hill would be airborne, even before the air raid sirens sounded. Later the valley was filled with barrage balloons and big guns, as the area was a gateway to London and RAF Biggin Hill was a major and vulnerable target onto which any unused German bombs could be dropped after raids over London! The German planes would come in low and howling. The kids all felt that if they could hang up nets they could catch them.

Some local households did their bit for the war effort by billeting the allied airmen. Brasted House was requisitioned to house Canadian soldiers, as were many others. Harold remembered the Canadians did not like the statue of General Wolfe in Westerham and they turned it around to face backwards. They even put ladies' underwear on it. What an interesting sight that must have been!

Harold moved back to Brasted around the age of sixteen and has lived at 1 Algernon Terrace ever since. As he reached eighteen years of age, he joined the 1st Battalion Royal West Kent Regiment. He is very proud of his regiment and has made a hobby of collecting regimental memorabilia. He told me that during the war in Burma, five hundred men from the regiment successfully held up about three thousand of the ten thousand strong Japanese 15th Army, to keep the Indian border open. He was too young to fight in the Second World War, but finished his army career in Cyprus before returning home.

By trade Harold was a master joiner, as was his father and grandfather before him. He worked for himself and took great pride in his workmanship. All of the projects he worked on came through recommendation and he made everything by hand. He had blade sharpeners to keep his tools in tip-top condition and would sharpen Mr Rich, the chimney sweep's circular saw when he was busy logging during the winter. Villagers would also arrive at his workshop to have their knives sharpened when they were blunt.

His carpentry jobs would vary from the smallest task to building barns and working in large houses in the district. He helped to upgrade properties in Algernon Terrace and described how the cottages had small black hearths to cook on and little coppers for the washing. The only sinks were decorated, white porcelain, with just a three inch depth. He mused on how large families managed with such simplicity. He would often personalise his work by including his initials in the finished articles. Most houses had sash window cords and he was kept busy repairing them. By his reckoning, there are countless weight boxes balancing window sashes with his initials inside them. "There must be hundreds all over the district," he said. Recently he was called to Brasted House where renovations were underway.   A wooden panel had been taken down and there, behind, was his father's name, L F Cuckow and a little boy's name, H J Cuckow (that is Harold) with the date 1943. He had been at school when his father did the work.

He remembers his father telling him that, as a young boy he would swim in the River Darent. He, along with his little buddies, boys and girls would strip off and build a dam across the river to give themselves deeper water. As a result, the mill in Brasted would see its water level drop and furious adults would arrive to break their dams.   Sometimes they were caught in the act, but on many occasions they scarpered, escaping by the skin of their teeth. During this time, several springs were discovered beside the river, one of which had a very active flow of water. Lord Stanhope, along with other businessmen, stepped in and helped finance the digging of the Darent Valley Swimming Baths at the Recreation Ground. Many locals volunteered to help with the digging and, in 1913, the project was underway. The pool was dug at full size, with both a shallow and a seven foot deep end. It was river fed and absolutely freezing. Harold's father and grandfather helped by making the three diving boards. There was a high diving board, a shoot and a sprung diving board on the bank of the pool. Both men were asked to be involved with the opening ceremony, but Harold could not recall the details of their roles.

The swimming pool was well used and caused great rivalry between the Westerham and Brasted youths. There was much sadness when shortly before the closure of the baths, a boy drowned and the lack of lifeguards became a big and controversial problem. Sadly, the baths closed in 1953, after they became contaminated and were deemed dangerous. The contamination came from rubbish brought in from London, which was dumped into landfill inside the Recreation Ground and this sludge slowly seeped into the ground, affecting the quality of the river water used to fill the pool. A few years earlier, the outdoor pool was allowed to stay open during the polio epidemic. The water flow in and out of the pool was considered fast enough to expel any living infections though other indoor pools were closed in a bid to stop the disease spreading.

In his earlier days, Harold worked at the Recreation Ground and described how vehicles would drive up towards the river and release caught foxes. The same happens today with urban foxes from London being released in the 'countryside'. Sadly a number of these foxes and their offspring meet their end on the busy A25 as the traffic moves so quickly.

People too have to keep their wits about them, as the village is much busier than it used to be with traffic. Harold can recall a much more peaceful time on the roads. Days before the motorway opened in 1979, he walked with his family from Westerham to Brasted on the new motorway carriageway. Many local families did the same. It's not to be recommended nowadays of course, as even breaking down on the motorway can put you in major mortal danger from other vehicles hurtling towards you!

Harold described how the village hall would host a monthly social gathering. For one pound (£1) you would get a countryman's supper, consisting of cheese and pickle rolled up in French bread with salad. Live music was played and many danced the night away. Often a talented gentleman, with an electric organ, would play through the evening, before returning to his daytime job of driving for Bowsers coaches, in Westerham. The hall was open from 7 p.m. to 11.30 p.m.

There is a granite stone wall next to Harold's property which was once the boundary of The Bull Inn car park. It was not demolished when the new houses were built there in 2013. Harold explained that the wall enclosed the Bull barn, which was home to some bullocks. The wall was protected by a preservation order and cannot now be removed. In the 1970s, there used to be a chicken farm between Harold's garden and The Bull Inn car park where Ken Reeves, a village postman, kept forty or fifty chickens to supply the village shops. The local children were encouraged to collect the eggs for him. His farmland was rented from Miss Wells, who lived over the road, at what is now Old Orchard.

Harold's reflections about today's world and how things have changed, is one of sadness that no one sits and talks. In his childhood days, people would gather at the pub and have a pint and a chat. A lot of families had no husbands or fathers at home as they were undertaking military duties, with perhaps ninety percent away fighting and maybe sixty percent never coming home. Everyone had to work very hard to support and help their families as there were no government handouts and no National Health Service until 1948. A visit to the pub and a game of shove ha'penny or darts was a highlight to relax and find a release from the stresses of the day. Friends would stop by without needing an invitation and he knew most people in the village. There were village dances, Women's Institute (WI) for the ladies, flourishing church meetings, with outings and socials. There were no televisions or computers and the art of conversation thrived. Now, he watches young people just one minute from their homes, playing on their phones. Even in groups they don't talk to each other, as they are all so preoccupied with themselves.

Harold is a great animal lover and has two cats in the house, four rabbits, two canaries in his lean-to and six hens at the end of his garden. The wild birds fight over his seed-filled feeders, completely ignoring any humans passing by. His garden is a mixture of home-grown vegetables and many colourful flowers. There are no solid, six foot fences, only wire mesh at his boundary, just as it always was. In his garden are comfy chairs for Harold to invite guests to come and sit and pass the time of day. But for the noise of the passing traffic, Harold's visitors are then transported back to a social age gone by!

May 2016

Neil Taylor

Neil Taylor was born in April 1935 in Wimbledon, the son of Robert Cecil Taylor and Evelyn Florence, née Carson. Robert always moved to follow his work, mostly as a builder and sometimes as a farm worker and Wimbledon had been a temporary location for the family. The family moved to Sundridge when Neil was around three years old and the following year they moved to a bungalow in Coles Lane, Brasted. However, they were soon on the move again, this time to a brand new house; 13 West End. This was close to his uncle George at number 20 and his sister, Aunt Flo Standing at number 24, both siblings of Robert.

In 1940, Neil's mother had twins and the huge coachwork pram she wheeled them in was heavy and not very manoeuvrable. She struggled to get it up the front steps to the house, with the last step being so deep, the pram just would not go up it. The back door was also impossible to access, as it had a long step down, with a small path immediately in front of a garden shed. This meant that the pram could not be taken out into the back garden at all. As a result, Robert decided to move his family overnight into number 10; a house which was still standing empty and was on flat land. When Mr Warwick, the rent man, arrived on Monday as usual, he was confronted by an empty number 13 and had no idea where the family had disappeared to!

The West End houses were originally built for the sole use of Brasted parishioners, but there were not enough of them seeking the available accommodation, so Sevenoaks Rural District Council had to look further to Sundridge and surrounding villages to fill all the properties. As a result, several of those houses stood empty until they were officially filled, which is why Robert and his family, had the opportunity to do a quick house swap!

The family settled into the village where Neil has lived ever since. Harold (Harry) Taylor, Neil's grandfather, worked for a while at Court Lodge Farm for the Edgar family. He drove the Shire horses that ploughed the fields. Neil remembers walking up to the fields to give his grandfather his lunch of bread, cheese and either an apple or an onion. He carried a small canister of cold tea. If it was raining, Harry would tuck himself under a hedge, with a hessian sack over his head for shelter as he took his break.

Neil started school in Brasted where he was rather prone to earning himself the cane. The headmaster, Mr Warner would open his desk drawer to reveal at least a dozen canes. The offender was asked to choose his cane and the boys knew that the thickest cane would hurt the least. Mr Warner must have known that too as he then simply picked his favourite weapon, a cane that had split from over use and then been fixed with any number of sticking plasters holding it together. He would stand flexing it before commencing with a boy's punishment. Neil figured out that if he put his hands on the boiling hot radiator pipes the cane somehow didn't hurt so much. One day at school, young Jonny Rich was shaken so hard by Mr Warner that he took the skin off his shoulders. Next day his mother walked up to

Mr Warner and shook the living daylights out of him!

Every few days, two strong boys were chosen to take a wheelbarrow up to Heverswood in Chart Lane, where they were loaded up with potatoes and vegetables for school lunches. The boys loved that duty, as they were officially excused from lessons. However, the children considered the dinners were notoriously horrible and cost one shilling and five pence halfpenny (1s 5½d) per week. Miss Rolfe of 3 Thorne Cottage was the cook and Mrs Annells, from 2 Cypress Cottages, was the assistant cook. The children thought that the cabbage was always overcooked into a mushy, yellow looking pile. However, they were still expected to eat it and if the meal was uneaten when school lessons started, that child would be left still sitting in front of his plate.

Heverswood and the gardens

For the last six months of his schooling the senior Brasted children were transferred to a new school in Westerham. Local businessmen George Bowser and George Alderson were in charge of the transport to and from the new school. One morning, Neil was running around in the playground, as boys do and suffered a severe asthma attack. At 9.30 a.m. he was sent home and had to walk back from Westerham to Brasted. He remembers having such difficulty breathing that he sat down under a hedge to recover. He was still sitting in the hedge when the afternoon school transport rolled past him without stopping. Children would simply not be treated like this now with the duty of care rules we have in place today.

Neil suffered badly from asthma attacks and missed a lot of schooling. That lack of learning was compounded by his mother developing cancer and needing to be looked after by all the family. She died in 1947 and Neil was not allowed to attend her funeral. He was left in the care of Mrs Day at home in West End. However, he found a way out and snuck up to the church and hid behind a tombstone. Unfortunately, he was discovered and dragged back to school where he was duly caned again. This time he was told that if he wasn't with Mrs Day then he had to be at school and nowhere else was acceptable.

To help cope with the asthma and stay fit, Neil was a keen swimmer. He was a frequent visitor to the Darent Valley Swimming Baths at the Recreation Ground where he could buy a season ticket for two shillings and sixpence (2s 6d), which enabled him to swim every day between 11 a.m. to 6 p.m. Then when everyone went home from the baths at the end of the day, he used his season ticket which allowed entry to the swimming pool out of hours. He recalled that the pool was fed by eleven fresh water springs. It was twenty-five yards wide and fifty yards long with a gravel bottom. For a whole year he would swim every single day, even breaking the ice first if necessary. If he dived in to complete a width, it would only take him one stroke to get to the other side and then he would rush back shivering to the changing rooms. In Spring, the Electric Light Company would be called in to start the pump to empty the pool for cleaning. It took about three days to fully empty the pool and then it could be cleared of grass, weed, frog spawn and anything else that covered the drains.

At weekends, he felt it was no exaggeration to say hundreds of cyclists from various clubs would spend the whole day at the pool. It was so packed with visitors enjoying the water and picnicking that there just wasn't room for any ball games. He remembered two people drowning at different times, one being a vicar's son and the other happening just before the baths closed. In the end, Durtnells, the building company in Brasted, wanted to buy the swimming pool, but Sevenoaks Council refused and it was closed down in the early 1950s.

School swimming lessons with the Churchill School in Westerham, were held in a swimming pool attached to the St Botolph's Church of England (C of E) School in Chipstead Lane, Chevening. Each class was packed onto the steam train at Westerham Station and travelled to Chevening Halt. They walked from there down to the school. Neil always had to go, but was made to sit and watch for fear of an asthma attack in the water.

The Second World War provided plenty of escapades for young boys. One Sunday lunchtime they watched the Luftwaffe fly over, just above the trees. They could see the pilots looking around and waved at them! No one was scared; it was just the thing to do. However, the aircrew soon dropped their bombs and John Groom's Children's

Home, over by the Pilgrims Way, was damaged that day. A V2 rocket later fell in Madan Road, Westerham on Sunday 11th March 1944, causing widespread damage and one fatality.

Neil's family only went into an air raid shelter once and that was in Mrs Dailly's garden, next door. It was a reinforced hole in the ground that was damp, smelly and dirty. The tiny space was lit by a paraffin lamp and there was a fire burning for heat. "It was horrible," said Neil and after that the family took their chances with any bombs that might fall. In Brasted there were two barrage balloons, one behind Heverswood Lodge and the other in the field behind the church. Neil would stand outside his house and watch the Spitfires from RAF Biggin Hill engaging in dog fights with the German planes. Instead of going to bed at night he would stay up and watch the tracer bullets dance across the sky, as the Battle of Britain unfolded above him. Later in the war, doodlebugs (V1s and V2s) also passed over him as he looked up, watching with boyhood interest.

The army requisitioned many properties in the area for use by the troops. Brasted Hall was taken as either an officers' or a sergeants' mess. Neil was not quite sure which. The house, now known as Lindertis, was called Booseys (after the Boosey family who lived there) and during the war it too was requisitioned and squaddies were stationed there. Every day they would march down the street to their mess for meals. The canteen was in the current coffee shop by The White Hart pub car park. All the local kids were allowed in there and were given loads of jelly and blancmange.

When the army suddenly decamped from their village quarters, they left behind large quantities of live ammunition. "There were thousands and thousands of rounds everywhere," said Neil. One school lunch break Neil, Jackie Davis, Trevor Fisk and Gerald Annells went over to Brasted Hall with the intention of filling their pockets full of it. However, Gerald chose to collect dried peas instead for his pea shooter. They arrived back at school with their trousers falling down round their legs. They tried to hide the bullets in their socks, but were caught and made to empty their pockets in front of everyone. Out came three piles of bullets and one pile of dried peas. They all had a good caning, but poor Gerald had a double helping from the harsh Mr Warner as he thought he had stolen the peas. Neil and his buddies would jam bullets into tree stumps and strike them with a hammer and nail to made them go off bang. Unfortunately, one exploded so seriously it damaged Neil's hand badly and he still bears the scars today from this scary explosion!

In the school garden the children were taught gardening skills and how to grow their own vegetables. There was an air raid shelter there and the onions were hauled up onto the shelter to dry in the sun. A more unusual use for the shelter was to force others up a ramp to walk across the shelter. Affectionately, known as walking the plank, they had to drop ten feet at the other end! The boys would have carpentry lessons and sometimes they were tasked with clearing the shed of all the sawdust and mess. On one occasion they discovered a bottle of red liquid and were convinced it was hidden wine. Poor Ron Day was made to sip it only to discover it was mahogany varnish. He was so ill he had to be sent home.

Outside of school, Neil played the usual childhood tricks. He described the antics as good clean fun, without hurting anyone. They could play marbles on the main road and would move aside if a vehicle came along. In West End they played 'knock down ginger'. They used a pin, a washer and a length of cotton. The pin was stuck into the putty around front windows. The washer hung loose and the boys would hide behind huge bushes of golden rod (scientific name, Solidago) that grew in all the front gardens. They would tap on the windows and quickly haul in the washer and pin. When the residents came to their window or door, obviously they could not see anyone and must have looked very puzzled. Meanwhile, the boys were hiding in the bushes trying desperately not to laugh too loudly, so they didn't give themselves away!

In those days no one locked anything up. One day, passing Brasted Hall Annexe on the corner of Church Road and the High Street, the boys noticed that the owner had parked his Morris 8 outside. They tried the door and lo and behold, it opened! They did no more than push it up Church Road to Mill Farm where the Day brothers farmed. They carried on casually walking around the block and when they arrived back at the house, the owner was frantically searching for his car. The boys offered to help (of course, they did) and set off up Church Road. On reporting back to the owner they had found his car and its whereabouts, he gave them each half a crown (2s 6d) for their help!! Nice work if you can get it!

On occasions, Neil would go up into the fields and catch both adders and grass snakes. He would find a forked stick to pop between 'their eyes' and then either hold them behind their head or by their tails. It would take some effort not to alert them with the vibration from his steps as they sunbathed in the fields behind West End[10]. For fun he would show them to anyone who might be interested and for an added bit of mischief, he'd go off and find Aunt Flo and wave them in front of her. Being scared of the snakes, she would let out a fearful gasp. Well, that was all the reward Neil needed! With nowhere to

---

[10] Editor's note. The grass snakes have always thrived in Brasted and even now are found in the fields adjacent to West End and in open grassland around the village.

keep them he eventually had to release them back into the fields.

Neil recalled that Mill Farm had a cowman called Mr Baker, more casually known as Dasher. He lived in West End and would walk home for lunch every day. Passing the field, he would open the gate and the cows never strayed until he returned shouting "come on, come on". The cows would then walk through the gate by themselves and up to Mill Farm to be milked – that was an event to behold.

In similar vein, Mr Shorey of Streatfield House had a small herd of ten to twelve cows that grazed in fields at Brasted Chart. Each day he would walk them down, through the High Street to his small farm in Rectory Lane. The local children would watch and happily help with herding them along. These days his farm has gone and Pym Orchard has been built on the land. It is a friendly close of bungalows built for the older residents of Brasted. Opposite Pym Orchard is Tanners Hill, which is possibly where the slaughterhouse was once located.

It was quite a prank to spy on Arch Day and his brother Fred delivering milk from a horse and cart. The local children thought nothing of giving the horse a good old whack on the backside, sending it bolting up the road! As Neil said, "it hindered them, never helped them, but it was clean, mischievous fun!"

After his school years, one classmate, David Warwick, stays in Neil's memory. He was called up for army duty, but refused to go. David did no more than walk into the woods with a shotgun and blow his trigger finger off! David was not only strong in character, but had great physical strength. He was the 'strongman of Brasted,' who could bend metal and break items; feats which amazed the other boys. Sadly, David met an untimely death while still in his thirties.

He worked at the ballast lake in Chipstead and one day was caught and crushed between a tug and a pontoon as he tried to jump from one to the other.

Neil left school at the age of fifteen and started his working life at Markwick's store in Brasted. He delivered groceries and goods using an old-fashioned bicycle with a large tray at the front. Three times a week, the bicycle was laden with five two-gallon paraffin cans for delivery around Puddledock Lane in Toys Hill. He had one can in front, one each side of the cycle frame and two over the saddle. No room for Neil then! He had to walk all the way up there, pushing the bike beyond The Fox and Hounds pub. The only relief was to be able to cycle back down the hill. He learnt to dress the shop windows, including stacking hundreds of cans of baked beans.

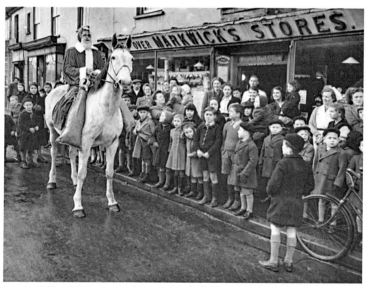

Father Christmas arriving at Markwick's store, Christmas 1946

They were good days and food was supplied to the shop by the wholesalers in bulk and was not individually packaged as it is today. The butter was supplied to Markwicks in a large block and needed some skill to cut it, pat it and sell it, all at the right size for the customers. Half a pig would arrive and it had to be boned to be sold as bacon. Sugar and many dry goods came in sacks to be weighed and sold over the counter. Blue bags were for food and grey bags for supplies, like soap powder. Mr Luxford was the manager and he lived over the shop.

Neil left Markwicks to work as a tea boy for the builder's merchants, Ransom and Banks, in Dunton Green, with the promise of an extra penny (1d) an hour. They undertook a large contract in Aylesford where Neil had to fill a cauldron of water and boil it either on an open fire or by primus stove. While the cauldron was heating, he would go to all the workers and take orders for their needs at a local shop. It could be tobacco or postal orders or even doughnuts for their break. By the time he returned the water was nicely boiling. Finally, having washed up and cleared away, his duties were completed by 3 p.m. and he needed to fill his time until the finish of the day. Fellow workers asked him to sit on the front of a bulldozer directing it through marked obstacles on its way through the site. It was a bit hair-raising with the blade just below him. One day he was spotted doing this by the manager and instantly sacked on the spot without argument even though it had never been his idea in the first place!

After that he returned to Brasted to be a 'grease monkey' for Mr Florey at Locomotors, part of a group of twenty one garages.

Again these were enjoyable days and Neil learnt many new skills to set up his future working life. It was a great place to work and Neil would also operate the petrol pumps part time at the garage on the corner of Chart Lane. While working there Neil applied for his provisional driving licence and Mr Florey did all he could to help with lessons. The company had a contract with Southern Counties Dairies in Gravesend where they used electric carts to deliver milk. Neil was encouraged to drive them to and fro to practise for his driving test. He passed his test at 10 a.m. on a Wednesday morning and the very next day Mr Florey sent Neil out at 3 a.m. on a vehicle collection job. He was given trade plates and money for food, drink and petrol. At Riverhead he had to hold up his trade plates, looking for a lorry to stop and give him a lift to his destination. That day he was on his way to The Bull Ring in Birmingham to bring back a Humber Hawk car for a local nurse who was buying it. His first job was a baptism of fire, quite an eye opener and the start of an eventful career based around driving.

While working at Locomotors that Neil had a scrape with the company sign – literally! Neil was sent to Chatham to collect an articulated lorry from the Better Bread Company. He had never driven one before and was a little shocked to be told it was, "round there in the car park". He didn't feel confident to drive it out of the tight spot, so the company foreman drove it to Rochester Airport. This gave Neil a straight shot at the roads. Everything was fine until he reached Brasted and had to manoeuver the truck under the company sign that formed an arch over the entrance. He lined it up and went for it, only to end up with the arch sitting fairly and squarely on top of the lorry. He reported his predicament to Mr Florey who shrugged and said the lorry still needed to be in the yard! So, the metal sign ripped the top of the lorry open like a tin can opener. The company repaired it, with Mr Florey commenting, "You never meant to do it. It's called an accident."

Neil was sometimes hired out as a driver and this was the case when the local baker, Percy Fuggle was knocked over by an army lorry. He could not deliver his goods, so Neil was hired until Percy recovered. Mr Florey lent Neil the money to buy his first motorcycle, which led to his passion for them and many more followed. He and his buddies would start in Brasted and race at top speed to Quebec Square, Westerham. It was a good thing no one was playing marbles at the time, as they screamed down the road at eighty miles an hour! He did have one nasty accident when a cat ran out in front of him and Neil was sent flying through the air without wings! The motorcycle was a write-off, but Neil carried on with his day, and it wasn't until much later that his leg simply seized up and he was unable to walk. The doctor cut his boot off only to find it was broken in three places and Neil had to stay off work for three months and there were no sickness benefits in those days! Another story was one of a visit to the hairdresser Paddy Donoghue. Paddy was a horse racing fan, so half way through a haircut, he dashed off home to watch an important race. Half hour or so later Paddy returned and finished Neil's haircut!

Neil remembers George Alderson of Brasted as a wonderful man. He lived at Church End House near St Martin's Church and ran several businesses which included being the local coal merchant for the area. The coal was delivered by steam train each night and loaded into bunkers near the station for onward delivery. Mr Alderson ran a local taxi with Tom Lawrence as his driver and hired out vehicles. He encouraged Neil to drive his coaches to practise for his PSV (Public Service Vehicle) licence, again opening up his future career. So Neil borrowed a coach to practise and then took his test, driving all over the lanes in the Weald. He had to accelerate away on a hill with a matchbox behind the tyre. If the matchbox was flattened it was an instant failure. That test went well. The instructor measured the distance between the parked coach and the curb. It had to be six inches so passengers could step down onto the pavement. That test also went fine. Eventually they drove back into Sevenoaks and it was Neil's bad luck to meet a lorry, transporting long pipes, coming the other way. The lorry and its trailer were one hundred feet long and they met at the narrow bend between the town fountain and Sevenoaks School. There was no way to pass so the instructor said that he had two choices. He could reverse, but by then lots of cars were lined up behind him, or he could drive onto the pavement. Neil asked the instructor to tell the cars behind him to reverse, as Neil knew he needed an attendant to do that while he stayed at the steering wheel. The instructor refused. Neil had no choice, but to mount the pavement to give the long lorry the chance to pass. That solved the problem except the examiner instantly failed him for driving on the pavement and they headed straight back to his starting point. Poor Neil, he was set up to fail no matter how the problem resolved itself!!

Neil told of how George Alderson was also a generous and kind man. Every year he arranged a Christmas party at the Village Hall for all the local children under the age of fourteen. Every child was given a present and they could eat and drink as much as they wanted. He also took the Young Farmer's Club for an outing to Bexhill every year and paid for their transport.

Neil played darts for The Stanhope Arms pub and the local men formed a cricket team and played for fun at the weekends. They used the field outside the second lych-gate of St Martin's Church. Before playing they had to remove the cowpats to avoid unsavoury accidents! One day George Alderson stood at the lych-gate watching the game and afterwards called Neil over. He proposed that Neil could rope off two cricket pitches on his own land for the team to use. The men had to mow it and George would supply the mowers and petrol. George had his own nine-hole pitch and putt course and the deal was to mow that for him as well. However, visitors would not be allowed to wander around his garden or go into his greenhouses where George kept his prize collection of camellias. He donated one hundred pounds (£100) for equipment and a trophy to be presented yearly for the best catch of the season. So, that was a deal and the wives would use The Stanhope Arms kitchen to prepare sandwiches and tea for the breaks. Although it was always for fun, they would play teams like the Westerham Brewery, Redland Tiles and Marley Tiles. All games finished by 7 p.m. to allow the ladies and children to play mini cricket and ball games before the end of the day.

In 1975, Neil moved jobs to the Post Office and delivered the local post. To augment his income, Neil was offered a part-time job by Dick Johnson at his BMW garage, after he'd finished his post office duties for the day. That led to a full time job offer, which he accepted, but having tendered his resignation from the post office, the garage job failed to materialize and Neil moved on again.

That led to lots of driving jobs including delivering for Westerham Brewery, then an Ind Coope and Double Diamond brewer. He would drive to Beckenham to deliver beer to Westminster Bank's Sports Ground, for their annual sports event. It was illegal to sell beer after midnight so Neil would go back and load it all back onto his lorry. They would always save him a crate of beer as thanks for his trouble and hard work.

Finally, he re-joined the post office, which was where he was working on the night the hurricane struck on 16th October 1987. Poor Michael Fish of the London Weather Centre became infamous the day before with this quote. "Earlier on today, apparently a woman rang the BBC and said she had heard there was a hurricane on the way... well, if you're watching, don't worry, there isn't!" Well, if you remember, there definitely was, and during it Neil from Westerham Post Office and Colin Howard from Biggin Hill Post Office were busy sorting mail at the main Sevenoaks mail delivery centre. As they worked they could hear the wind getting noisier, the doors started slamming and the building began to creak. Finally they were told the mail lorry from Tonbridge could not get through and they were to finish and make their way home. Neil made it to Bessels Green where a huge tree was down, completely blocking the road. Strangely, there at 2 a.m. was a woman out walking her dog and he told her, "you shouldn't be out here," as a dustbin crashed out from an alleyway in front of them. He turned round and tried the route through Dunton Green towards Chevening. Trees littered the roads and sometimes he was driving over the treetops. It was still hopeless so he abandoned his van near Bessels Green and scrambled home on foot. Next day he walked all the way back again to collect the van.

Among Neil's observations on how different things are now, his most emotive thoughts were directed at many of today's young people. "They don't know what hard work is!" he mused.

Neil retired in the year 2000 and now, he loves to sit on a bench at his back door. He feeds the foxes and pheasants and has a bird feeding station made up of fifteen bird feeders and bird baths dotted around his garden. He loves to see the blue tits, great tits, lesser spotted woodpeckers, sparrows, robins and wrens. A well-earned quiet moment in this oh-so-changed world.

July 2016

John Bellingham

John Paul Bellingham was born in Shoreham, Kent, in August 1935, the youngest of three children. His brother, Richard, was born in 1920 and sister, Violet Patricia, born in 1922. Their parents were George Edwin Bellingham and Violet May Wilkinson. They were married in the West Ham area. John was named after John Paul Jones, a Scottish pirate. This hard man had a chequered and at times brutal career. He went to America where he joined their Navy. His exploits in the Revolution against the English led him to be known as the 'Father of the American Navy'. John's father must have admired this man greatly and John Paul Jones was clearly one of his favourite characters. Perhaps he viewed him as a tough, gritty pirate, who took no prisoners, as a fearless, canny and daring leader of men and these were the characteristics he wished to impart to his son. This seems to be the case, as John was an inquisitive and astute young lad. He served in the Army from the age of eighteen, was a keen athlete and went on to forge a successful career in management.

Coincidentally, there is another association with pirates on John's mother's side of the family. Violet, John's mother was born in Wapping, in April 1896. She used to say she was from 'Wapping Old Stairs', close to the Thames. It was a place where pirates were taken to be chained, until three tides had washed over them. There is also a song,

'Your Molly has never been false, she declares, since last time we parted at Wapping Old Stairs'.

Violet had another interesting family connection and one that raised her family high above pirates. It was rumoured that her mother, Annie May Hogman, was related to the Swedish Royal family. Certainly, Annie's father, John's great, great grandfather, Andrew Hogman was born in Gothenburg, Sweden to Swedish parents. He came to England as a mariner and married Ellen Reardon, in 1866 in Whitechapel.

John's father, George, was born in Ticehurst on the 14th February 1887. He joined the Grenadier Guards in 1906 and became a well-trained professional, where he was famously drilled to fire fifteen rounds per minute. The Guards were the only regiment known to achieve this. Part of his duties were guarding Buckingham Palace and Windsor Castle, where they each carried ten rounds of live ammunition, until one night! An army mate on duty at Windsor Castle reacted when he was sure he saw movement in the grounds. In a flash he raised his rifle, fired and seriously injured a statue! Live ammunition was banned after that episode! George took his discharge in 1912. For two years, he was in the reserves and when First World War started he was called back. Sadly he had a very hard war. He was sent to France with the 2nd Battalion Grenadier Guards. They were dispatched to Le Havre on the 13th August 1914 and sent directly into battle against the Germans, in North West France. The men took up positions in the trenches and George and his army comrades were subjected to the feared and dreaded gas attacks. On the 23rd August 1914, five hundred men were commanded to attack the German lines. With bayonets fixed they obeyed orders and for King and country they went over the top and were annihilated. Staggeringly, George was probably the only survivor. He was certainly the only Grenadier Guard captured by the Germans that day.

George was sent to the Doeberitz prisoner of war camp: his war was over. George never talked about his experiences, but John's mother described to him how his father had suffered. The prisoners were kept in freezing conditions, in tents housing five hundred men. They had no shoes and were left up to their knees in snow. They laid branches on the floor, as the only protection from the freezing ground, both to walk on and sleep on. All prisoners were forced to work and barely fed in return. George was starving, along with many men who died beside him. He managed to get to know one or two of his German guards and sometimes they gave him a little extra food. The prisoners were forced to break the ice on a lake and twice George fell into the freezing water. Each time he was pulled out by his German captors. He was later marched to Riga Concentration Camp in Latvia.

When the prisoners were finally liberated, George had wasted away to less than ten stone in weight. He never spoke of the horrors he saw, or the terrible things he suffered there. George was damaged by his treatment in the camps and being gassed in the trenches. His health deteriorated and he died in 1948 aged sixty, having spent only thirteen years with his youngest son. Violet voiced the hope, that having guarded the gates of Buckingham Palace, he would guard the gates of heaven!

When John was born in Shoreham, George, was working as a gamekeeper for Lord Dunsany, a military man and creative writer.

Part of his duties, were to shoot the prolific rabbit population in order to supply the London markets. George was so experienced with a rifle, he was known to simply shoot from his hip. In the end, he had seen so many dead rabbits he could no longer face another and they never graced the family meal table. His skills included shooting mistletoe out of the trees at Christmas. It beat all that ladder climbing!

John aged two with his parents

Soon, the family moved to Scords Cottages in Toys Hill, where George worked hard on Scords Farm, close to The Tally-Ho pub. John's brother, Richard, was a nursery gardener, working for Charles Fleming's nursery. They were busy growing fruit and vegetables, but Richard was soon called up for military service. Violet, John's mother trained visiting workers in the art of hop picking without too many leaves. All the hops went to the Black Eagle Brewery in Westerham, to make beer which was then sent back to The Fox and Hounds and Tally-Ho pubs in Toys Hill.

Again they moved, this time to a bungalow in French Street. Called, The Bothy, it was a large property with a marvellous kitchen garden that ran the length of the building. The accommodation was better and there were greenhouses in the garden, where George could grow all the vegetables he needed to feed his family. John recalls that during the Battle of Britain he heard a German plane had crashed close by. His young boy's curiosity prompted him to walk through the woods to investigate. The reality of the tragic consequences of war were suddenly and harshly brought home to him when he saw two parachutes hanging in the trees and two German airmen hanging limply from them. He was only five or six at the time and the police quickly ushered him away from the scene. On another occasion, he was walking to Toys Hill through the woods and the whole area was covered in silver foil strips. It must have looked like Christmas decorations to a boy. In fact, the German planes had scattered them everywhere, to interfere with the local radar signal. The reflection of the foil, known as chaff, was designed to confuse the early and more basic radar systems used at the time. It was impossible to identify how many planes were in the sky as the foil rained down across the area. Although it was the British who discovered this system, the Germans used it with equal success.

One casualty of the war was Weardale Manor, built in 1906, in Toys Hill. It was owned by Philip Stanhope, Baron Weardale and his wife, Countess Alexandra Tolstoy. Although they seldom used it, they had hosted some earlier gala events there to entertain their guests, which included members of the German hierarchy. Therefore they knew the exact location of the manor. After the couple died, it suffered years of neglect and the landmark was taken down, in 1939, brick by brick.

John's family would walk from French Street to The Fox and Hounds pub in Toy's Hill and while they went inside, John, too young to join in, would sit outside with a three penny (3d) bag of crisps and a bottle of Vimto! What a treat for a young boy! John's mother told him that on a clear day, you could see all the way to France although that is not proven fact. However, Toy's Hill is one the highest points in Kent.

John started school in Brasted and walked there each day from French Street. He and his friends had their moments of naughtiness. He received canings from Mr Warner, the headmaster, but he cannot recall his boyish misdemeanours. Miss Amy Cronk was one of the teachers he remembers well. At 10 a.m. each day, she would eat her ten penny (10d) bun, while checking her students work. While chewing her bun, she would carry on talking and the unfortunate minor she was addressing at the time, would be sprayed with regurgitated crumbs - a most unpleasant experience! She also carried out punishments and used the thin edge of her ruler to smack any small, open hand that had displeased her - ouch! Each morning started with thirty minutes of mental arithmetic. There would be geography and history lessons and woodworking in the playground. In one history lesson, John pronounced the River Thames as the River 'Thaymes' making all who heard him burst out laughing! The children had swimming lessons at Chevening School's open air swimming pool. They had to jump in regardless of the weather, even when it was freezing cold, and John remembers how it felt on his young body. He also recalls that sports lessons were at Sundridge Recreation Ground.

The family moved again to a cottage at Colinette Farm, in Chart Lane. Mr and Mrs Aspen were tenanted to the farm, and grew crops and reared cattle. John helped with jobs on the farm for threepence (3d) a week. One of his tasks was to dig up the mangel beet crop, considered one of the best crops for feeding dairy herds. It was very hard work and consideration for the herd was not in John's thoughts as he tackled the job! George, was employed as an ostler, looking after the farm horses. As the harvest finished the hay was made into tall haystacks. A small white farm horse was chosen to walk in circles all day turning the cogs that operated the conveyor belt on the grain elevator. It raised the bales up to the top of the stacks. With the long task finished, the horse was released and John was asked to ride it back to the stable. This horse smelt freedom and took off galloping with John hanging on. He managed to throw himself off and the men caught the horse, somewhat amused by the event. The farm horses were strong, sturdy creatures used for pulling farm machines, such as the thresher for gathering in the crops. There was no automation to help on the farm. John remembers that George continued growing vegetables and keeping chickens, always helping to feed his family. At Christmas, his father would mark the festive season by sourcing a goose for their special dinner! Despite the hardships of the times, the family always sat down to a midday meal. Fortunately, George was good friends with Bells, the butchers, in Westerham. They often gave him a little extra meat beyond the ration to take home to his family.

As John walked home from school one lunchtime, there was a terrific thunder storm overhead. A shock went right through him as lightning struck Chart Lane, a short way ahead. It instantly dried the soaking wet surface and John commented, "I wasn't half scared". 1947 was a particularly snowy winter and John made himself a wooden snow plough to help everyone out. He hauled it from Colinette all the way down to the village through Elliotts Lane and then back up again. When his mother saw the post lady she remarked, "Some good Samaritan has done a path for me," and his mother smiled.

At night the skies were so dark that John would see shooting stars rip across the sky and on quiet nights, when the moon lit the sky, the peace and twinkling stars were sublime. John and his buddies would try to catch the many bats that flew around. Of course, they never had a smidgen of success

Whatever money John earned, he gave to his mother. There were the exceptional treats though, like a penny (1d) roll and a ha'penny (½d) bun from Cowlards, the bakers. As a real treat, John, would buy a tin of Horlicks tablets from Hebbs, the village chemist and eat them all as sweets. Rosie Rice, had her sweet shop and John would go in and buy ten Players cigarettes. Rosie knew they were for his mother, so she would sell them to him.

John had two black rabbits as pets and the family also took in a little dog they called Trixie. She had been bombed out and was running around wild. Although a lovely dog, she did not last long when she bit someone who had come to visit their house!

With the war still being fought ferociously overhead, John often watched the planes fighting over Biggin Hill air field. He missed many school days at this time and would spend them with the air force officers stationed nearby. These men had three barrage balloons to watch over. Two satellite balloons were near Colinette, both located in the woods. The Irish corporal in charge of the group not only let John stay around, but would also share his food with him too. This was one example of the many kindnesses shown in those times of food rationing. There were occasions when John was put onto the back of a balloon and floated upwards, a hundred feet or so in the air. Health and safety obviously wasn't a consideration in those times! A scary episode occurred when a doodlebug became entangled in the wire of one balloon and John remembers the whistling noise, screaming down the wire. The officers threw him into their dugout, until the doodle bug had crashed, somewhere beyond them. At night, John would go out to watch the fighting wearing one of his mother's saucepans on his head for protection. Shrapnel would streak around him, but his saucepan kept him safe. In the cottage, the family had a Morrison shelter and John would sleep in it at night.

John became a choir boy at St Martin's Church where he was paid threepence (3d) a week. The rector, Reverend Henry Longuet - Higgins, gradually stopped paying him and John decided no pay, no play and gave up. The rector would call at the house, to see why he was missing from church. In order to avoid him John would hide under the table, out of sight! When attending the church on a Sunday, he sometimes rang the one bell pulling on the rope in the entrance to the church. His sister, and Jean Burgess, would both volunteer on the rota to clean the church. Sunday school offered outings and John enjoyed a trip to Hastings, in one of George Alderson's coaches.

After George died, Violet and John had to leave their tied cottage at Colinette Farm. They were due to move into a new house, but the building wasn't completed. Major Pym stepped in and found them a flat at Valance while they waited. In 1951, they moved into their new home in Thorns Meadow, Brasted.

At the age of fifteen, John left school with an offer of an apprenticeship at Durtnells, the village builders. However, he chose instead to join Fred Still, who ran the village blacksmiths. He started work each day at 7 a.m., with Eric Norman and Bert Peters the blacksmith. They built trailers for tractors and road tines for the steam rollers. These were long spikes, fitted to sink into the road surface and tear it up as the rollers moved along. It took a fourteen pound (14lb) hammer to strike the ends, to draw out the points. A local farm would send, "the biggest white, Shire horses I had ever seen, Hengist and Horsa", to have new shoes fitted. The floor boards of the forge had to be removed as the huge horses heads went up through the ceiling joists. The gypsies would bring their horses along for second hand-shoes, but would not always be ready to pay! Bert would threaten, "If you don't pay up, I'll get my man on to you," and summon one point nine metre tall (six feet three inches), John. "I was only about seventeen, but their short arms soon reached into their long pockets."

One day, as John was working the curse of a thunder storm struck again. He ignored it and got on sawing angle iron to its required length. Just as it broke off and fell to the floor, the forge was struck by lightning. It ran down a metal pole and lit up the metal all around him, bright red and live. Just seconds before it would have been a tragedy! Sometimes John would get metal splinters in his face and would have to visit Dr Ward to have them removed. He remembers that the doctor would pull out a tatty, old case full of glasses. He would try each one on in turn until he found the pair that could magnify the splinter best. Only then could he start work on removing them. John also recalled that when he was called out on an emergency, the doctor could drive as fast backwards as he could forward!

In 1953, the Village Hall Committee commissioned the blacksmiths to make commemorative iron gates for the front of the Village Hall. The gates were designed to celebrate the Queen's coronation and the intricate ironwork was all handmade. John cleaned the welds, primed the ironwork and painted them black. They have perfect swirls and curves and as the gates shut, they bear the initials 'ER' and '1953' as shown in the picture below. They are still there today, but are generally kept open so most villagers never see the beauty of their work! Sadly, John was called up to the army, in 1953 and missed the installation ceremony.

The Village Hall Gates at Brasted

John was an excellent athlete and competed in a number of sports. He trained with two friends, Bill Boyd and Gordon Allan and together they became proficient gymnasts. They trained themselves and practised regularly at Brasted Chart Village Hall. They gave displays of their splendid skills all around the area, even attending outdoor events, performing entertaining turns. Bill was a roofer and would practice at work, lifting himself up and balancing upside down on the scaffolding. It must have made an interesting sight! When John was called up he could no longer take part, but Bill and Gordon continued and even appeared on television.

With his call up papers, John thought to follow his father into the Grenadier Guards. However, his mother, recalling the awful conditions George had experienced, fiercely opposed his choice and John joined the Royal East Kent Buffs[11] instead.

Stationed in Canterbury he had been busy training for service in Kenya, but, "the powers that be, must have known about my father and they stopped me." Instead, John found himself assigned to the armoury, as permanent staff. He trained hard in marching and three days a week he marched to Canterbury Cathedral. It was about two miles away, so was a fair distance to march in ceremonial dress and heavy boots! At 11 a.m., he and several others would march into the Warrior's Chapel, also known as the Buffs' Chapel, where two books of remembrance are kept. They would conduct a short ceremony and turn a page in each of the books, followed by prayers. At times, the crowds were so thick it was difficult for John to make his way through.

When he came home on leave, John would find a reason to walk up the High Street. Mr Stott, from his café and sweetshop, would rush out and give him a bar of chocolate, to take back to camp with him. He looked forward to that tasty delicacy.

---

[11] The Buffs were one of the first infantry regiments in the British Army and got their name from the colour of their uniforms.

Every evening, John would go to the army gym to keep himself fit. Afterwards, it was a trip into Canterbury with his army buddy, Barry Woodward. Sometimes, they would go to Tankerton, on the coast and Barry would swim to the Isle of Sheppey and back. John accompanied him for part of the way, but Barry was a more experienced swimmer and able to swim the distance readily. He had swum the English Channel and been a winner in the Morecambe Bay, ten mile swim. He was honoured in a big celebration in London, but it fell on the exact day that John was demobbed, so he missed that occasion as well!

Leaving the army in 1955, John went back to the forge where Dick Turner was now in charge. John ran it for a while, but got fed up with the low pay and lack of recognition. By now, he had married Jean Wood, from Dunton Green and he had a family to support. He chose to move and joined Fisk and Dailly, working on vehicle bodywork repairs. They had a garage behind The Kings Arms pub, in Brasted High Street. For leisure, he liked to meet his friend Charlie Bailey and enjoy fun evenings drinking in The Kings Arms. Ever the sportsman, John, Trevor Fisk and Bob Day, Arch Day's son, would play football for the Brasted and Sundridge team. He played badminton in the Kent championships and was always fond of a game of golf. With a twinkle in his eye, he told me all his activities are why he has had three new hips!

John remembers the stories of Mr Hutty driving to The Stanhope Arms pub every day, in his Austin 7 car. Out he would come, totally sozzled and drive his car haphazardly down Church Road. From time to time, he careered into a ditch and would turn his car upside down, onto its canvas roof. Everyone would rush to his aid and put the car back on its wheels. Off he would go again unscathed, unruffled and uncaring, heading for home. Luckily for him there were no drink driving rules in those days!

John moved jobs to Stormont Garage, in Otford Road, Otford and worked in their body shop for twenty-one years. During that time, he started as a worker bee and rose, through well-earned promotions, to the management team. Stormont Garage was finally taken over and John found himself telling the new staff everything he knew. He felt they were amateurs and not competent at all. Disillusioned, he handed in his notice and quietly said that he gave the new business three years. Right on the button it went bankrupt, three years later.

John remembers all of the shops in the High Street as he grew up. Starting opposite the old Brasted School, first there was Fuggles the bakers, then the International Stores, both before reaching The Kings Arms. Next came Wisteria House and Brasted House, where Mr Eberlie lived. There was a shoe repairer, Mr Jones, where Barrington's antique shop is now. While John was at the forge, he helped convert part of that building to make way for the Barrington family and their business. They were tasked with fitting metal joists to the ceilings, for the extension. Next came Mrs Evans the greengrocer, and Paddy O'Donoghue, the hairdresser. He also recalls Cowlards the bakers, Stotts and another grocers shop, and finally Markwicks.

Back down the other side of the road was Malpass the butchers, Shoreys, also a butchers. Maudsleys, the paper shop and next door a third butcher! Rosie Rice had her sweet shop, before Hebbs, the village chemist. The fishmongers, run by Mr and Mrs Kimber came next, before Mount House, where Lady Kilmaine lived.

So many people have commented on how it was never necessary to leave the village for the supplies they needed. It is not hard to see why supermarkets thrived, offering most of these commodities under one roof. However, the supermarket revolution has led to the eventual decline of these little, individual village shops and diminished much of the character of old Brasted.

These days, John only drives through Brasted where he sees his workplace, the old forge has gone. The Kings Arms has gone and so has The Bull Inn. All the things that were familiar to him and made life good. To this soldier, time marches on, but still the old memories remain.

August 2017

April Williams
née Barnett

April's father, William Edward Barnett was born in Sutton, Surrey, on the 9th April 1906. Soon his family moved to Ide Hill where he grew up. Alice Elizabeth née Willis was born in Brasted on the 30th May 1908. William and Alice met and courted in Brasted and were married in St Martin's Church in 1934. April Amy Barnett was born in April 1938 at 18 West End, Brasted. Her sister, Shirley Alice, had been born two years earlier while her parents rented 3 Bull Cottages, Church Road, Brasted. The sisters looked quite different, as Shirley had brown curly hair like her mother and April had fair straight hair like her father.

The Staples/Willis Family Tree

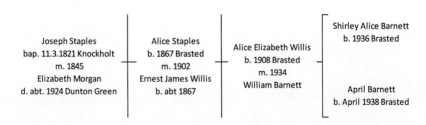

Joseph Staples
bap. 11.3.1821 Knockholt
m. 1845
Elizabeth Morgan
d. abt. 1924 Dunton Green

Alice Staples
b. 1867 Brasted
m. 1902
Ernest James Willis
b. abt 1867

Alice Elizabeth Willis
b. 1908 Brasted
m. 1934
William Barnett

Shirley Alice Barnett
b. 1936 Brasted

April Barnett
b. April 1938 Brasted

One of April's earliest recollections was the new council house the family lived in. West End was a cul-de-sac with the houses built around a green, where the children could play. There were many young families and it was a good place to grow up in. The neighbours next door were the Forester family and they had a daughter called Susan. She was six months younger than April, but they became good friends and playmates. The mention of Sue made April smile broadly as their friendship has lasted all of their lives.

Another of April's early memories was being wheeled in her black pram to meet Shirley from Brasted School. The big, old pram had a central panel that could be removed allowing her feet to dangle down. This was perhaps the forerunner to the all-in-one pram/pushchair and car seat that these units commonly come in now. Her sister could hitch a ride as they were both pushed home.

April was a war-time child, and clearly remembers the war years, but never being frightened. She feels they all just lived a normal life and carried on without any obvious fear. It was in the background of everything, but life just went on. She remembers that the adults longed to have their lights on and the blackout curtains removed. The darkness all around must have been depressing. However, in April's mind she thought that when the war ended, the whole world would light up and there would never be night time again! What a wonderful childlike vision! Everyone had to blackout their windows. Some families had windows permanently black and others had frames that could be fitted at night and removed again in the morning.

April remembered that an incendiary bomb dropped into the front garden of their house at West End. It was designed to cause fires, but mostly for the family, it messed up the garden and damaged the front path. April, Shirley and mother, Alice, were all under the stairs, so no one was injured. When their father, William, heard that a bomb had come down, he hopped on a bus from Westerham and rushed straight home. He was so relieved to find his family perfectly safe, if not a little shaken. The path was repaired, but always had a section of new cement that marked the garden for its unfortunate experience.

Initially, during bombing raids, the family took shelter under the stairs, but an air raid shelter was later installed in the garden. The girls would go into it when the siren sounded, but William never did. April still remembers it smelling musty and damp. Sometimes, they would watch the planes fighting in the sky with screaming engines and gun bursts rattling out. The planes would spew black smoke from their engines as they battled.

William and Alice in their courting days

April started at the village school during the war and followed a family tradition of her mother, two uncles and her grandmother; all attending the same school. The teachers were to be feared and the headmaster was a real tyrant. He would cane a child at the drop of a hat, and most of the children lived in fear of him. April was never caned, but was certainly lined up with the others and threatened with caning.

When the air raid siren went off during classes they all filed into the shelter in the playground. "It had a horrible mouldy, damp odour," she recalls. They all had to take their paper and pencils for drawing, while waiting for the all clear signal. Then, they would file out, back to the classroom and carry on with lessons. On each coat rack there was a gas mask provided for every child. Fortunately, April cannot remember them ever being used!

William worked in forestry during the day, but at night he was an ARP Warden. He had a uniform to wear and a helmet to protect himself. In April's memorabilia is a map of Brasted with all the wartime fire hydrants marked for quick access in case of need. On reflection, April feels he must have been very tired at times and that her mother must have worried horribly[12].

The family had close relatives with Aunty Amy and Uncle Ernie Willis, living in Rose Cottage, Church Road. They looked out for each other, and her aunt and uncle featured hugely in the lives of the Barnett family. As April patiently explained, Amy was the sister of her father, William Barnett and Ernie was the brother of her mother, Alice Barnett née Willis.

During the war, Aunty Amy and Uncle Ernie opened up their house; Rose Cottage, to army wives. Their husbands were billeted across the road in a large house and many wives came to visit. The Cottage only had two bedrooms and many of the wives must have slept on

---

[12] ARP (Air Raid Precautions) Wardens were appointed during the Second World War to protect civilians from the dangers of air raids. Their main role was to patrol the streets during the blackout to ensure that no lights were visible to enemy planes. They also organised and staffed public air raid shelters, distributed gas masks and reunited family members separated in the rush to find shelter from the bombs.

the floor, in any space they could find. Aunty Amy had been in service before her marriage and she was a superb cook. With so many visitors, meals were served in relays. The ladies sat around the table, which also converted into a Morrison indoor bomb shelter, when the siren sounded. Many of the visiting ladies travelled long distances from around the country to visit their husbands. The A25 was always full of army lorries crowded with soldiers. They would throw out sweets to the children as they drove past. Amy was certainly one of the many unsung heroes of the war effort. She also worked full-time for many years, at the laundry in Sundridge. On a rota, she would also take her turn fire-watching from the roof of the laundry building.

William and Alice would attend dances in the village hall and arranged to help entertain the many soldiers stationed up and down the village. April and Shirley were never left at home, and April remembers standing on the soldiers' feet while they danced around with her. In fact, William took his girls everywhere to keep them all together. They would go to the cinemas in both Sevenoaks and Westerham. However, April recalls that Shirley hated the old black and white films with Charlie Chaplin and Old Mother Riley. She would cry and could hardly wait to get out of the cinema and on the bus home.

Old Mother Riley was an Irish washerwoman and charlady character, played by an actor called Lucan whose given name was Arthur Towle. His wife played Old Mother Riley's daughter, Kitty. It was both a drag act and a double act. Lucan was voted sixth biggest British box-office star in 1943, with his performances. He and his wife Kitty McShane gave Jimmy Clitheroe his break in 1939, in an Old Mother Riley pantomime called 'The Old Woman Who Lives in a Shoe'. Jimmy Clitheroe was a famous comedian who entertained with his popular radio programme until 1972.

April clearly recalled Victory in Europe Day[13] (VE Day) and the joy and celebrations that swept across the country. There was a party on the West End green, for all the families on the estate. There was lots of food, singing and an enormous bonfire that lit up the night sky. Everyone stayed up, and April can remember holding her father's hand and walking across the green at two o'clock in the morning, desperately trying to keep her eyes open. The searchlights were flitting across the sky and it was an amazing event. The piano for the party belonged to Aunty Amy and was carried up the road from Rose Cottage. It must have been quite a task, but it certainly enhanced the joyful celebrations.

The family would spend a lot of time with Aunty Amy and Uncle Ernie. April has particularly happy memories of special Christmases spent with them. Aunty Amy would serve up the most fantastic food. April's grandad, William George Barnett (born 1877 in Brasted), bred rabbits, reared chickens and had an allotment for vegetables. The table was never short of food. Both mother Alice, and her grandmother Amy Barnett, would subscribe to the Christmas club, known as the 'Slate Club', at The Kings Arms pub, in the High Street. That paid out before Christmas each year. It was a tradition to ride the bus to Croydon and visit Kennards, a large departmental store in Surrey Street. It was always beautifully decorated during the Christmas season. There they would buy all their presents and carry them back on the return bus. If time allowed they looked at the open air market stalls, outside in the

---

[13] Victory in Europe Day was 8th May 1945. It marked the formal acceptance by the Allies of Nazi Germany's unconditional surrender and thus the end of the Second World War in Europe.

street. It was a fun expedition for the family.

For some reason Uncle Ernie was known locally as 'Caleb'! Whatever his name, he enjoyed his regular outings to The Stanhope Arms pub. He would cycle up and then return drifting down the hill until his bike finally came to a halt back at Rose Cottage, all the while happily singing, "You are my sunshine, my only sunshine," etc. One day he came out of the pub to find his mates had heaved his bike up on the top of a lamp post. No one can remember how he managed to get it down!

William George Barnett

In 1947, when April was eight, her mother died unexpectedly and tragically at home. Children were not expected to attend family funerals so April and Shirley stayed with Mrs Wickenden, a kind neighbour. She must have been taken to school that day, as Granny Barnett picked the girls up and took them back to Rose Cottage. However, April clearly remembers seeing black stockinged legs walking up Church Road to the funeral. The bereaved family never again returned to West End.

The following Sunday, all the family attended a memorial service in the village hall. St Martin's Church may have been under repair from bomb damage, because the service would usually have been held inside the church. To this day she still wonders if the actual funeral was held at the graveside only. She watched her father break his heart, the girls had never seen him cry before and it was a shock. In the hall, April remembered her uncle, Bill Willis giving her a big wink when he caught her eye. He and Aunty Brenda, also lived in West End, but for whatever reason the families did not have much to do with each other.

William and his two daughters moved into Rose Cottage. Amy and Ernie never had children of their own and, as ever, lovingly welcomed the family. April would usually spend her days in the cottage, but slept at 2 Bull Cottages next door, the home of her grandmother Amy Barnett. Rose Cottage only had two bedrooms, so this arrangement worked well for everyone.

Rose Cottage had been in the Staples/Willis family for a long time. Joseph Staples was christ-ened on the 11th March 1821, in Knockholt. He was originally

Joseph Staples (left), Elizabeth (centre) and Alice with an unnamed gamekeeper about 1900

apprenticed to his father, learning the family business of thatching. However, by the 1861 census he had moved to Brasted, where he was employed by Lord Stanhope on his Chevening Estate. By the 1871 census he was a gamekeeper for the estate; a position he held for the rest of his working life. In moving to Brasted, it seems he acquired the lease of Rose Cottage as part of his Chevening employment deal. Even after retirement he stayed in the cottage and after his death in 1903, his daughter Alice (born 1867 in Rose Cottage) and her husband Ernest James Willis took over the lease on the property. In turn the cottage went to their eldest son, Ernest Joseph Willis (Uncle Ernie).

After the Second World War, Ernie and Amy had the opportunity to purchase Rose Cottage, for one hundred and fifty pounds (£150). Even then, they sometimes struggled to meet the mortgage repayments, as salaries were equally small. It still had gas lighting even then. There was one mantel in the kitchen, one in the living room and one in the bedroom. The lounge did not have a gas mantel and had to be lit by candles as did the rest of the cottage. April remembers taking a candle to her bedroom every night, even when she lived in West End. It also had an outside toilet, so in cold weather they had to wear coats to walk around the corner, into the garden. The three terraced Bull Cottages had an outside toilet block, located some way down the gardens. They also had an outhouse each for the copper and cylinder used for washing clothes. You certainly had to prepare for the walk if you were desperate to 'spend a penny'! Ernie made a wooden arch around the front of Rose Cottage and picked some honeysuckle out of a hedgerow. He planted it and watched it grow for his wife, Amy.

William, would help at the annual horse show and gymkhana, held in the grounds of Combe Bank. It was his job to build the jumps for the horses. Horse transport and visitors would turn up from all over and folks would enjoy a day out with their picnics and a beer tent. April and Shirley always enjoyed the entertainment.

In the recreation ground was the open air swimming pool, fed by the river. Although freezing cold, the children loved it and spent all their spare time there. It had wooden dressing rooms and a shower that could be reached by climbing lots of steps. The baths had a marvellous wooden slide with three tiers of diving boards. There was a large lawn, where they could sunbathe, when the weather permitted.

Mr Strickland was the pool attendant for many years and taught lots of the children to swim. He used a broom handle with a rubber tyre on the end, for beginners to cling to. Once learners could swim with some confidence, he left them alone to enjoy themselves. At the beginning of the year, the water was clear and clean, but as the summer went on it became murky and streaked with green slime. The odd frog would appear and maybe a few tiddlers waylaid from the river. It didn't seem to do anyone any harm.

Shirley and April also belonged to the Junior Red Cross Society. It met regularly in the village hall, where they were instructed not to go up on the stage, but stay in the main hall. That was a challenge, and someone always managed to get onto the stage sometime during the meeting. The lady looking after the Hall would shout at them to get straight down. Sometimes, the village boys would creep in and turn all the lights off, leaving them in darkness. This resulted in screams from the girls, which only encouraged the boys to do it again! They learnt a lot from the lessons and had fun doing so. Shirley, April's sister, became a midwife off the back of these lessons and their friend, Ann Carter a phlebotomist. It provided a number of pathways for girls who wanted to follow a medical career. The courses taught everyone so much and certificates were earned as they passed each stage.

The Hall was also used to put on plays to entertain the adults. The plays often stemmed from the Red Cross courses and the girls ended up in all sorts of bandages – well wrapped and with stitches; stitches from laughter that is! The audience would equally be left in tears of laughter and the curtains could not be closed until it all subsided. Aunty Amy and Granny Barnett were always there to support the girls.

At the age of eleven, April left Brasted School to be one of the first year of students attending the new Churchill School in Westerham. They would be collected by coach at the bottom of West End and taken directly to school. However, it was soon considered that they all lived close enough to Westerham and that the local bus service could be used instead. Brasted School now taught juniors only, instead of taking pupils through their whole schooling years.

The Churchill School was mostly made up of concrete huts, where the lessons took place. It was fun at school as pupils came from all the surrounding villages. Everyone's social circle expanded as a result. All pupils were allotted a 'house' to represent in school. April was in Caxton house, coded blue. Wolfe house, was yellow and Sidney house, green. She could not recall the name of the red house. The houses competed against one another in academic achievements and sports. In addition, the boys would have a cross country running competition. The school also had a brand new domestic science room for the girls and the boys were taught carpentry in the school grounds. Sports day was held at Westerham Recreation Ground and so also were sports lessons; tennis and hockey! Oh dear, hockey! April was always put in goal and she hated it. It was certainly not the safest position to be in, with the wickedly hard ball being whacked at her! There was a drama group which staged plays for the teachers, governors and parents. April was given the main part in a school play, assisted by Derek Cronk and Alan Day; all Brasted children. Alan was her next door neighbour in Church Road.

Growing up and as young adults, April and her friends had an amazing amount of freedom. Their parents and Aunt Amy would pack up sandwiches and off they would ramble for the day. Within the village the Recreation Ground, swimming pool and the green in West End were the favourite playing places.

April and her friends would take their sandwiches and walk up Church Road and cross the River Darent, behind Bridge Cottage. That led to fields they called 'The Moors'. Alan Day, was a nephew of Fred Day, who had Mill Farm by The Moors and he let them wander all over his fields. A large oak tree had been cut down and the boys would climb up and sit in the hollow centre. They made wooden boats and floated them in the river. Inevitably they got themselves wet and Mrs Day would help dry them off before they went home.

Sometimes they would play in the river at the Recreation Ground. One side had a steep bank and the other was flat-sided. It was fun to find a tree branch and pole vault across the river, but success was rare and a ducking was normal. Thank goodness, for Mrs Day!

Their father, William sometimes assisted with the haymaking by The Moors. April was allowed to go up and help too. There was always more fun to be had in the village, including sledging in the fields during the winter. It seemed to snow more often then and leave a thick covering.

It was fun to ramble by the station and into the hills, to collect primroses and armfuls of bluebells – except that the bluebells always wilted before they could get them home! They collected blackberries in the autumn and in the summer, wild strawberries grew in droves around Colinette Farm. Grandmother Barnett and Aunty Amy would help collect both fruits. That led to a flurry of cooking, as they both went to work on many different dishes and, of course, jam.

Finally, it was time to see the careers officer at school, and prepare for the future. April stated she was good at the sciences and wanted to work in a chemist shop. So much for that, as she was found a job as a receptionist working for Wheeler, Brill and John. They were the local solicitors based in offices on The Green in Westerham. She loved the job which included answering the phones, collecting rents from two rows of houses in the town and doing the company banking. After a while, old Mr James Brill approached April with a proposition. If she went to evening classes and learnt typing and shorthand, she could become a secretary. So she did and became their secretary.

After a further couple of years, April felt the need to stretch her wings and looked for a job in London. Aunt Amy took her to an interview with The General Electric Company at Bankside Power Station. She was given the job and went back to evening classes again, for further English and accounting classes. For a while it was fun to catch the bus to Tubbs Hill, Sevenoaks. There, along with others she would fly into nearby Sevenoaks station and jump in the guards van, as the guard held the door open. A steam engine pulled the packed train on into London. However, April found her health was suffering during this time, and her doctor ultimately suggested she should leave smoggy London and come back to the countryside. That was fine by her, as she was fed up with the bottom of her skirt and her petticoat always being dirty from sitting in the guard's van!

Janet Waters, another friend, suggested April should apply for a job at Fort Halstead where Janet already worked. April took a job as a typist and stayed there until she married. It was a top security job which needed her to sign the Official Secrets Act. Even during our talk she felt she could not describe her job, even after all these years! Every day her bag was searched, as she was checked-in through the security barriers. At the end of the day, all used typewriter ribbons were put into a sack and taken away to be shredded. During the lunch break, April could walk around the boundary fences enjoying the fresh air and wonderful views. She remembers it was a good crowd to work with.

Brasted held an annual carnival for a while, and for several years the Barnett family entered into the spirit of it. Uncle Tom Barnett, William's brother, lived in Sundridge. He had an old lorry which he offered as a float. One year, the family chose Beauty as their theme and the lorry was decorated accordingly. William raided the female wardrobes and dressed himself as a teenage beauty, with makeup and lipstick. April had an evening dress with a fancy hat to top it off. Shirley was a bathing beauty, and her husband, Ron, dressed as a bride. They had to be cautious, as the lorry drove around the village. It was so old, there were holes in the flooring and they had to be careful not to fall through. For all their efforts, they won the best float competition and were awarded a cup for their accomplishment.

At the age of twenty, April married and joined her husband, Ted who was stationed at RAF Benson, in Oxfordshire. He was in the RAF for five years, and came out the same week their first son was born. They had returned to Rose Cottage, while they looked for a place of their own. It seemed rather fitting that Robert came along at that very time. Ted found a job in Noah's Ark, Kemsing, working for a garage. It had a tied cottage across the road where the new family moved in and continued to expand. They never returned to Brasted, but April has never been very far away from her roots.

She does still maintain her connections though and for seven years she arranged the annual school reunions. This year, 2017, she finally decided to let someone else take over the reins! Her first reunion was at The Stanhope Arms. It was a lovely occasion, much appreciated and enjoyed by everyone. They sat around a big table and traded stories, while tucking into a pub meal. About twelve to fourteen people attended. Old mates, Joyce Furst came along with Mary and Ernie Swift. Then there was Pam and Ann Carter, Sue (Forester) and her husband, Geoff Wells and Donald Ingram. It was all deemed a great success. Ernie Swift was teased about his nickname 'Pedro'. It was taken from a song called, 'Pedro the Fisherman' a song he was always whistling. The name fitted him perfectly.

The second year was at The Bull Inn and the usual crowd turned up all smiling. Suddenly, in walked Trevor Fisk, Derek Cronk and Gerald Annells. With a cheeky grin, Gerald gave April a big kiss on the cheek. The landlord was wonderful and opened on a Monday, especially for the reunion. It grew ever more popular, until numbers reached about forty old school friends. How wonderful that they all keep in touch every year!

What does April think has changed the most about Brasted?

The loss of the shops where you could buy anything. As they changed hands and became antique shops, the heart of the village was ripped out.

Most people of April's age had to leave the village as no houses were built, either by the council for rental or private sale. It broke up families who had spent generations in and around the village. This is still happening today and is a sad reflection on the loss of family life and families helping each other.

When the village was deprived of the railway in October 1961 by British Railways, then under the chairmanship of Dr Beeching[14], it was a grievous loss to villagers who could have the most wonderful days out. Westerham was in one direction and Dunton Green in the other, with easy connections to London and Hastings. April knew the old steam engine as the old 'push and pull' and it left a deep hole in village life, when the line was closed.

May 2017

---

[14] Dr Richard Beeching was Chairman of British Railways from June 1961 to June 1965. In 1963, he published the first of two reports on reshaping Britain's railway network which led to the sad, lamentable loss of many railway lines nationally.

Jane Smithers

née Pierce

Jane's story is one of two halves, first we will start with Jane and then her family, the Aldersons who have been associated with Brasted for nearly two hundred years.

Jane Pierce was born in June 1940 at Woodlands, Combe Bank, Sundridge. Her parents were Charles (Charlie) William Pierce and Joyce Marie née Alderson. Joyce was the sister of George Albert Alderson of Church End House opposite St Martin's Church, Brasted. Although Jane lived in Sundridge as she grew up she spent far more time at the big house, Church End, and really only seemed to go home to sleep at nights. They were a close and loving family.

An early childhood memory for Jane happened during an afternoon walking with her family along the railway line near Combe Bank. She remembers picking wild flowers in an area now close to the M25 motorway. Suddenly, the air raid siren howled and they scurried into their shelter. There was a huge BANG and the shelter shook, glass broke and the door jammed. Local people came to help them escape and luckily no one was hurt. However, Woodlands was in a bad state, with glass everywhere, the windows had blown in, doors were damaged and the house well shaken. It was a lucky thing that the family were tucked safely inside their shelter.

During that same afternoon, July 1944, a bomb exploded by Church End House. It was in the area of the current church car park that it exploded causing much damage around it. Uncle George Alderson owned a small holding next to his house where two new houses have recently been built, Beechcroft and Tudor Rose. The small holding took a major impact and the horse in the stable was killed instantly. There were also turkeys being fattened up for Christmas. They had their feathers blown off and had to be put down, as they were all in a state of severe shock. The church was badly affected and the building undermined, with stained glass windows shattered, the roof damaged and cracks appeared in the walls from damage to the foundations.

St Martin's Church in winter from Church End House

The winters were very much colder as Jane grew up and one of the delights of winter was ice skating on Combe Bank Lake near the school. Jane would stand and watch experienced skaters spin and dance while gliding across the ice. On waking up in the mornings at home, the inside windows were covered in ice and Jane would etch pretty patterns into them. There was no central heating and coal fires had little effect before being re-stoked after dying down through the night.

As the branch railway line to Westerham ran close to her house it was fun for her and her brother to take a basket or sack and watch the engine pass by. Big, black, shiny bright lumps of coal would fall on the track behind it and they would happily scoop it up. It burned so well and was a treasure hunt of fun to collect.

In similar vein, Oveney Green Farm, in Sundridge would harvest swedes and cabbages from their fields. Again some would fall off the laden trailers and they were taken home to be cooked. The family looked forward to them and as Jane said, "they were gorgeous."

Mr Arthur Archer ran The Stanhope Arms beside Church End and his son Robert and Jane would play bat and ball outside the pub. They could hit their ball back and forth with little fear of traffic as the road was so quiet then.

As Jane still lived in Sundridge she went to school at the Combe Bank Convent. The nuns were not keen to accept her though as she was of the Church of England faith and not Roman Catholic. Uncle George solved the problem by offering them as much coke and coal as they needed from his coal merchants business!

Tragedy struck the family in 1957 when Jane's elder brother Edward Alderson Pierce died in a cycling accident. He was a talented student and was close to finishing his studies at the Kent Farming Institute in Sittingbourne. He finished a lecture and was cycling back to his digs over a newly tarmacked road covered in loose gravel. The bike skidded and Edward flew over the handle bars head first. At first he was thought to have concussion, but by the next morning he was dreadfully ill and his mother Joyce was summoned by the Institute. She called an ambulance, but Edward passed away before it could reach the hospital. He was nineteen and on the threshold of his career. His studies in farming work had earned him all the college cups and future success was guaranteed. Henry Steven of Oveney Green Farm, had already offered him a job as his farm manager. The shock of this catastrophe left his parents, Joyce and Charlie heartbroken.

After school, Jane chose a career in catering and signed up for a two year course at Lewisham Technical College. She achieved her City and Guilds award and hoped she could instantly be successful in a managerial role. As her instructor put it, "Oh Jane, you cannot run before you can walk!" So she took a job at Emily Jackson House, newly reopened in Eardly Road, Sevenoaks. She cooked for the patients in shifts of 6 a.m. – 2 p.m. or 2 p.m. – 8 p.m. It was a depressing place with many patients critically ill. Still, she must have cheered them up one Christmas when she cooked a huge turkey. It would barely fit in the oven and when it was cooked she needed help to lift it out. They took it up to the ward and carved this delicious feast in front of everyone.

From there she moved on as the assistant catering manager to St Helen's Hospital, now known as Conquest Hospital, in Hastings. She was duly promoted to catering manager and moved around various hospitals linked to St Helen's. Various jobs followed, but catering finally lost its appeal and so a job change was needed. She was working for the Ovaltine Company in Upper Grosvenor Street, London and decided to walk around to Selfridges to see if they could offer her a job. She knew she could not sit in an office for them, as her jobs had always kept her active and on her feet. "So," they said, "how about being a store detective?" "Well," she thought, "I would be walking around, so I did!" She took staff training and has many untold stories of protecting the store. However, the best part was meeting her future husband John Smithers who was a buyer in the menswear department. They courted and Jane became Mrs Smithers in 1968.

She and John emigrated to Perth, Australia soon after their marriage and again Jane took a job in security. However, John found himself homesick and missing the history and culture of his own country. Their foreign foray lasted a year and back they came. John returned to Selfridges and they returned to Brasted to have their first son. Her family persuaded them to take the top floor of Church End House as it was 'a lovely place to have a baby'.

So after all these adventures Jane was back in the area of her roots. They ultimately bought Meadow Cottage in Church Road where they could be close to the rest of her family.

In October 1987, Uncle George became very ill and Jane left the family home to return to the flat and look after him. She described an old barometer on the wall in the house and how every night she would automatically tap it and look at the dial. On this night the needle was right down in the corner and she thought her tapping had finally broken it. During the night she awoke up to a terrible roar, like a jet plane. Doors slammed and a window blew open and broke. The unpredicted 1987 hurricane had arrived and only the barometer had correctly forecast it. She crept down to George shouting out that she was on her way. They stayed up all night close to a fire, still alight in the grate and giving out a little warmth. The power had failed and subsequently stayed off for several days. Together they listened to the wind revving up and then quietening down and then howling all around them again. The next morning she called John, as the phone was still working, to see how he had fared down the road. He had heard nothing and slept right through the night. Saying goodbye, he then drove his car out of the driveway to find he was totally blocked in by fallen trees and instantly reversed back home. Church End House lost tiles from the roof and, of course, a broken window. More painful for George was the loss of his large pine trees lying in a heap in the garden. They had been planted by his father many years before.

John and Jane later moved back to Church End House to care for her uncle in his final year. They again had the top floor flat and George stayed downstairs. She would be cautious moving around at night and always called out to George that it was only her. There was a good reason for this. He always kept his shotgun by him on the bed. The house had previously suffered burglars who had broken into the property while George was inside. They had chosen the items they wanted to steal and moved them outside to the lawn. Somehow, they must have been disturbed, as they left them there and scarpered. So the shotgun that had previously only hunted rabbits and pheasants was ready for bigger action. As George said, he could, "shoot them in the legs where you are allowed to! They are not coming in my house again." George finally passed on the 22nd December 1988 at the age of eighty five and is buried in St Martin's churchyard.

John and Jane took over Church End House, with its beautiful interior and wonderful garden. It had been filled with magnificent furniture, collected from sales and auctions by Uncle George Henry and her grandfather George Albert. There were many souvenirs of the past collected thoughtfully over the years. Walking through the kitchen gate, the house wall was covered in horse shoes, an old frying pan, a coffee grinder, a corn grinder and many more knickknacks. They did cause a little difficulty, as car rallies would come to the property searching for objects on their treasure hunt wanted lists. Identifying treasure hunt objects on the outside of the property was fine, but strangers coming into the private gardens to locate them was too much to put up with!

Church End House

On the garage wall were more mementoes of the Alderson family. A large black sign hung on the brickwork advertising:

G. Alderson
Coal, Coke and Forage
Merchant
Motor Cars and Carriages
Carting Contractors

There was also an old petrol pump on the driveway, which was later bought by a friend of George's and has since been restored to working order. In the garden were two wells, one real and one ornamental. Each had a large bell hanging over it. The smaller bell was a fire bell from a Westerham fire engine. The larger bell was later sent to a chapel school in South Africa.

Jane would often see the local rector, The Reverend Anthony Curry, who was a multi-talented man. He played the organ beautifully and would take pupils for lessons in London. In the early morning of the 4th November 1989, Jane looked out of the kitchen window and saw smoke drifting up from what looked like the roof of the church. She knew Tony Curry was always cutting the grass, strimming and trimming the churchyard and she hoped the smoke was one of his fires. "No," she uttered, "it can't be," and she urgently phoned the rectory to report her sighting. On the other end of the phone, was Ann Curry, who was a slightly edgy character and sharply told her that they already knew of the fire and the fire brigade had been sent for.

John was out taking their youngest son to Sevenoaks. When he returned, he rushed into action and, along with others, went into the burning church to rescue what he could. He described entering the church and seeing brilliant colours, bright and dazzling, all being reflected from what was by now the roaring flames. He helped a fireman lift out the lectern with its brass eagle on top. The fire had already scorched it, but it was later restored and returned to the church.

The road was filled with fire engines sent from all over the area. The police closed Church Road and then they popped in and out of Jane's house to use her phone to give progress reports. Someone went to the village shop and bought bread, sandwich fillings and milk to make tea in the Church Hall building in the car park (long since demolished). Jane helped and she says the day passed in a flash as they all worked together to support the services, including ambulance men on site for any injuries. Everyone was terribly shocked by the devastation.

The brass lectern in St Martin's Church that was rescued by John Smithers

It transpired that the fire had been started by a man who had entered the church the night before, soaked through from pouring rain. The bell ringers had been practising that evening, and the church doors were open. He took his wet clothes off and turned on an electric fire to dry them. He then left the building, but evidently he had not turned the fire off again. Slowly through the night the fire took hold with no one knowing. The police asked Jane if she had seen anyone around the church, but then they discovered a man standing watching excitedly as the flames leapt into the sky. The police arrested him, but afterwards he was judged mentally unstable and no charges were ever brought against him. Jane later donated funds to restore some large, ornate cupboard doors inside the church in the name of her mother.

While the church was closed for rebuilding, Church End House was occasionally mistaken for the rectory. One day a lady knocked on the door and announced, "I've come because I want my baby baptised and I wondered if it could be done in the bird table in your garden?" Was she serious? Oh yes, but also unlucky!

The church services moved to Brasted School which had recently been vacated, as it had amalgamated with Sundridge School. Jane would help with the teas and one day she found a most wonderful white table cloth, the perfect item to cheer up the plain table. It looked so nice until Ann Curry arrived and was most put out, saying, "That is the altar cloth and must come off immediately."

The Alderson Family

William Alderson was born in 1805 in Holtby, Yorkshire. He met and married Mary Greenwood in St Martin's Church, Brasted in November 1829. Their six children were mostly born in Brasted where he was recorded as being an agricultural labourer. However, by the 1861 census, William had become a farm bailiff for Heverswood Lodge and was living on the estate. He died there on 6th May 1885.

William, the second son of this family was born in 1835. He followed his father into work as a farm worker. His census records have him recorded as being the only child born outside Brasted, in Frant, Sussex although his family must have been there for a very short time. He married Louisa Palmer of Sundridge again in Brasted Church in July 1857. His six children were all born in Brasted.

George Henry Alderson was the fourth child born on the 7th February 1863. His early career can also be followed in the ten yearly census documents. In 1881, the family lived in Chart Lane and George was an agricultural worker, as many men were in the area at that time. In 1891, he lived in the Westminster district with his mother Louisa. His occupation was described as a coachman and groom. Things changed and in 1898 he and Louisa had taken on the tenancy at The Bull Inn in Brasted. He married Fanny Jeal in Brasted in 1902 and their children, George Albert and Joyce Marie were both born in the pub. George Henry had taken over several horses and carts stabled on the premises left by the previous landlord, Richard Berry. Richard had gone to Sevenoaks to be a livery stable keeper, where he hired out horses from his new premises. The acquisition of the horses and carriages, kept at the back of the pub premises enabled George to develop a business of hiring them out.

George provided most of the horses for the Sundridge Fire Brigade, which was once stationed where the Sundridge village store now stands. The firemen could be called out all over the area. The horses would be used to haul the fire cart to fires ranging from houses to hay stacks. In 1912 he acquired the local coal delivery business and started to successfully supply the coal and coke needs for the local community as well.

In the same year many local properties were auctioned off by the executors of the Colonel William Fearnon Tipping estate. He had lived in Brasted Place from where his father had secured the purchase of many Brasted properties, restored them and rented them out. George bid and successfully acquired Church Cottage. He then had it renovated and extended and renamed it Church End House. It became a classic Kent tiled house, large and attractively built, with The Bull Inn just five minutes' walk away.

It was the perfect base for his expanding businesses and provided plenty of room for his young family. However, his occupation was delayed as the renovations were taking place. When the property was returned to him, his family were finally able to move in.

In 1920, George Henry modernised his horse carriage business and replaced them with motor vehicles. The horses were retired to live out in the freedom of the fields. Inevitably, this talented business man expanded his enterprise and bought and operated a fleet of coaches.

Brasted Station and George Alderson's Coal Yard

As they all required regular maintenance he built a garage for storing parts and repairs. The coaches proved very popular and were hired for journeys all over London and the south. His business enterprises always needed updating and modernisation was moving ahead at a rapid pace.

By the time the 1939 census was taken, George Henry was seventy-six and described himself as a retired farmer. That said, he was still approached by the government who asked him to use his farmland to grow food, to help the war effort. George Henry died on the 27th December 1946 having had a very successful career as a victualler and entrepreneur. Fanny inherited Church End House and owned it until her death on the 17th May 1951.

George Alderson's first Ford taxi in Brasted

A point of interest for Church End House or Church Cottage as it was known earlier, was that in 1898 Charles Victor Benecke and his wife Marie Mendelssohn had rented the house. She was the daughter of the German composer, Felix Mendelssohn. It seems the house and particularly the drawing room hosted a lot of talented musical gatherings, from this families connections.

Jane remembered her grandfather as always wearing a thick apron, with his ruddy face looking over it. The Bull Inn was heated by an open fire and from time to time George would roast rats over it and the locals would eat them!

Jane's uncle, George Albert, born on the 22nd September 1903, had already taken over the running of most of the Alderson businesses by the time of the 1939 census and he inherited the house after his mother's death. He was already a well-respected member of the Brasted community. He had two marriages, but sadly both ended in divorce.

Jane's mother, Joyce ran a small dance school at Church End House for local children. They learnt ballet and ballroom dancing in the large dining room. Joyce had been taught by Dame Marie Rambert who had a ballet school in London called Ballet Rambert. Marie Rambert was born in Poland to a Polish father and Russian mother. As a teacher she was strict and she would swear at her students in broken, heavily accented English. She was a harsh disciplinarian, but would have been pleased that Joyce continued to share her dancing knowledge.

Joyce also took the Sunday school meetings for the children in the church. The rector was the Reverend Hugh Longuet - Higgins and Jane well remembers that his sermons would to go on forever.

Joyce once met Sir Winston Churchill while out riding her horse near Chartwell. He was known for his bricklaying skills and was busy working on a wall. The horses were frequent visitors to the local blacksmiths on Brasted Green.

Before World War Two, George and his sister ran a tennis club in the grounds of Church End House, which had plenty of room, as the property sprawled over five acres. They had to stop, however, when the Army subsequently requisitioned the property. The Army also requisitioned two of George's lorries along with their drivers, Mr Hall and Mr Forester. They were sent to Shorncliffe Barracks, Folkestone for war duty.

George was a hugely popular man locally, kind and generous. He is remembered with affection by everyone who speaks of him. However, he was a humble man and used to say he was only a tradesman! George would take a pony and trap to Brasted Station just before Christmas every year. There he would meet Father Christmas off the train and they would trot down Church Road. The pavement was lined with people and Father Christmas would throw sweets out to them, as they passed by. The end destination was Markwicks, the village store where Father Christmas was set up with tubs of toys to give out to the children.

George had a dance band and jazz group that were hired out for parties. George played the drums and they often performed at the village hall on dance nights or for weddings. He would also organise fireworks in his field each November 5th. All locals were welcome and the event was always eagerly anticipated.

Winston Churchill was a client of the coal business and a notoriously bad bill payer. George went in person one day to collect his dues. Winston appeared in maroon slippers, with his initials sewn in gold thread. The two men become friends and Winston gave him an old top hat and a coat. George hung them in his kitchen, to make it feel like Winston had just called in to visit and could be found somewhere in the house. Finally they became too dusty and had to be taken down.

George had a passion for gardening as his father before him. His prized possession was a collection of sixty varieties of camellias, kept in his greenhouse. Eventually, they grew so well they pushed out the greenhouse glass, but were so well-treasured they were never consigned to the garden.

The Alderson family had a lot of influence in the village, both in employment and entertainment. They took much pleasure in sharing their generosity and talents wherever they could. The village is poorer for the loss of this family!

September 2016

Pamela Day

née Giles

Pam Ann Giles was born in August 1942 at 2 Cacketts Cottages, Brasted Chart. Her parents, Charles Leslie and Doris née Balderstone had both moved to Brasted for work. Charles came from Newhaven and was one of eleven children. His father James worked on the Newhaven to Dieppe ferry crossing. Charles came to Hann's Grocers, in Brasted High Street, to take up a master grocer's apprenticeship. Doris came to Brasted for the country air and took a position of work for Mrs Mary Jackson, at a large house called Philippines in Ide Hill. She was one of nine children from Ilford, Essex.

Their wedding took place on a wintery day in Ilford, on the 14th March 1937. Without sophisticated camera equipment the white wedding dress against the white, snowy scenery was impossible. The following week they dressed up again and returned to have their official wedding photographs taken.

Charles was in the army when Pam was born. On leave for the first time since his daughter was born, he arrived home and quickly fell asleep. "Aren't you going to look at your daughter?" asked Doris indignantly. With a small baby and the war so intense in Kent and

Charles and Doris Giles

London, from time to time Doris would stay with one of her sister's, Mabel, in Ipswich. With Charles on a fleeting visit a quick decision was made to christen Pam in Suffolk. So, on All Saint's Day, 1st November 1942 the service took place in St Thomas Church, Ipswich. Doris had four sisters and none of them had children of their own. Pam was the much loved niece and they spoiled her whenever they could.

Back in Brasted Chart the barrage balloons drew Pam's attention. 'Mummy, there are elephants flying in the sky!' was her observation.

Living in number 1 Cacketts Cottages was the Woodgate family with children Valerie and Trevor. At number 3 was the Rixon family and their son Brian. All the children were of a similar age and grew up as instant playmates. They had the freedom of the local woods and could climb trees and busy themselves with hide and seek. Building dens and camps was easy using the fallen branches and twigs.

Pam aged about three

Doris and Auntie Elsie with
Valerie Woodgate, Brian Rixon,
Pam and Trevor Woodgate

The cottages were built on a downhill gradient, with number 1 attached at a right angle to the other two. It was also the highest cottage on the hill, so Pam's first floor bedroom was in line with the downstairs sitting room of number one. As Pam lay in her bedroom with her window open she could hear the radio playing as Ambrose Homewood listened in the evenings. If she went to bed early she could hear the football results on a Saturday.

From the Giles's cottage back bedroom, Pam and Val would open windows and communicate. Not by shouting, but using a walkie-talkie made of tin cans (or beakers) and a piece of string. Holes were drilled though the bottom of the receptacles and string was passed through each end and knotted inside them. When the string was

204

pulled taut they could speak to each other and their voices vibrated down the string and came back at the other end in the magnified voice of the speaker. Children might laugh today as their fingers press a button and they speak to their mates on mobile phones.

Pam started at Brasted village school when it taught all ages up to school leaving age. At the same time Mr Blezard, the new headmaster, also arrived. The school was short of staff and the infants found themselves without a teacher. The older children were tasked with looking after them and counting heads in the mornings and afternoons and ringing the school bell at the right times. They must have seemed very grown up and important to the tiny new starters!

Early maths lessons were achieved with the help of an enormous glass jar of shells used for counting practice. This was accompanied by the smell of delicious food coming from the kitchen close by. The first Christmas term saw Pam being chosen for the part of Goldilocks in the Christmas play. Her beautiful flaxen locks made her a perfect choice although Goldilocks is not often associated with any Christmas entertainment! To perform this play all the desks were pushed together even though they varied in height. Everyone tried hard not to trip or fall down the gaps. However, poor Pam wailed her heart out, but was soon forgiven when she went down with pneumonia an hour or two later. Not the best way to greet her Christmas that year!

The nit nurse, although an excuse for altering the school routine, was not a welcome visitor. She was a very stern lady and her nails scratched as she searched heads for those dreaded little creatures. A clinic was set up in the Village Hall for teeth inspections and in fear Pam and her class mates would scuttle across the road hoping the dentist's drill was not for them!

Mr Blezard seemed to relish in giving out lines, usually in the form of 'I must not chatter in class,' to be written one hundred times. If not done by the following day, and written within school break times, he would double the punishment. Pam says she never did achieve the target and it didn't occur to her to cut down on the talking!

One day Pam was punished by Mr Blezard. No child had to do very much to feel his wrath and Pam cannot remember why this happened. What she does remember is being put under his desk in the cubby hole to sit in quiet contemplation. After much thought it seemed a great idea to tie his shoe laces together and she did! He certainly stumbled, but whatever happened next is a blur.

School days, on the whole, were a happy time. The end of the day always finished with the singing of 'Now The Day Is Over' and a great crashing of chairs as they were thumped on top of the desks ready for the cleaners.

Pam took her eleven plus exam and found herself off to Tonbridge Girls Grammar School to complete her education. On leaving school she took up a successful career in London. However, that provides more tales, but perhaps for another story.

Meanwhile life continued in Brasted and Brasted Chart for Pam and her friends. Mrs Bremner of Thatches on the Chart originally started the Brasted Fellowship Group. She was active in the community and on one occasion had the local children dress up as walking whist cards. Many pillowcases were converted by mothers and the result was perfectly impressive.

Children dressed in their whist card costumes

Mrs Woodgate, next door, attended the Baptist Chapel facing Church Road. Doris decided it was suitable for Pam too and she joined the congregation. Pam enjoyed Sunday school and the organised children's parties. Outings were arranged to Bexhill and Hastings and the more you attended the chapel the cheaper the tickets were for the trips. The participants took a sandwich for the day out and they always stopped at the nearest Baptist Chapel for afternoon tea as they returned home. For the Mothering Sunday service Pam would go to Chartfield Farm at Colinette and pick masses of primroses to decorate chapel. When the Harvest Festival service was due Doris and Charles would pick apples from their garden. Doris would polish them so hard you could almost see your face in them!

On snowy days the little gang of friends would take their sledges out. The Chart was limited as trees grew everywhere. Pam clearly remembers one occasion when they hauled their sledges up Hogtrough Hill to a field above Pilgrims Way. To make the adventure more fun and little more dangerous, they built a snow jump that they hit at speed and took off! The next barrier was the barbed wire fence between them and the road! In summer a flat part of Chart Lane became their tennis court where little or no traffic interrupted them.

Brasted Swimming Pool was a place to spend many hours during the summer months. Fed by fresh water from the River Darent, it was always very cold and in the early part of the season you could find yourself swimming amongst tadpoles! There were separate changing rooms for the boys and girls, built of very knotty wood with single compartments in each block. The girls had to choose their base within extremely carefully, as the boys took to poking the knots from the outside to create a peepshow! The pool was finally closed in 1953 mainly due to health and safety reasons, but the changing rooms were used by the thriving Tennis Club for some while after until they were also demolished.

Pam and her friends would enjoy putting their sweet ration coupons together and then visit Mrs Stott in her sweet shop. They would ask her to count out two or three hundred sweeties for their coupons. The whole intention was to get the most sweets for their allowance. The smaller the sweet the better!

Somehow, Pam was volunteered to deliver papers to Brasted Chart during her school holidays, when the regular man, Mr Ingram was not available. He would use his car which was easy, but Pam had to walk to Maudsleys the newsagent in the village to collect the papers. They would come in two separate bags. She then waited for the 413 bus and loaded up her bags. The driver would obligingly stop at the Chart village post office to allow Pam to drop off the bag for the lower half of her round. He waited until she boarded again and took her on to the start of the round at the top of the Chart. Off she trotted to complete her round in two halves with a little help from the bus driver!

To earn extra pocket money Pam took a Saturday job at Woolworths in Sevenoaks. She was assigned to the sweet counter which seemed appropriate after her practice with Mrs Stott! The managers were happy that their staff could help themselves to a few sweets, but judged that they would soon get sick of them and not bother again. The sweets were protected by a glass counter and the boys would come in and wrap on the glass for attention. She held her own and refused to serve them until they said please. Pam wisely saved her money for when she might need it in the future. As it turned out she was able to buy her first season ticket to London when she stared work in the big smoke!

At the age of sixteen, Pam joined the congregation at St Martin's Church. She learnt to ring the bells with Fred Budgen and Bob Sherlock. Then, she was invited to join the choir along with several other lady singers and is still busy singing today. The rehearsal times clashed and Pam chose the choir over the bells. She has been an enthusiastic supporter of the church having volunteered for the Parish Church Council, where at various stages she has undertaken the rolls of secretary and treasurer. For any occasion Pam has actively supported our village church.

In 1961 Brasted held its carnival and Pam was elected as the carnival queen. The procession passed through the High Street and onto the Recreation Ground where many events were organised. There would be a baby show and dog show. Aunty Elsie, Doris's sister always came and was game for anything including the testing tug o' war competition.

Pam had always known Robert (Bob) Day, the son of Arch and Annie. Bob was the last person in Brasted to be called up for National Service. One day, Annie suggested that Pam write to Bob, so she did. That Christmas a card dropped through her letter box from the army base in Cyprus. With Bob's writing on the front she tore it open and started to read a card that announced, happy Christmas to my brother. Surely there had been a muddle so she rushed the card to Annie who calmly explained that 'brother' cards were the only Christmas cards Bob could find in the NAAFI and everyone had one!

Their friendship grew and on a beautiful afternoon on the 14th September 1963, they were married by the Reverend Cosgrove, in St

Martin's Church. The service was carefully planned for 3 p.m. to fit around milking and milk rounds that Arch was committed to at Mill

Farm. Mr Jenner, the taxi driver from Westerham turned up at Cacketts Cottage to take Pam and Charles to the church.

A large reception took place at the Village Hall for about one hundred and ten guests. Mrs Louie Ring, the caretaker, made salad dishes, while Uncle Dennis made a splendid three tier wedding cake. He was Bob's uncle and a baker by trade. Doris was cross with herself because she forgot to have sherry to hand as guests arrived, but no one else noticed. The entertainment was provided by Bert Mombrum, a one man band. He set up his drums and accompanied records played on his record player. They spent their honeymoon at a Shanklin hotel on the Isle of Wight. The first morning Pam pulled back the curtains and there walking up the driveway was a work colleague and her husband!

For the first time Pam left Cacketts Cottage and went to live at Vale Cottage a little further up Chart Lane. Originally, they rented the beautiful cottage in its magnificent location, but later were able to purchase it. They undertook a large extension and Bob manicured the garden until it looked like a park. Full of wildlife, it is visited by many birds and mammals including Roe and Fallow deer who may not be so welcome through their desire to eat bushes and flower buds! Still the peacefulness and serenity of the cottage and garden are always evident.

Pam remembered her first Christmas as Bob's wife and a visit to Mill Farm to see Arch and his brothers at work on their dairy farm. It was a frosty morning and Arch announced, "We have our first Christmas calf, but it is a male and will soon be a meat pie!" Farming began and ended right there for Pam.

The hurricane of 1987 saw the Chart hit hard by the catastrophic winds across the woodlands and properties. Bob and Pam had two cats at the time and Pam woke wondering why the cats were making such a noise. She pulled back the sitting room curtains and the wood at the bottom of the garden was gone. She rushed to Bob who could not believe what she was saying until he saw the devastation for himself. From their garden they could clearly see Foxwold House and garden for the first time ever. As the wind blew from the south west, all the trees on the boundary of their garden blew over into their property. Pam's comment was that they acquired a lot of new vegetation that day, but all of it was lying on the ground! They spent the next week cutting up and clearing trees.

One month after the hurricane Arch and Annie Day were due to celebrate their golden wedding anniversary. Pam had a freezer full of prepared food and the hurricane caused power cuts for many days. A friend still had power and saved the day by taking the food before it defrosted. The celebration successfully took place on the 21st November 1987 in the old hut, in the church car park.

Both Pam and Bob involved themselves in helping and supporting St Martin's Church. On the day of the fire in 1989, Jane Walker phoned Pam to report seeing the rising smoke. Pam walked to the bottom of her garden and could instantly see the same destructive black smoke wafting upwards into the sky. She rushed back and called Bob at his workplace as he was a churchwarden. He rushed to the church, but the devastation was a shocking reality. The next day, Pam and Bob went to the morning service at St Mary's in Sundridge, but it simply highlighted their overwhelming sadness for their own church.

Bob attended well over one hundred meetings (not that he was counting!) while the church was repaired. The triumph came when

St Martin's Church ablaze on 4th November 1989

The aftermath of the St Martin's Church fire

The restoration committee outside the newly restored St Martin's Church

The congregation returning to St Martin's Church

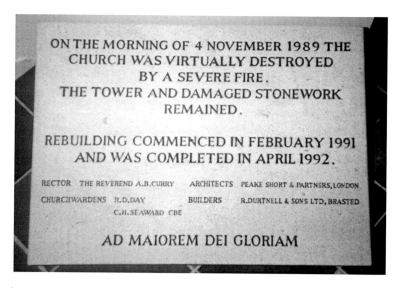

ON THE MORNING OF 4 NOVEMBER 1989 THE
CHURCH WAS VIRTUALLY DESTROYED
BY A SEVERE FIRE.
THE TOWER AND DAMAGED STONEWORK
REMAINED.

REBUILDING COMMENCED IN FEBRUARY 1991
AND WAS COMPLETED IN APRIL 1992.

RECTOR   THE REVEREND A.B.CURRY   ARCHITECTS   PEAKE SHORT & PARTNERS, LONDON

CHURCHWARDENS   H.D.DAY   BUILDERS   R.DURTNELL & SONS LTD, BRASTED
           C.H.SEAWARD CBE

AD MAIOREM DEI GLORIAM

the congregation marched up Church Lane in 1992, from the empty Brasted School and reinstalled itself in the newly renovated church.

Pam today is as active as ever in the village. She has a wonderful memory and fondness for life in this village, some of which she has kindly shared in her 'story'.

What changes has Pam seen in the village? Sadly her comments were how life has changed for the worse.

With the loss of shops there are far fewer people out and about in the High Street. Reverend Bertie Talbot used to park his car and just walk up and down passing the time of day with all those he met.

Families did not have cars and tended to stay in the village for entertainment. Dances at the Village Hall were packed with excited local residents.

Commuters have replaced a lot of local families as improved mobility has meant easy access to trains, roads and other towns to work and socialise in.

House prices have increased excessively. Children of village families have not been able to afford local housing. Families now live far from each other and the sense of family togetherness has gone.

April 2018

Ian Brown

Ian's family came to Brasted with his grandfather, George Brown Senior, in 1912. George moved into Heverswood Lodge and was employed as the head gardener for the Heverswood Estate. He arrived with his five daughters and one son. Brigadier-General Harry Anthony Chandos-Pole-Gell owned the Heverswood Estate, along with his wife Ada. They must have kept George busy, as the estate was large and in 1923 Harry lent his grounds to a Brasted Church fête. It was well supported, with many familiar villagers' names both helping and attending to make the day successful. In 1926 the estate hosted the British Empire Day celebrations. The school children attended, including some from Toy's Hill, brought by George Alderson's charabanc. Once assembled, the children marched from Brasted Green to Heverswood. Sports events and entertainment were organised for them. George must have been very busy in the gardens, particularly when these special events were held.

George senior was a great supporter of the Sundridge and Brasted Horticultural Society. He would enter his produce and became a much-respected judge at various shows in the district. He is also credited with being the instigator of Brasted Sand Pits. He needed sand for his gardening projects and found it in the pit area. It went on to become a thriving business.

George senior and his family
L. to R. George Senior, Peggy, Beth behind Georgina, George junior, Mary Purdie,
Lou and Jean

George senior left Brasted to continue working in Chobham, Surrey in the service of Brigadier General Harry Chandos-Pole-Gell. He died in hospital in Wendlesham, Surrey in 1942. He was brought back to Brasted and laid to rest in St Martin's Churchyard. His wife Mary Purdie Brown followed him in 1950 and they are buried together; once again reunited.

Ian's father was George Adam Brown, born on the 12th April 1913. After leaving Brasted School, George started work at Bond's Garage in the village. In September 1927, aged fourteen and a half, he had a dreadful accident, which scarred him for life. He was charged with burning rubbish at the garage. He found a forty gallon tank, mostly filled with oil, which he thought would encourage the flames. He

218

used a rake, intending to tip a little from the tank, but it fell over completely, spilling out all its contents. Part of it soaked the clothing on George's arm and leg and he was horribly burnt, as a result. PC Giles and Mr Sharp rolled him to extinguish the flames and Dr Ward attended his wounds.

On a trip to Westerham, for a New Year's Eve dance, George met Edna Phyllis May Tough. She was working at the Vestey Estate as an upstairs maid. At work she was known as 'Peggy' and that is how she was always known in Brasted. Her father, Charles, had taken a vehicle mechanics and chauffeur training course with Rolls Royce and he was also employed on the estate, driving the magnificent Vestey family Rolls Royce. George would visit the estate to maintain their generator and of course, see the lovely 'Peggy'. In 1937 George and Edna married, close to her family home in Egham, Surrey. Returning to Brasted, George continued to work for Bond's Garage.

Charles Tough, Peggy and the Rolls Royce

When World War Two began, George started working for Sevenoaks Council as their only mechanic, fixing and maintaining ambulances, ARP vehicles and all other service vehicles in the Sevenoaks' fleet. It was classed as a reserve occupation, as the shocking, disfiguring burn wounds on George's leg must have precluded him from any military service. He worked at Dunbrik Depot, Sundridge which, even now, has a garage for council vehicle maintenance.

In August 1942, Ian was born at number 10 High Street, the house at the end of Alms Row, across from the school. Making his entry as a breech birth caused lots of trouble and may explain why he was an only child! One of Ian's first memories, aged three, was being caught by a blast from a flying bomb exploding in Brasted Chart. He was propelled backwards into the living room, but fortunately was not badly hurt. George and Edna billeted three airmen at number 10. They worked at the Sundridge barrage balloon site, in a field off Combe Bank Drive. They had a depot where damaged balloons were repaired. Ian would visit them, but was too small to ride up on the repaired balloons. Ian clearly remembers seeing strips of silver foil hanging from trees and scattered on the ground. Like John Bellingham, he also witnessed chaff scattered by German planes, but this time over Sundridge. Designed to confuse the local radar systems, it either swamped the radar with images of the possibility of multiple planes flying past, or it could utterly confuse the radar screens with so much interference.

After the war, George junior moved on to his own motor mechanics business at Park Garage, behind the White Hart cottages in the High Street. He chose the name for the parkland at the rear of the garage. At first, he rented his workshop from George Alderson and everything went smoothly until George Alderson wanted to sell the property, as a bus depot with workshops. He planned to sell his small fleet of coaches as a going concern. After some negotiation, George Brown managed to buy the property and secure his own business.

Ian started his schooling in Brasted, although very little of it stands out in his memory. He says he has run late for everything all his life and school was no different. He did get into regular trouble for his timekeeping, even though he only lived over the alleyway! The only other event that came to mind was about his gym bag. His teacher swung it towards him from the peg and he grabbed it as it went flying past. The teacher accused him of snatching it, although he had not deliberately jerked it at all. For punishment Ian was made to stand on a box next to the chalkboard. Beside the box was a piano with a pot of chalk on it. What was a little boy to do to entertain himself? Quietly crunch up all the chalk in his boredom, of course!

The school still had its old air raid shelter, which by now held all the gardening equipment. Ian remembers being tasked with cleaning the tools, which was a job he relished. The shelter had no windows so no one knew what was going on inside! The tools took a long, long time to clean, what a great chance to avoid lessons!

In 1953 Ian and his parents moved to a bungalow called Clova in Coles Lane. Grandfather, George senior bought it immediately after it had been built and named it after the beautiful valley in Angus Scotland, close to where he was born. However, not long after, George senior moved away to Surrey, as a result of his employment with the Chandos-Pole-Gell family. The bungalow was rented for a number of years until George junior and his little family moved in, when Ian was eleven. Ian and his family would take holidays in Scotland and explore the country his grandfather loved so much.

A sad memory for Ian was one of the lady that moved into number

10 when his family moved out. She went to the hardware store to buy a length of rope. It must have seemed odd when she asked the shopkeeper if it was strong enough to hold her weight! She was returned home and hanged herself with it in the old outside toilet. Everyone suffered her sadness at her terrible ending.

Ian went to the Churchill School in Westerham in his senior school years. He would travel on the 'Westerham Flyer' steam engine, standing on the footplate, blowing the whistle all the way, as they went along the tracks. In the summer months he would cycle to school. On one occasion he was busy chasing the bus along the A25, with his head down, pedalling like mad. Suddenly his pedal caught the pavement and he was thrown up in the air and landed on top of the railings by the allotments. His bike didn't fare any better and was too damaged to be ridden! Both had to be limped home!

In Westerham he met his best friend, Roger Gale and much fun was to be had together. The woods in Brasted and Westerham made for wonderful play areas for the boys. They made themselves bows and arrows and later upgraded to swords. Next came air pistols with which the boys could play commandos, chasing one another down. Ian was never hit, but there was one incident that did not go well. Each gun could only shoot one pellet, but Roger grabbed an unfired gun and his thumb was over the barrel as it went off. The shot planted itself in his thumb leaving him jumping up and down in pain. His mates simply fell about laughing - boys. The pellet was successfully removed and certainly did not dampen the passion for commandos! Ian went on from this to be an accomplished target shooter and travels all around the area to shooting ranges to test his skills. This includes Bisley Shooting Ground, in Surrey, the most exclusive premier centre in the country.

In his teenage years, Ian would take holidays with Roger and his family. They usually went to the beautiful Ringstead Bay, in Dorset. His father would rent a small boat from the local fishermen and the boys would play in it all day. On one occasion they rowed out a long way, but the tide turned and they had a scary struggle to row back. It took them twice as long and left them completely exhausted. They learned a great deal of respect for the ocean and its tides that day.

Flying model airplanes was another hobby to be enjoyed in the local fields. They were mostly gliders or rubber band-launched planes. Ian did graduate to radio-controlled planes, but they could take a year to build and then fly out of control and crash! One even ended up in the top of a tree.

Having left school, Ian went on to Bromley Arts College to study fine art and stone carving. He was particularly talented at stone masonry. In a college project, everyone in the class was given a stone to shape, which would eventually become the master's driveway boundary. Ian was top of the class and, as a reward, he was asked to reshape everyone else's stone to match his! Later, Ian made the cap stones for a well at the Cowen family property in Sundridge. He also carved the Clova name plate that is still on the bungalow today. In the life-class the students had models to draw, one of whom was Quentin Crisp. Quentin is well-documented as a colourful character, but he spent over thirty years modelling in art colleges in London and the surrounding counties.

At college Ian met his lifelong partner, Ann Kay, from Sevenoaks. Ann has drawn and painted many wonderful pictures of Brasted buildings, both old and new. They are a fine and accurate record of the village.

While Ian was at college, the studio opposite George was rented by a couple, called Bernard Ashley and Laura Mountney. Better known as Laura Ashley, this is where their company started to build towards the multi-million pound empire it became. They had started their business in a chicken house in Limpsfield before moving into Brasted. In the studio they designed and printed fabric using pots of dye, in their small premises opposite George. Disaster stuck when Brasted flooded and the dye pots fell into the water causing streaks of colour flowing like a rainbow into the street! This may have prompted them to move on to their amazing success!

At the age of sixteen, Ian wanted a sports car when he passed his driving test. The solution was to build himself an Austin 7 special. He found a complete Austin 7, which he took apart down to the chassis and rebuilt it from there. He rebuilt the engine and gear box and made a tubular frame. The frame held aluminium sheeting to form the new sports body. He fitted hydraulic brakes to improve the original poor braking system. Then he painted it with lightweight, blue aircraft paint in the hope that being 'lighter' the car

Ian with his converted Austin 7

would go faster! The paint had barely dried on his masterpiece when someone came along and made him an offer he couldn't refuse and he sold it! Later, Ian achieved his sports car dream when he made himself a Lotus Super 7 kit car and this time he kept it!

After college, Ian chose to work for his father, even though George thought it might be better for him to work at another garage. Forty years later Ian retired, still working at Park Garage with George! Cars were fairly simple to work on as they were all manual controls and all parts could be repaired or replaced. Now cars have to be connected to computers to diagnose what is wrong or how they are running! The garage worked on many Vauxhalls and British Leyland cars, but tried to avoid foreign cars like Renaults and Citroêns. Again they were more difficult and sourcing parts was harder. Still, business is business and they could hardly turn anything away.

In 1959, City Timbers, a local woodyard, was destroyed by a huge fire. Ian and George heard explosions and saw the smoke rising high

After the fire at the City Timbers woodyard

into the sky. They rushed from Clova to find City Timbers well ablaze, next door to their garage. The fire brigade were already on the scene and Ian was handed a hose to train constantly on the garage petrol pump. Many men from the village helped to remove piles of timber

225

to stop the fire spreading to the garage. City Timbers was razed to the ground, but Park Garage survived intact.

Not long before the fire, the splendid Riley Pathfinder, belonging to Charles Boise of Emmetts House, arrived with the front and wing crunched from a collision. Mr Boise had been watching tennis on the television and had then taken the car straight out into bright sunshine. Somewhat dazzled, he drove into a tree on the driveway and the car lost the argument! Unfortunately, the fate of the car was finally sealed with the fire at City Timbers. It was the only vehicle burnt out in the fire!

George junior finally retired at the grand old age of ninety and for Ian it was simply too late for him to take over the business. He retired at the same time and lives over the garage property in a flat he mostly built himself. Lionel Wood, an architect from Brasted Chart, designed it and Ian, with all his practical skills, only needed help when it came to installing the services.

Ian had a wonderful dog, a huge Great Dane / German Shepherd cross, called Boris. He had many dark spots on his grey fur, with the obvious drawback being that it was impossible to tell if he was covered in oil or not! Boris was a good garage dog, but when he had had enough of the workshop, he would disappear and take himself off home to Clova. He loved no more than to sit beside Ian in his open top, Austin - Healey Sprite and feel the wind fly past him. One day Boris noticed a sports car in the High Street and jumped into the passenger seat. When the owner came back Boris defended his position and barked and growled at the poor man. Ian had to come to his rescue and remove Boris so the owner could drive away.

Ian and Ann share a passion and hobby for horses and owned one each. They would often ride around the area and join Paddy

O'Donoghue and his daughter Jill for hacks around the district. Paddy soon found many more horse owners to join in and the usual objective was to ride flat out wherever possible. Ian's horse was a big bay called Mounty whom he describes as a lovely animal, but a little lazy. On the other hand Ann's horse, Sophie, was more spirited and a greater challenge. She was also a bay with a white foot and a pretty white star on her forehead. They would ride out all over the district when the roads were safer and less busy than now. They had friends who ran the old Railway and Bicycle Pub by Sevenoaks Station and could ride there to visit them. The pub had stables at the back where Mounty and Sophie could be left before returning home again. In Brasted they were stabled at Mill Farm and had the run of the field beside St Martin's Church. On the day of the fire in the church the horses were in that field. Ian and Ann arrived to find clouds of smoke hiding them. Ann called and the two horses galloped out of the smoke, like something from an atmospheric movie! They led them past all the emergency vehicles and popped them safely into their stables.

At The Stanhope Arms the landlord, Bob Shaw, had an archery range in the back garden. If the target was missed Ian and Ann would find arrows littering another field they rented for the horses, behind the pub. Sadly, the pub fell on hard times and Bob owed money to the village paper shop. After a long saga of non-payment Bob decided to pay what he owed. His method of delivery was somewhat unorthodox as he chose to tie the cheque to an arrow and shoot it through the upstairs bedroom window of the newsagents!

Sophie liked a little kick and would kick out at the stones in her stable. This led to one episode when a local man wanted to stand his brand new caravan on a cement base in the horse's field. He was told he could park there, but the caravan would need a fence around it, to save it from Sophie's attentions. Well, he didn't! So when Ann passed by The Stanhope Arms the landlord caught her and said, "You should have heard the noise last night!" Sophie had taken the challenge and dented the caravan all the way around it. The owner was furious, but he had been warned!

During the hurricane in 1987 Ian awoke to the noise of falling fir trees on the main road. There were no trees in the immediate area of his flat and luckily nothing was damaged. In the early morning the main road was impassable and Ian had no tools to clear it. The best bet was to go back to bed to get a little more sleep!

How has Brasted changed and is it for the better or worse?

Ian felt all his friends had moved away and the village has become a dormitory place for people who work in London and further afield.

With so much traffic on the A25, Ian has difficulty finding a gap to pull out of his drive and has to wait patiently for a long time.

"In my day the shops were proper shops and now they are nearly all antique shops," commented Ian.

Horse riding is impossible on the main roads or country lanes, as there are too many cars and drivers make little allowance for horses. Riding around the district on bridle paths is also challenging, as many have been blocked to stop horses using them. Complaints were made that the hoof prints and horses themselves were a hazard to walkers. Maintenance is down to the landowners and they do not want to do it.

February 2018

Terry Everest

Terry Everest was born at 1 Haines Cottages, High Street, (now Spring Cottage) in January 1944. He has a wealth of fond memories about his family, particularly of his father and growing up in Brasted. His father was George Friend Everest and mother, Rose Emma née Blackman, who was born on the 27th September 1910, in Cranbrook, Kent. Rose lost her mother, also called Rose, in 1912. Her father, Dennis Blackman, remarried and Rose had stepsisters. Interestingly, they all called her 'Em' and no one used her name Rose in their household. Perhaps as her own mother was Rose, one has to wonder if Dennis could not stand to hear his lost wife's name after her passing!

George was born on the 20th December 1905, close by in Dunton Green and died in 1998 whilst living in West End, Brasted. He was the eldest child and all his siblings were born in Chimneys, a tiny cottage in Alms Row, Brasted. Terry remembers that the family was large with three boys and four girls. Every night, the boys, George, John known as 'Tubby' and William, were each tucked up on the landing to sleep.

The Everest Family Tree

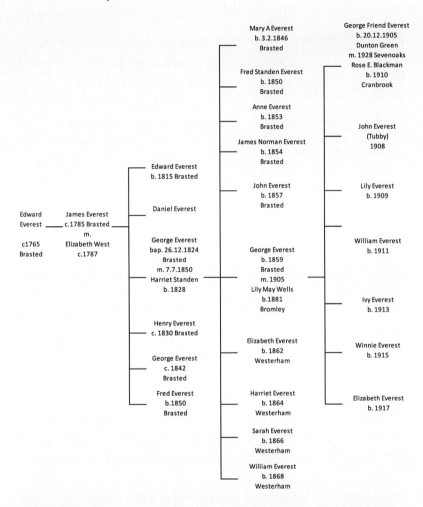

At Brasted village school, George's headmaster was Tommy Hubble, who happened to proudly sport a beard and handlebar moustache. When George was in trouble the punishment was severe even if late for the start of school. Kicking balls out of the school yard was a terrible crime. One day, George was in trouble and received the cane and was then locked in the cupboard, a punishment that would finish a teacher's profession these days. George went home and told his dad who explained exactly what to say to Mr Hubble the following day. "My dad told me to tell you that if you ever do that again, I can pull the whiskers of your moustache out, one by one." Well it worked, as the hirsute headmaster Hubble never did it again!

Terry's father George was one of many local lads who volunteered to dig out the swimming pool in Brasted Recreation Ground in 1913/14. Terry remembered swimming in the river-fed pool as a boy and his descriptive comment said it all, "it was bleedin' cold!" Mind you, despite a bit of discomfort Terry, didn't complain, as he did all right out of it, collecting up all the farthings (¼d), pennies (1d) and threepenny bits (3d) would fall out of the pockets of the other swimmers as they changed behind the huts.

George and Lily May Everest
taken about 1910

Terry also remembers that his father suffered the terrible experience of seeing his own father (Terry's grandfather), die in front of him, when he was just ten years old. George had to leave school to help his family and went to work at two local butchers' shops; Doves in Sundridge and Shoreys in Brasted High Street. George also had a paper round and would deliver papers on his bike. Close to the paper round there was a field where swedes were grown and, miraculously they would often end up in the Everest pot for dinner! He would willingly take a farthing bread coupon to Mr Fuggle, the baker, in the High Street. Mr Fuggle would ask George if he would like a humbug sweet. "Yes, please," was the instant reply. That trip to the bakers was always a highlight and a task to volunteer for.

The village had thirteen shops that sold everything anyone could want as well as a resident doctor and dentist. Mr Francis, the village dentist, was the lucky man that finally removed all of George's teeth. Certainly one of his more painful moments. As with most villages in those days, everyone knew everyone else and no one locked their outside doors. During the Second World War, George was an ARP warden[15] and could mostly be

Signatures 'of the few' at The White Hart

found inside The White Hart pub with the servicemen doing their bit for King and country!

Terry recalls that his father later worked at the chalk pit, by Hogtrough Hill and was the foreman there for many years. The land was rented from Lord Stanhope and at the official opening the manager, Mr Lloyd, asked George to carry out the official ceremony. During the war, the pit was partly run by Italian prisoners of war and it was a bugbear to see that they were given everything they needed including the best cakes! Still, George could amble to the pub at

---

[15] ARP (Air Raid Precautions) Wardens were appointed during the Second World War to protect civilians from the dangers of air raids. See also April Williams' story, Footnote 12

lunchtime for a few pints and then again on his way home, he could call in and sink a few more. George's daughter (Terry's sister) was the office telephonist at the pit.

George and Rose married in 1928, and settled into life together in Brasted. They had four children, with Terry being the third child.[16]

Terry described how the horse and carts would go by Haines Cottage and if they left a dropping, Rose would rush out and collect it for her garden. He went to school in Brasted where Norman Blezard was the headmaster. Like his dad, Terry was often in trouble at school. Terry got ticked off for fighting and was known by the nickname 'bruiser'. His mum Rose always told him, "get in there boy, hit first and ask questions later." This was advice he never forgot. One year he was chosen to be a robin in the Christmas play, but his outfit was too big and kept falling off. In frustration his teacher marched off, telling him to put it on himself. It looks as though Terry secretly enjoyed irritating his teacher and he seems to have been quite successful at it! However, he didn't say if he managed to appear on stage properly dressed in his costume!

Terry had many scrapes as a youngster and remembered that rubbish was dumped in the Recreation Ground, after the war. It was brought down from London. At about the age of five, he and his friend Roy Evans, found paint pots with paint still in them; yahoo what treasures! Finding their 'inner artist', they set about repainting

---

[16] Editor's note: George was my neighbour for eleven years and after his wife Rose died in 1992, he carried on, but never stopped missing her. On the day Rose died, she and George were attending a funeral at St Martin's Church. She was feeling ill and sat down for a while in the tower entrance. As if heaven had arranged it, she died peacefully right there, in our beautiful church.

the rocking horse in the play park area, in multiple colours. Roy was whacked by his father for his efforts, and Terry was read the riot act. The rubbish tip has long since been grassed over, but it is still under the right hand side of the Recreation Ground, between the old oak tree and the river. Terry remembers his excitement as a child when the A1 fish and chip van used to pull into West End, ringing its bell. He told me, "all the little boys would rush out and queue eagerly along the curb," awaiting their turn to order. Another fun hobby was to fish for trout in the Darent River, from the bridge in Church Road. In those days, the trout could be eight or more inches long.

Terry remembers having a pet rabbit that suddenly disappeared one day. His father told him it had died, but Terry soon realised it was in the pot cooking for dinner. He would wander up to the old forge in the village where the carthorses would arrive for new shoes. He loved the smell of the work going on inside. Sometimes he would fill his sister Betty's wellington boots with water, then tip it out again. When she needed them, she had to walk off squelching with each step. Ah, brotherly love! He was well known by the station guard, at Brasted railway station, and could hop on the steam train to Westerham for free. Often they had to haul the Westerham station master out of The Rose and Crown, so the steam train could return up the tracks again!

Terry was very proud of the fact that his dad George was the first person in West End to own a colour television and in those days it was a great way to get everyone together. All Terry's friends and the local kids would come round and sit in the lounge, watching it with the family.

Terry left school at fifteen, and started work at Court Lodge Farm working for Mrs Steven. He loved the job, but soon afterwards had a terrible motorbike accident, which ended that career. He was riding on the back of a friend's bike, returning from Streatham Ice Rink. In Sundridge, a car pulled out in front of them. Terry was bucked off and flew over the handle bars, crashing at speed, head first into a brick wall. His helmet split in two and Terry had shocking injuries. He was deaf in one ear and, for a while, it was thought he might lose the sight of his right eye. Worse still, he had a huge hole in his skull, which needed surgery to insert a metal plate over it. If we think that is a shocking injury now, years ago it was far more serious.

Terry then became a pest control officer, and was sometimes called to Hever Castle. He would set to work and Lord Astor would ask for "a little poison here and a little poison there". Around Christmas time, he would tell Terry to go and see Charlie, who would have a brace of pheasants put by for him. By now, Terry had married Marjorie Dowlen and they had adopted a rescued Jack Russell terrier, from Viking Oak Kennel, an RSPCA sanctuary. They called him Tinker and he would go to work with Terry, often wrapped around his neck. Tinker had fallen on his feet with Terry and lived to be over twenty years old. Tinker started a long line of adopted pets, as Terry and Marjorie took in all and sundry, who needed a good and kind home.

Terry spent the majority of his career working for the local council. Much of that time was spent driving the lorries for the refuse collectors. He did this for forty-five years before his retirement.

During his life, Terry has often taken on extra duties. At the age of sixteen, he joined the Territorial Army for two years. He then opted to become a special constable and tells of two lovely stories from this period of his life.

In 1982, the Pope visited Canterbury and Terry was sent down to assist in patrolling the event. The Pope left and all was calm until he and another officer heard girls screaming. They rushed to the scene, ready to sort out whatever the problem was. However, they had to skid to a halt, when they realised the fuss was over Prince Charles, slowly leaving in his Jaguar car.

On another occasion he was at Chevening House, a property bequeathed to the nation by Lord Stanhope and used by government ministers. During a charity event attended by the local celebrity Gloria Hunniford, Terry was able to walk straight up to her and ask for her autograph. The general public were held back and could only look on with envy. There was a balance to this story though, as the Queen's Guards turned up to go on parade in full uniform, and sometime during the afternoon, two bear skin hats were stolen from their coach. Where were the constables, one might ask?

Terry is now the Verger for St Martin's Church, a task he has been doing for twenty-one years. Here's to the next twenty-one in quiet, enjoyable retirement!

June 2016

David Edgar

David Gordon Edgar was born at Park Farm in August 1947 with the village doctor, Dr Ward and midwife Nora Maylam, in attendance. His parents Joy and Gordon had married and moved there in 1946. As a boy David would walk down to the River Darent and fish for sticklebacks, catfish and latterly trout. At first light by the farm, it was possible to see fifteen to twenty trout fry. In 2015 he pulled a full-sized trout out of the river below Park Farm towards Westerham. The river was much deeper in his young days and he was able to swim in it.

In 1958/59 the farm flooded badly, washing away a bridge that connected the land on either side of the River Darent. Until the bridge was replaced, milk churns had to be taken across the river using a temporary bridge, strong enough to walk across and run a tractor over, but not strong enough for milk lorries to use. A permanent, stronger bridge was rebuilt over the original bridge, which is still lying on the riverbed. The land around Park Farm has long been subject to flooding and in the late 1980s/early 1990s the National Rivers Authority sent in JCB excavators to reroute the river around the meanders in the river as it wove through the farm. It was thought a straight river would drain downstream more quickly and

237

help prevent the problem of flooding. The meanders are still visible when the water level is high. This solution eased the flooding problem for the farm, but allowed water to flow into Brasted village faster and possibly adds to the flooding around Brasted Green and Rectory Lane.

David remembers being taken to Swans haberdashery shop in Brasted and being fascinated by the huge inglenook fireplace. That was a far greater draw for a little boy than buying anything in the shop.

Although farming was hard work, there was still fun to be had. One day Gordon was sowing grass, kneeling down, drilling seed into the soil. A bus driver pulled up and opened his window and shouted, "Ain't up yet!" By the age of at least ten, David was driving tractors on the farm, even if he had to stand up to reach the pedals!

Sometimes the local steam railway engine would stop on the tracks near Park Farm and the fireman or train driver would walk over and buy eggs. David would often hop aboard the train with them and ride on the footplate to Dunton Green. There he had to tuck down, out of sight of the station master, until the engine started back down the tracks to Westerham via an unscheduled stop at Park Farm. Close to Brasted Station was a small siding where a repair dolly was kept. He could ride on that too, but never when a steam engine was on the lines. The last train at night would steam by at 10 p.m. Day old chicks would regularly arrive at Brasted Station for the farm. The station master would keep them inside his house, comfortable and warm, until Joy or Gordon could collect them.

David attended school at Sevenoaks Preparatory School, by the Vine in Sevenoaks. At first he travelled by bus and later he would cycle. He left the school at the age of thirteen. From there he went to

Cannock House Grammar School in Chelsfield, Kent. When David was about fourteen every child in the class was asked to write about their weekend. At the time Gordon was unwell and in Middlesex Hospital. David, his mother and the cowman had to run the farm themselves and it was a full-time job. The teacher read his essay and in astonishment asked David, "Did you really do all this?" Yes, of course he did!

This meant he had little time to make friends in the village, as Park Farm was some way from the centre of Brasted. At the end of his schooling, his family insisted he came home to help on the farm instead of going to college. They felt they could teach him everything he needed to know. So, at the age of seventeen, David joined the family farming business.

David and his father Gordon worked hard together and built up the farm to increase the milking herd, improve facilities and take on more land and farms. They started to grow maize and silage for their cattle to make the farm completely independent of outside suppliers for foodstuffs.

In 1958 the family bought land from George Alderson that was later sold on to become Westerham Golf Course. The fields were originally intended for George's nephew, Edward Pierce to cultivate after his farming college education was completed. As his sister Jane Smithers explained in her story, Edward had a terrible and untimely accident in which he lost his life. The Edgar family used the fields to grow their winter maize. It did so well the crop grew over their heads which made for a good yield, but it made harvesting a little challenging. Sometimes local deer would trample the crop and badgers would steal the ears, but that is just country living! Joy and Gordon would pack a picnic and the family would walk up the hill near Valence School and sit watching the fields when they had a rare relaxing moment.

In the early days Park Farm only had thirty three cows, which was the maximum for milking twice a day, as the process was manual and took so long. The milk went into buckets and was then poured into churns before being collected by a small tanker. Once a milking session had been completed, everything had to be hand scrubbed ready for the next one. It was hard manual work. The family took forty gallons of milk each day to the Day brothers' Mill Farm dairy, as they could not produce enough milk from their own small herd to supply their business. In 1969 a milking parlour was built at Park Farm to speed up the milking process. Milk churns were phased out and the farm was unable to supply the Day brothers with any more milk. The Day brothers retired and Gordon and David expanded their business by taking over the tenancy of Mill Farm which adjoined Park Farm. The building of the milking parlour and the automation of the milking process allowed them to buy two new herds, a total of one hundred and twenty five cows. Through a 'breed and feed' programme on the farm, they finally pushed the number of cows up to one hundred and sixty. Even with the parlour and automation, milking took five hours at both ends of the day. The new process also enabled them to put in a tank that held four thousand, five hundred litres of milk: sufficient capacity for two days' production. The second of the newly acquired herds were Ayrshire cattle, which were then crossed with Friesian Holsteins to improve the milk yield further. A milk tanker would arrive each day to empty the tank of milk. In the early days it was a simple four wheel tanker, but these days it's a huge vacuum tanker with capacity to collect milk from many farms.

At first the priority for good milking cows was the hardiness of their feet. Black hooves were considered the strongest as the cows spent so much time on concrete floors and in slurry. Ayrshires had black feet and were an ideal choice. Holstein's complimented the Ayrshires, as all their energy goes into milk production. The next priority was the efficiency of conversion of feed into quality milk production. The third element of production was the condition and quality of the buttermilk produced. The farm always had one or two bulls, at least one being an Angus bull. The breed has a smaller head and body and was ideal for a heifer's[17] first calf. She could calve easily and in subsequent years she could be put to the larger Holstein Friesian and thus produce larger calves without difficulty. Ideally, cows will produce only one calf a year. A cow expecting twins is undesirable because the birth can damage the mother and render her unable to continue breeding safely afterwards. At Park Farm, cows are currently kept for ten to twelve years providing they stay fit, can still calve and do not suffer from mastitis. This is far longer than the national average. The cows are given all they need and their welfare is always at the forefront of their management.

Currently, farmers can import bull semen from almost anywhere in the world, including USA, Australia and Europe. Specific semen can be chosen to improve any herd; perhaps in beef production, or butterfat, A1 milk, or even the longevity of calves.

Some time ago vets compared racehorses to Holstein Friesian cows. A horse converts its energy into power through running whereas the Holstein Friesian converts its energy into milk production. For a cow to deliver forty, fifty or sixty litres of milk, it uses twice the energy of

---

[17] A heifer is a cow that has not borne a calf, or has borne only one calf.

a thoroughbred horse making it the perfect breed for dairy farming.

In 1974, pegs were laid on the land that had been the Westerham to Dunton Green railway. These pegs mapped out the future course of the M25 motorway that was completed in 1979.

Building the M25 Motorway in the 1970s

While this new project was taking shape, David would drive his cattle across the wide expanse of mud and watch the construction of the motorway with its huge unwieldly vehicles and busy workforce. David had to be careful that the cows didn't wander off and make their way down to Westerham!

As part of the construction, a nine foot, six inch wide underpass was built to allow farm vehicles and cattle to pass under the motorway. David would never have thought then that farm vehicles would get so big that the underpass would be unable to accommodate them, but with farm vehicles now a minimum of three metres wide the underpass can no longer be used. Instead, the tractors have to use Church Road and somehow navigate around all the parked cars to reach different parts of the farm! However, the motorway has eased congestion within the village as, before it opened, the traffic would regularly come to a standstill from Westerham to Park Farm. The main volume of traffic was successfully relocated to the motorway and to this day the A25 jams have not reoccurred, except on those days when the motorway is closed or part-closed by crashes or repairs to the highway.

In 1994 David purchased Starborough Farm, Marsh Green near Edenbridge. It was a lovely farm, but wheat prices hit rock bottom and it was a long way to travel to and from Brasted daily to manage the farm. In 2002 it was sold. Farming is dependent on its market prices and for many reasons these fluctuate and can render crops unviable!

In the 1940s and 1950s farming magazines would often photograph Court Lodge Farm where David's grandfather, Reginald Edgar farmed. David has some wonderful photographs from that time, some of which are printed below.

1941 – Shorthorns in Home Paddock by Court Lodge Farm.

Reginald Edgar leading the horse and Alf Fry ploughing in 1946

'Autumn, the corn goes in at Court Lodge Farm'.

Alf Fry on Court Lodge Farm 1942. The picture caption read, 'In setting out 500 tons of London refuse 'Shoddy'[18] on Mr R.G. Edgar's farm at Brasted a gold ring, a two shilling piece, half a crown and 8d. in coppers came to light.'

---

[18] Shoddy is made up of inferior quality yarn or fabric and was used as a fertiliser.

Alf Fry on Court Lodge Farm 1942. The picture caption reads, 'Not every horse and waggoner can back a load of barley through so narrow an opening. Our photographer saw this handy bit of work on a Kent farm.'

A thresher machine at harvest time Sep/Oct 1945 at Court Lodge Farm with three Italian prisoners of war on top of the thresher

Gordon Edgar working on the farm in 1946

Gordon Edgar on his 1939 Bedford truck

Reginald sold Court Lodge Farm in 1950, along with all the farm stock and equipment by auction. He then moved on to Knights Farm in

Lingfield. Court Lodge Farm was taken over by Bob Steven and the family farming business was centred on Park Farm.

David learnt to ring the church bells when the Reverend Bertie Talbot asked for villagers to volunteer in the 1970s. Bertie's sons Patrick and Stephen both rang and together with David had "the best instructor in Kent", namely Bob Sherlock. Bob was the tower captain and David's daughter, Melanie also learnt to ring the bells, starting when she was eight. On the day of the fire at St Martin's Church in 1989, Bob phoned David at 4 p.m. and arranged for the ringers to ring the church bells at 5 p.m. Smoke was still rising from the main church as the bells rang out, but the tower with its six bells had been saved and was not damaged.

In 1987, the hurricane struck the area and wreaked havoc in its path. The previous Saturday David had listened to a Kent Radio broadcast that had recorded how much rain the area had suffered. They advised that all animal stock should be moved to safety away from rivers, including the Darent. David moved his stock to higher ground, but the real danger came a few days later from hurricane winds and not flooding!

David was woken at 4 a.m. and says he remembers the events of the day like it was yesterday. The farm had lost its power and he could see flashes all the way across the hills to the south, which must have been the power cables coming down. The farm had a small, petrol driven generator which, when fired up, enabled the milking to start in the dark. Lit only by a torch, a cow was identified as in trouble with calving at the same time. The torch was perched on the water tank as assistance was given and almost inevitably it fell into the tank!

The A25 was obviously blocked, so David collected a chainsaw and with his father Gordon operating the Matbro farm forklift, he started to cut up the trees by the sandpits. He did enough to enable his father to drag them to the side of the road with the forklift truck. He then attacked the fallen beeches on the far side of Brasted up to New Road. Again he cut the trunks into manageable sections so they could be moved off the road. He could hear the still standing beeches cracking behind him while he was cutting. A sense of fear crept into his head, as he realised at any moment one or more of those trees could have fallen and crushed him. Nevertheless, he continued up the A25 to the other side of Sundridge and that opened up the road to traffic. David's wife had a solid fuel Rayburn and cooked a welcome breakfast on it when they got home.

The Valence School entrance was opposite Park Farm and the fir trees lining the drive had all fallen in the wind. The night staff could not leave and the day staff could not reach the school. No supplies could be delivered either. So, the next job for David and his father was to clear the way through to the school. Again the yellow Matbro machine was able to push the large trunks away from the access road to clear it, so the school could function again. Next it was onto Chart Lane which ended up giving David nightmares on the state of the road. They cut and hacked, but everything was a tangled mess and perfectly hopeless. The task was simply too great for two men and a forklift alone. Word went round that the army was being called in and finally David and his father could step back from their huge efforts.

As a measure of the damage caused that night, a fifteen acre field on the now Westerham Golf Course had trees down all around its perimeter and David counted two hundred and seventy fallen trees. The soil was so soft after all the rain and when the winds came the trees simply heaved straight out of the ground. At times the gusts were so strong that the trunks and limbs of trees snapped off. The clearance task was immense and the damage done that night was immeasurable.

Shortly after the millennium, Nick Moon, an experienced member of the Kent Archaeological Trust was given permission to use a metal detector on part of the farmland. The land including Park Farm is owned by the Chevening Estate. It was formerly the estate of Lord Stanhope whose line ran out of heirs at his death, in 1967. He gifted the Chevening Estate to the nation for use by the government.

It is well known that the Romans had villas along the River Darent approximately every half a mile from Westerham downstream to the Thames. The river was much deeper then and the Romans could row up river from the Thames to at least Otford. So Nick started to explore an area of particularly rich soil, with woodland and of course, access to good water. David turned the earth over to help discover any deeply hidden artefacts and Nick found a Roman nail, which confirmed the knowledge of local Romans. However, much more exciting was the discovery of an iron age, gold coin. Over a period of several years many more coins were discovered with the total numbering over fifty. These were quarter staters and full staters, all gold and all dating from 10 B.C. David had the pleasure of digging up one of the coins himself and being the first to see it in over two thousand years. The river area had long been inhabited and these coins were thought to have been minted for Dias or Diras who ruled Kent in the first century B.C. He was a sub-king under the Tasciovanus of the Catuvellauni tribe. The coins were taken to Tunbridge Wells County Court where it was declared Celtic treasure trove and they are currently displayed in the British Museum and Chevening House.

During this time Nick explained to David why we bank in 'banks'. Before such financial institutions were available, moneyed noblemen would need to secure their wealth when they went to war or left their homesteads. It was normal to locate a safe place often in raised ground (a bank), where the site could easily be identified when the owner returned home. If he never returned, the location remained unknown although with modern metal detectors these places holding old treasures are now fairly often rediscovered. Banks still bear the same name, but we no longer have to dig big holes to store our treasures when we need to leave our castles, or rather our houses these days!

David lived at Park Farm for sixty-three years and finally retired from farming in 2017 - well maybe! His son James has taken over and the farm continues to modernise and grow, but was that David just driving by in the tractor? David is keeping busy with an allotment and doing splendid work clearing the St Martin's churchyard of

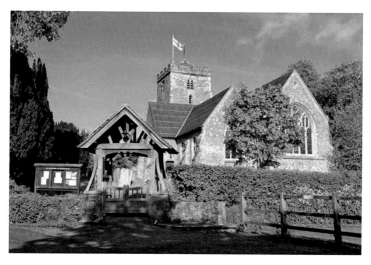

overgrown trees and weeds. He still rings the bells when needed and is a great volunteer and asset to the village. He says he has always enjoyed being in Brasted, being part of the church and now knows more people in the village than ever before.

With Brexit under way and the UK negotiating to leave the European Union, David voiced his concerns on the future of farming. He recently listened to Michael Gove MP, the Secretary of State for Environment, Food and Rural Affairs. He suggested widening the borders on cultivated fields to encourage flora and fauna. Park Farm already sets itself a policy of six metre borders, but making it wider cuts production. As David says, "How can the UK feed itself if it doesn't use every inch of available farmland?" In 2008 Bob Steven left Oveney Green Farm in Sundridge and David and his son James acquired it. They found the corners of fields completely unploughed with the theory that they were simply too fiddly and had poor soil. They set about ploughing and planting and everything grew well. It is farm policy to spread slurry on the fields to fertilize the earth. "You should put back what you take!" as David says, "and productivity stays balanced and results in good healthy crop growth".

David then laughed as he remembered on one occasion he was taking slurry up Church Road. It spilled out just as he was passing a vending cycle bike on which a gentleman blended tea. A sticky, smelly splash and the vehicle was covered! So David summoned his son and together they cleaned up the vehicle and washed the road. Timing is everything!

David takes his responsibilities towards the natural world seriously. For instance, the farm identified a two acre patch of poor soil and instead of abandoning it, planted wild flower seeds and thistles. In a similar vein, contractors for hedge cutting now recommend it is done every two to three years. David disagrees and likes to trim hedges every year. That way the hedge thickens in the middle to give shelter and suitable nesting for small birds. He now slopes the top of the hedge from the middle down on each side. This stops the crows and magpies settling on top and stealing young chicks and eggs.

This consideration for nature along with the serious business of farming is something the inhabitants of Brasted never see to appreciate. Great care is taken with animal husbandry, crop growing and balancing the needs of nature by our premier Brasted farming family. A few years ago David walked around Strawberry Hollow, a field just north of the Pilgrims Way. It had at least fifty different wild flowers, some of which were orchids. The beauty of nature is still there just for the looking.

When considering changes in Brasted, David says it is sad that it has deteriorated socially and people are too busy dealing with their own families to socialise with their neighbours. Children go to activities outside the village and have to be driven to take part in them.

Most of the shops have disappeared, including the transport café where many drivers could gather together for a break while enjoying cooked foods and drinks.

On a positive note, the motorway gave much relief from the constant traffic jams that plagued the village. It is still better now even with so many more cars on all roads. If the motorway is closed for accidents David, along with many locals, knows not to use the Pilgrims Way as an alternative route. If you do, as he says "it is a lost wing mirror day, due to it being so narrow!"

January 2018

Juliana Stewart

née Budgen

The Budgen family, first came to live in Brasted when Juliana's grandfather, Walter John Budgen and his wife Jessie set up home in the village. Walter was born in Bletchingley, Surrey the son of Jesse Budgen, from Godstone, a farm worker. Country life and farming was embedded in his blood, as the tradition went back through many generations. The family soon moved on and Walter's younger siblings were born in Knockholt. Walter had an early career at Grey's Stud Farm, in Knockholt, before the farm moved on to Newmarket, but Walter chose to stay behind in this area. He found employment with the Dark family, at Court Lodge Farm, Hogtrough Hill, Brasted. He and his family moved into Court Lodge Cottage, which was tied to his new job. Walter and Jessie lived in the cottage, for over forty years, until they finally moved to retirement housing in Pym Orchard, off Rectory Lane. Pym Orchard is a small complex of single storey dwellings close to the High Street and bus services.

Walter, born 26th September 1889, married Jessie née Seaman in 1913, in St Mary's Church, Westerham. Jessie was from West Barsham, Norfolk and had moved to Brasted, to work in service, for

Richard Durtnell and his wife Clara. Her job was to care for their three younger children, Geoffrey, Nora and Richard. Jessie lived-in with the family, in the house called Constables, on the corner of Rectory Lane.

Walter and Jessie had three children, with the youngest being Frederick, father of Juliana. Fred broke the family tradition of farming through his mother's link to the Durtnell family. He was offered an apprenticeship with the village builders, as a plumber and heating engineer. In the 1939 census, his occupation was shown as a fully qualified plumber and heating engineer, whilst his father Walter's occupation was given as a farm tractor driver.

As a young boy, Fred had an amazing soprano voice which was much admired in the choir at St Martin's Church. He once sang the solo part in The Messiah, to the joy of the congregation. However, all that changed when his voice broke and he took up bell ringing, in the church tower, instead. He and his village buddy, Bob Sherlock, both became proficient bell ringers and travelled the country on 'bell-ringing excursions'. They were both members of the Ancient Society of College Youths and regularly attended

Fred Budgen bell-ringing

the Society's annual formal dinner in London. Fred and Bob rang the bells with Mr Edwin Lewis, who was a well-known and talented teacher of campanology. He held the office of president of the Central Council of Church Bell-Ringers. Edwin lived in the old Rectory, off Rectory Lane, a house later occupied by Sir Malcolm Muggeridge, the journalist and satirist. George Alderson would entertain the bell ringers with parties at Church End House.

Fred is mentioned on boards hanging in the bell tower along with Bob Sherlock and Edwin Lewis. These boards commemorate the achievement of either ringing a quarter peal, or full peal on the bells. A full peal takes nearly three hours and is a test of concentration and physical energy. The peals are usually done in commemoration of an event such as a remembrance for someone, the sovereign's birthday or a church festival. Edwin Lewis is noted as ringing and conducting seven peals, in Brasted, between 1935 and 1951.

Fred also held the post of Chairman of the Village Hall Management Committee. The committee's major task was to upgrade the neglected village hall building, starting with the kitchen. The plan was for every household in the village to contribute something towards the works. After the renovations were completed, the hall could be let for functions. When the

Fred Bugden's appeal for help

plans were submitted to the Parish Council, a licence for music and dancing had already been applied for, to restore interest in the hall. The kitchen is still put to good use today, although the hall is now challenged by the much newer, Brasted Pavilion, in the Recreation Ground.

Juliana's mother was a pretty, fair haired girl from Scheveningen, in the Netherlands. Her given name was Aasje Taal, but she was known as Ans. She came to England having experienced very difficult family circumstances, during the war years. The Germans invaded the Netherlands on the 10th May 1940 and quickly overwhelmed the country. They swept into Scheveningen and seized both houses and land, displacing many families. The area had strategic importance for the Germans as a district of The Hague with wide, sandy beaches. The Hague was the seat of the Dutch parliament and just to the south was the Hook of Holland with its shipping industry and open

Ans Taal

waters to the North Sea. The Germans occupied a prison, known as the 'Orangehotel', in Scheveningen, where resistance fighters and Dutch dissenters were held. Up to twenty five thousand prisoners were detained there during the war years.

They also used Dutch captive labourers, to build a large network of tunnels and bunkers along the Scheveningen beaches. It was all part of the Atlantic Wall project to conquer and control the seas around mainland Europe, stretching from Norway to the Bay of Biscay. As the Germans occupied the area, many industries were lost, including the fishing industry, on which the Taal family depended. The locals were starving and the Taal's had eleven children to care for, they were desperate for food and general supplies. Ans and one of her sisters, would cycle out regularly around the Netherlands, trying to purchase food on the black market. They could be away for days, sleeping rough wherever they could, often in farmer's barns. Once, they were shot at, by German soldiers. These were difficult and dangerous times! The family had no income, so eventually all their savings went on black market essentials.

After the war, Ans and her sister moved to Westerham, in the hope of a better life for themselves. They found work in a large house, where Ans was the cook and her sister, the children's maid. One of their cousins, Jacoba Taal, was already living nearby in Ide Hill, having met and married, an English soldier, Robert Probert.

One New Year's Eve party, Ans and Fred met and became an item. Having fallen in love, they travelled to Holland to marry in 1948. Ans' family must have been delighted at the perfect match. They returned to Brasted and settled into married life, having three children, Juliana, young Freddy and Marina.

Juliana Frederica was born in May 1949, in Langton Green Nursing Home and taken home to Court Lodge Cottage. Juliana inherited the beautiful features of her mother, and was named after the Dutch Queen, Juliana. It is a lovely name and a wonderful representation of her Dutch roots. Her Dutch heritage has always played a large part in her life.

Sometime later, the little family moved to a flat in the same Constables house that Jessie had worked in. The building had been converted into three flats comprising of one rather splendid downstairs apartment and two flats upstairs. The family lived on the first floor.

Every second year in the school holidays, Ans would pack up her children for the summer, in Scheveningen. They would book Mr Harris, a Sevenoaks taxi driver, to take them to Liverpool Street Station. The train would take them on to Harwich, in time to catch the night boat, to the Hook of Holland. Although the family would spend all summer there, Fred could only join them for two weeks, using his annual leave from work. At the age of twelve or thirteen, Juliana actually did the journey by herself. Fred took her to Liverpool

Street and saw her off on the train. Children today would never be allowed such freedoms for fear of 'terrible things' happening! Juliana remembers the family had a golden cocker spaniel, pet dog, called Lulu on whom Ans was not so very keen. During one holiday she was left with Walter and Jessie and never came home when the holiday was over. Probably no guesses as to why and did Ans have a little smile on her face? No doubt Lulu loved living with Walter and Jessie enjoying the open countryside.

The Brasted Coronation Party in 1953

In 1953, a Coronation party was held on the Village Green. Ans made her family traditional Dutch costumes to wear. However, the flat was on the opposite side of the road to the Green, and Juliana had to walk across in precarious clogs. She remembered being scared of the road in case a car came by, as she could barely shuffle along. At the party Mr Watts, the butcher, roasted venison on an open spit. There was music and entertainment and a big occasion was enjoyed on the day. Juliana and her family did not have a television, but were invited to a Squadron Leader's house at the back of the Green, to watch the ceremony. The television was most impressive with wooden doors that had to be opened. When her family finally bought their own television, it too came in its own cabinet, but did not have those lovely doors on the front!

Fred had an allotment behind Court Lodge Cottage, where he grew all the vegetables his family needed. The Durtnell family kept pigs in their yard, behind their offices and Juliana could pop over to see them. Behind Court Lodge Cottages were watercress beds and every Sunday the family had a large fresh bunch at teatime. Fred would clear out the beds each spring. Water cress collectors had a contract and would arrive at the stream in their Land Rovers each weekend to harvest a crop. The clear water would spring from the rock bed, as it drained off the chalk hills of the Downs. Juliana could paddle in the water, which was about six inches deep. A little closer to the railway tunnel were the sheep dip pens, beside the stream. Water was diverted and filled with chemicals before the sheep passed through, one at a time. No one fancied paddling in the water below that spot!

Juliana started school at the age of four in Mrs Gurteen's class. She was always her favourite teacher and Juliana recalls the kiss curls neatly tweaked around her face. Once, Juliana, Martin Wood and Susan Hughes were invited to her house, in Solefields Road, Sevenoaks. Their respective mothers put them on the bus in Brasted and the conductor put them off when the bus reached the Solefields Road bus stop. The children were only aged five! Once there, they shared a cosy tea with Mrs Gurteen. Her next teacher was Mrs Catlin, followed by Miss Rowe and Miss Pink, and in the top class Mr Blezard, the headmaster. Miss Pink lodged with Mrs Stott, at the sweet shop in the High Street.

At the age of ten, Juliana lost her mother when Ans died suddenly and Fred was left alone with his three children. For eight months he struggled on, with one year old Marina living in Sevenoaks, with Fred's brother Walter and his wife Elsie. Juliana and young Freddy stayed back with their father. This situation had to be resolved, and through the Dutch Church, Austin Friars, in the City of London, Fred found a housekeeper called Cornelia. Another Dutch lady, she stayed for six months, but later returned for a longer period. Finally, in 1968 Fred and Co (Cornelia) had touched each other's hearts, and they married in St Martin's Church.

Back to Juliana, who continued her schooling despite the family's loss. Her main memory from the top class, was of Mr Blezard teaching them The Ancient Mariner, oh hum! He went on and on, only interspersed with The Lady of Shalott. During her last school year, 1960, they celebrated one hundred years of Brasted School. Each child was asked to dress in Victorian costume and Juliana went as Queen Victoria. She had to make her own costume, using one of her grandmother's old dresses.

The school nativity play was performed in the village hall, where they streamed across the road dressed for their parts. Rehearsals were always in Mr Blezard's classroom, where they pulled the desks together and climbed on top, to practise being on the stage. Maybe health and safety rules are not so bad these days!

Dinner had to be eaten off the same desks. The school had a kitchen and the cook was Mrs Edna Seale with Mrs Annells assisting. Juliana described the gypsy tart as being utterly delicious and much darker in colour than the current pale representations found in the shops. It truly had the texture of a thick layer of sticky toffee. Another favourite was the hot water crusty pastry used to make meat pie. Juliana was not fond of carrots and was caught by Mr Blezard mashing them into her potatoes. She was scolded for the mess on her plate. Lent pie was on the disgusting side of the menu. With a pastry base, it was made of solid semolina, with a thick skin on top. Scattered with the odd sultana it would be left for the whole afternoon, in front of the children who had not eaten it. At 4 p.m., Mr Blezard would finally clear it away. A board went out each day, showing the milkman the number of milk bottles needed for the children attending that day. There were about one hundred children in the school at that time. Drinking sun-warmed bottles of milk containing one third of a pint was a test for any child during hot summer days. All milk had to be drunk and not left!

One Christmas, Juliana and her friends Jane, Tessa and Pat went carol singing to Mill Farm. Mr Day answered the door and told them to come back at Easter. So they did, but Mr Day did not answer the door so they went away again empty handed!

Often they would walk around the churchyard and Juliana told me of a wall, dotted with children's graves alongside it. Each had short poems to the lost child. The path through the church and out to the fields, was well used by the local villagers, as the quickest route to the railway station.

With such freedom in her childhood, Juliana and her friends could wander around the area all day. If she was out and spent her bus fare she would simply have to walk home.

Juliana remembered one family outing to Greenwich to see the original nineteenth century clipper Cutty Sark. Sadly, the ship was devastated by fire in 2007 and completely rebuilt. The new ship was reopened to the public in 2012, but is now mostly a replica of her former self.

Senior schooling was at the Churchill School in Westerham. Juliana could go by bus, but most often caught the train. Sometimes they would travel 'first class' by climbing into the overhead, rope luggage racks and other times they were allowed on the footplate. If they were a little late, the engine driver would wait for them. At Beggar's Lane it was a treat to pull the whistle, to warn of the approaching train. If they missed the train completely, the fastest route home was walking along the tracks. They would beat or stamp out the fires on the banks, caused as the engine had gone by. The tracks were an interesting play area and Juliana and her friends had a pile of junk that had been laid on the tracks, to be flattened as the engine went over it. Halfpennies (½d) were carefully laid out and the engine would stretch them to the size of one penny (1d). Some would say creative accounting! They could then go to Mrs Stott's sweetshop, and hide the coin in a pile of real pennies. Their money could buy black jacks, rainbow drops, pear drops, anything peppermint and Juliana's favourite, liquorice.

During school in Westerham, the girls were asked to help raise money for the Winston Churchill statue, on Westerham Green. The school was supposed to pay for the plinth that the statue sits on. But, none of the parents seemed to like Winston too much and the fund fell short of its target. The school children were all sent home to ask for more money. It became known, when Winston died, that he owed money to many of the businesses, in the town, as he was a shocking bill payer! Maybe this had some bearing on why the funds were low.

More fun could be had by taking the bus to Sevenoaks, to visit one of the two cinemas: the Odeon, now known as the Stag Community

Arts Centre and the Granada. Later, the Granada closed and, as teenagers, the Odeon was their only choice of cinema. If the family went to Sevenoaks, Juliana and her siblings were given the treat of walking around Woolworths, looking at the toys, not buying any though! The best treat was a visit to the coffee shop opposite The Chequers Pub, in the High Street. Juliana could have ice cream and a wafer in a metal bowl, while her parents had tea and cake. Later with friends, Bligh's Hotel offered entertainment, with bands and dancing. If they missed the last bus, it was the inevitable walk home.

Sometimes the friends would take the bus to Bromley and walk to The Bromley Court, a night club that featured such artists as Georgie Fame, Eric Clapton and Ginger Baker. Shopping was best in Croydon, with its direct local bus route. Kennards was a lovely department store and in the cellar were ponies that could be ridden around a wooden pen. That was only if you could afford the money for such a treat. One day, Juliana remembered getting travel sick on the bus and she had to get off half way there. Once she felt better, she had to catch the next bus to continue her journey. When old enough, Juliana took a part-time Sunday job in Mr Maudsley's newsagents. Her job was to serve customers with their choice of sweets and tobacco. This gave her pocket money for some little treats in life.

On finishing school, Juliana went to work in Holland for four years. There she worked as an au pair in Amsterdam, for a year, before moving to Rotterdam. Fully fluent in Dutch, she found work with the Rotterdam Logistics Company and then with the Bank of America. The bank was typically American and sometimes the president of the company would send encouraging words to the staff, to be played on records! The door advertised its hours as '9 thru 5', which always rankled as it was not real English!

While working in Holland, Juliana met Keith Stewart, a merchant seaman from Chester. As romance blossomed, Juliana returned to Brasted. She found a job as a laboratory technician in Farnborough Hospital, now renamed the Princess Royal University Hospital. The journey to work was straight forward, with one bus trip to Keston Mark on the 705 Greenline and a walk the rest of the way. After a year she left her job and married Keith.

In April 1971, their wedding was held in St Martin's Church. It was a unique occasion, sharing the service with her Dutch family. They all came dressed in their regional Dutch costumes. The service sheets were printed in both English and Dutch. Juliana sang the hymns in Dutch, while Keith sang in English. The service had two church representatives; Reverend Bertie Talbot of St Martins and a Dutch minister, from the Dutch Church in London. It was conducted half in Dutch, and half in English. The reception was held in the village hall, but everything had to be finished and tidied away by midnight, as that was the limit of the hall licence.

By now Keith had joined the police force, and with no time for a honeymoon, they left immediately for Stalybridge, in Greater Manchester. Keith was a police officer for over thirty years and is an ordained minister for the Church of England.

So has Brasted changed and for better or worse? These were her observations:

There are no shops now whereas in her younger days there were two bakers, butchers, a Co-op at one end of the village and Markwicks the grocers at the other. There was a fishmonger, a bank, pharmacy and Swans haberdashery shop. The only antique shop belonged to Mr and Mrs Barrington.

Village people were once related to one another, but now families can no longer afford the price of local property. That luxury has been taken by people working in London and earning enough money, for expensive mortgages. This has caused the loss of so much of the community spirit that once existed between families and friends.

Villagers are so busy in their own lives no one volunteers to help run or assist any village activities. So many clubs and village events have been lost.

There are no facilities in the village for young people. They leave the village for schools and later entertainment. There is nothing arranged to keep them in Brasted.

The ability to enjoy freedom in Juliana's young life gave her confidence that she feels young people now lack, through over protective parents and life in general.

August 2017

Beryl Herpe
née Everest

Beryl's grandparents were George Everest and Lily née Wells. Sadly, George died before Beryl was born. She was told that he was on the roof of Wisteria House in Brasted High Street, when he fell to the ground and did not survive the accident. The Wells family have lived in Brasted for many generations, as have the Everest family. This was perhaps a joining of the oldest families of Brasted.

Beryl is the daughter of George and Lily's second son, John. He was always known as Tubby, which is even engraved on his gravestone, in St Martin's Churchyard. Beryl has never known where the name came from, he looked just great to her. The Everest family were good, working class folk, but had very little money to spend on anything more than necessities. Beryl remembered her father telling her that, between him and his brothers, George and William, whoever was first out of bed, claimed the only pair of shoes. That son was then able to attend school, whilst the others stayed home. If there was a hole in the sole, they stuffed folded newspaper into the precious shoe to cover it.

The Everest Family Tree

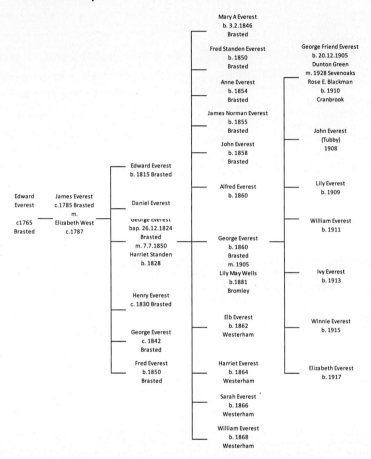

John married Beatrice Maud née Friend on the 19th of August, 1933, in Biggin Hill. They suffered the sad loss of a baby girl, before Beryl came along. She was two months early and weighed just three and a half pounds (1.6kg). Born in August 1936, at 2 Alms Row, the local doctor who attended her birth was Dr Kenneth Ward. Tiny, Beryl, was wrapped in cotton wool and bathed in olive oil. When Dr Ward came into any patient's home and the windows were closed he would say, 'fresh air is the best medicine' and immediately open one. He would always drive his car, at any time of the year, with the windows down and a scarf wound around his neck if necessary. Neighbour's daughter Joyce Cole would take Beryl out in a doll's pram, to give her a dose of fresh air. Beryl was followed by her three brothers John in 1937, Tony in 1942 and Bryan in 1946.

Dr Ward also attended Tony's birth and told Beryl that if the air raid siren went, she was to grab two enamel bowls and hold them over the heads of her mother and new brother. She felt a bit left out. "I just had to obey, but what about me?" Then, she stayed home from school to look after them.

If the family needed to visit Dr Ward, his waiting room was the greenhouse in his garden. He would call his patients into his room as he needed them.

Sometime after Beryl was born, a new development of ten houses was built in Station Road. Known as Glebe Cottages, the family moved into number six. Beryl remembered and named all the neighbours in their little close:

In house number one, lived the two Miss Days, until one of them married Mr Knight and that Day became Knight!

House number two, belonged to Frederick and Charlotte Geal. He worked in a road-stone quarry.

Harry and Elsie Sanders lived in number three and they were the parents of Beryl's best friend Mary.

Mary later married Ernie Swift, whose parents, Edwin and Matilda Swift lived in house number four. Ernie would whistle the song

'Pedro, the Fisherman' to let Mary know he was outside.

House number five was occupied by Alfred and Mabel Greenaway and their son John. In the 1939 census, Alfred was a coalman possibly working in the station coal yard.

In house number six lived Beryl's parents John and Beatrice Everest with their family.

William and Amy Day were the occupants of house number seven. William was a gardener for Mrs Norah Arnott, of Tanners House, Rectory Lane. She was the mother of Lady Wilhelmina Kilmaine. When William retired, he and his wife moved into a cottage beside Mount House, where Lady Kilmaine lived.

Number eight housed Charles and Doris Hyland with their children. Charles was a shepherd and stockman.

Number nine was the home of Basil and Margaret Firmager. Basil was a heavy goods vehicle driver.

Last, but not least, house number ten was the home of Grandma, Lily Everest with her daughters, Ivy and Lily.

John, Beryl's father, eventually moved to number nine next door to his mother. There, they made the gardens into one magnificent plot. They kept chickens and every vegetable they could grow, along with many flowers. His speciality was roses and particularly one called 'Super Star'. It has a lovely deep pink colour, with a wonderful strong scent. Roses grew everywhere in the garden and all of John's grandchildren remember his sage advice: "Don't prune the roses till the last week of March!" They always wait! John was a talented gardener and this filtered down through his sons. Bryan is a show judge and grows prize chrysanthemums and sweet peas. Bryan's son, followed him into gardening and grows show-quality flowers, particularly dahlias. John would also help look after the churchyard and mow the grass, Beatrice would help him. It looked beautiful when they had finished.

John would wander out into the fields to snare rabbits for their meals. Beryl's mother would tell her she was brought up on rabbit's brains - a real treat! Beryl's comment, "no wonder I am hopping mad!" Good thing, myxomatosis was not around then, as she would have had wild eyes too!

Father, John and Uncle George, both worked at the chalk pits by Hogtrough Hill. They would walk up the road together and climb into a lorry filled with chalk. It was part of their job to deliver it to farmers and spread it over their fields. The natural chalk was a rich source of fertiliser for the crops. Initially it had to be spread by hand which was back breaking work. Later, the lorry would tow a spreader which swept it on to the fields using a turning mechanism. Sometimes, Beryl would sit between the two brothers and enjoy seeing the farms and farmers. They would always arrive home with something, sweets or apples, the farmers were very generous and everyone knew each other well.

At the age of five, bubbly Beryl started at the village school. There were two separate classrooms and then a larger room, separated by a glass partition. She said, they must have been disturbed by the other classes, but that was just how it was! Mr Warner was the strict headmaster, but he never grumbled at Beryl. Mrs Warner would give Beryl small tokens for 'doing jobs' for her. "I've got a little present for you, dear," she would say. Miss Cronk, one of the teachers, would reward Beryl with gingerbread when she did some shopping for her.

She recalls spending a lot of time in the air raid shelter, in the playground. There she learnt to knit, now a lifelong hobby. They would knit the soldiers hats, with scarves attached. During the school half term, they were encouraged to collect rose hips by a government campaign. These were handed into school to be made into rose hip syrup. Stinging nettles were also harvested through the school as part of another government campaign. Green dye was extracted from the nettles for use in making camouflage fabrics. John was an ARP[19] officer during the war. Beryl remembered very little about it, except she was scared of him in his tin helmet.

The classrooms were freezing cold in the winter, as they only had a small fireplace to heat the room. The milk bottles would come in frozen solid and were put in front of the fire, to melt. Swimming lessons were held at the Brasted Swimming Pool, which made the pupils feel just like those milk bottles, frozen solid! Sewing lessons taught Beryl to hem and repair clothes. There were no irons at the school so the girls were taught to stroke a horse's tooth over their work to make it smooth. Cookery lessons took place in Dunton Green Village Hall. Beryl remembers making her first loaf of bread there. It was left in front of the fire to help the dough rise. She mused on this and said, "the lessons must have been very long staring at the rising dough!"

The school children would walk up behind Mr Strickland's gatehouse at the end of the village to a field for their sports lessons. The field was officially part of the Combe Bank School grounds. They would play stool ball, a game played in two teams. The 'wickets' were

---

[19] ARP (Air Raid Precautions) Wardens were appointed during the Second World War to protect civilians from the dangers of air raids. See also April Williams' story, Footnote 12

boards at shoulder height and the bowler would throw under arm, trying to hit the board. The other team defended the board with a bat and the idea was to hit the ball hard and score runs. It seems this game is mostly lost from school curriculums these days!

As the war time bombing increased, Mrs Warner called the school children together and told them they were being evacuated, for their own safety. They were all issued with new clothes to take with them. So, with baby John in her arms, Beatrice took her two children to the meeting point, at Blackcurrant Hill, on London Road, Westerham, to await transport. They were sent off together, to Sevenoaks train station. Beryl remembers hundreds of children, standing on the platform, as they waited to board a steam train, to London. The end destination was Truro Station, in Cornwall. From there, the little family caught a bus to Perranporth. They arrived exhausted at the village hall, in the middle of the night. They all had to wash in a big, old tin bath, before being tucked up, on fold up beds.

They were sent off to various homes, over a two week period and Beryl can still hear her mother saying, "we're not stopping here." Sometimes the houses were so crowded, there would be six people, in a shared room. Then, a telegram arrived, from her father, which simply read, *"If wife in need will come."* He arrived that very Sunday morning, having walked from Truro to Perranporth, with only blackberries to eat along the way. So, back to the train they went and it was heaving with troops. Beryl sat on a soldiers' knee, while eating cornflakes out of a box. As they got into Paddington Station, the siren howled and they were straight back in the thick of the bombing!

The church choir in the early 1950s

Once back home, Beryl started her usual routine of church again, going three times on Sundays. Starting at 8 a.m. for the morning service, 3 p.m. for Sunday school and 8 p.m. for Evensong. Sunday school was taken by Mrs Grosse, where the children were awarded stamps for regular attendance. At Christmas in 1948, Beryl was given a prayer book, as a prize for her good attendance. Her Christmas stamp was stuck inside the cover of the book, and it still has the price of seven shillings (7s) on it. Evensong was at 8 p.m. As they got older, Beryl and her brothers were all in the choir, so practices had to be fitted in during their busy week.

The village was full of good, kind people and Beryl knew them all. She mentioned some of the shopkeepers that have particularly stayed in her excellent memory.

Miss Rosie Rice had a sweet shop, next to Elliotts Lane. She was a lovely lady and had taken on the shop, after her parents died. She would take Beryl's sweet coupons. Her 'D' coupon would allow her one ounce of sweets and an 'E' coupon would buy two ounces. Beryl's favourite sweets were liquorice covered in a red, sugary coating. What fun it was to lick the sweets and then apply them to her lips like lipstick.

Mr Hebb, the chemist, a lovely kind and knowledgeable man.

George Harris was the blacksmith, at the forge on Brasted Green. Beryl loved the smell of shoeing horses and watching Mr Harris, bashing away at the forge.

Mr and Mrs Stott had a teashop and Beryl's mum, Beatrice baked gingerbread for them. They had a telephone and when Beryl went missing, Beatrice always knew that she was busy picking up the phone. "Put that down," she would scold.

Miss Helena Fuggle was wheelchair-bound, but Beryl would go into her bakery and watch her making bread. As soldiers marched through the village, Beatrice would send Beryl into Miss Fuggle, to see if she had any sweets, "for the poor souls". Beatrice did housework for Mrs Fuggle and Beryl still has the mop on a short pole that Beatrice would use. It is still in great condition at over seventy five years old!

Mr and Mrs Horscroft lived in a cottage behind the High Street, where Mr Horscroft mended shoes. He was disabled, with one tall boot for his shorter leg. Beryl would love to sit and chat to him.

Mr and Mrs Kimber were the village fishmongers. He would ride to the station and come back wobbling on his bike, after a few pints in The Stanhope Arms. Mrs Kimber had puffy, mauve hands from handling the ice packed around the fish.

John changed jobs and worked for Stratton Campbells, who had a timber yard in Rectory Lane. He would drive the 'timber bug' lorries, with trailers that had long poles, supporting an outer frame. Whole tree trunks were secured to the poles and then driven to the yard. There, a machine would be used to remove the bark. John made Beryl a trolley from pram wheels and she and her friend, Mary Sanders, would fill it with bark and drag it up the hill home. It was one of their only sources of fuel for the open fire. Another night, she and Mary would go to the coal yard at the station, to collect coal for their fires. It was a two-girl task to haul the filled trolley around.

Beryl's mother, Beatrice, did the ironing for many of the families in the 'big' houses in the village. She would carefully wrap the finished items in brown paper and Beryl would deliver them back, in her trolley, of course! Beryl knew many people in the village and this led to a job of shopping for the older residents. Again the trolley would come into its own, up and down the roads. Her customers would give her a ha'penny (½d) or a penny (1d), as thanks, which she squirrelled away for savings. Beatrice taught her to be careful with money and Beryl was encouraged to buy one penny (1d) stamps, from a machine outside Markwick's shop. When she had twelve stamps, she would exchange them, for two sixpenny (6d) savings stamps. She still has two of these blue stamps with the Union Jack flag on the front. When her savings reached five pounds (£5), she proudly opened a Post Office Savings Bank account.

Her shopping jobs had other benefits: as Mr Upton had a grocery shop and he would give her a pat of butter. Mr King was a baker, and he would give her a bread roll. Finally, Mr Malpass, the butcher, would give her a slice of corned beef. This was the time of food rationing, so these acts of kindness were indeed a treat.

Jessie Budgen lived at Court Lodge Cottages and Beryl remembers that she wore her hair in a big bun to keep it tidy. She would come into the village to put her son Walter's children to bed. Sending them on their way up the stairs, in the tiny cottage she would say:

'Up the wooden hill, down the sleepy lane,
Into fleaberry, and back again.'

Her ditty still rings in Beryl's ears.

Beryl's family would help with harvesting on Mr Steven's farm, at the bottom of Westerham Hill. The hardest work on the farm was digging potatoes. There were runner beans and peas to be picked too and strawberries, when in season.

In the field, between her house and the church, there was harvesting to be done with the hay. It was cut and Beryl and her best friend Mary, would turn it, to help dry it out. They would stack it up, waiting for the horse and cart to arrive, to take it to Mill Farm for Mr Day's cattle. Each year, Reginald Alderson, from Sundridge, would arrive and get to work. With his trousers tied below his knees, he would skilfully thatch the hay into two, perfectly beautiful haystacks.

Mrs Alderson of Church End House, would invite Beryl into her kitchen and ask her to sing. She would be rewarded with sixpence (6d). Father John and George Alderson were good friends and John played darts and golf with George, in his huge back garden. George, also had a cottage in Pevensey Bay and every time they could, John and his family took holidays there. The beach was only five minutes away and the family loved it. John would stand on the shoreline casting his fishing rod out to sea for many hours.

During Beryl's schooling, the time came for the exam to place one student into the grammar school system. Three girls went down to

Tonbridge to sit the exam. Beatrice advised Beryl that if she did not pass, she faced a life in service. She took the exam, but was beaten to the place by her school friend Ann Carter. So when Beryl left school she did start in service, but hated it and ran away!

So now what was she going to do? She hatched a plan and walked to the phone box, on the corner of her road. Phoning the post office in Sevenoaks, she enquired about being a telephone operator. They sent an application form and she was summoned to an interview. It was something of an ordeal, with lots of people sitting around a table listening to her reasons why she wanted this career. Anyway, she was thrilled when they offered her a job and she was sent to Windsor, for six weeks training. The post office provided a train ticket, but the 705 bus from Sevenoaks went directly to Windsor. It was an easy journey. Having arrived, the new recruits were asked to put their hands up, if anyone needed lodgings. Her hand shot up and so did that of a girl, called Carol Barlow. "Shall we share a room," she asked, and they did, in nearby Dedworth.

Beryl had turned up in her rather staid clothes, with laced shoes and a brown hooded coat. She never had the opportunity to own fashionable clothes. Carol said, "You can't go around dressed like that. Shall I lend you the money for new clothes?" She did, and Beryl got to wear nylons for the first time in her life. Their friendship was immediate and lasted for many years, until they finally lost touch. Needless to say, the borrowed money was religiously paid back every week until her debt was quickly repaid.

Each week of training ended with an exam every Friday, which Beryl passed every time with ease. She was assigned to Westerham Telephone Exchange and loved her job. It had an old-fashioned board and her district included the military base, in Biggin Hill and Winston Churchill in Chartwell. When a security call came through, she had to cover the keys with a box so she could not accidently listen in, or cut the call off.

One day, such a call was on her board and it simply went on and on. She daren't listen, but surely it was finished. She decided to call Biggin Hill and they passed her to the military exchange. A male voice assured her the call had finished, a long time ago. "Who are you?" asked the mystery operator. He thought he knew all the girls in the exchanges, but not this one. He continued, "I'll come on the bus and meet you outside The Kings Arms pub in Westerham". Beryl told me she didn't know who it was that she had rashly agreed to meet that day, but there in front of her, was a handsome young man. Beryl was only sixteen, and how could she know the young man standing there would be her future husband, Bernard Herpe. (Pronounced Her-pay the name is Guernsey/French.)

Bernard Adolphe William Herpe was from St Peter's Port, in Guernsey. Born in March 1933, his family were long-time residents of the island. When war was declared, in September 1939, the islanders seemed detached from events and life continued, much the same. All that changed, when the Germans invaded and occupied the Channel Islands, in June 1940. Bernie with his mother, one brother and two sisters, evacuated on the last coal barge out of the port, bound for England. Hundreds of women and children left the island, but no men were allowed on the boats. Bernie's grandfather stayed to witness the Germans sink his boat and push his car off the quay, into the harbour. Bernie's mother, Maud took her family first to Bradford and for a while they moved around. Bernie attended eight different schools. They finally settled in Oxted, staying with an uncle. Bernie found a job as a messenger boy, with the GPO, delivering telegrams. He later joined RAF Biggin Hill as a civilian switchboard operator and as they say, the rest is history...

Beryl transferred from Westerham to Brasted Telephone Exchange, at the Grey House in the High Street. She enjoyed working in Brasted. It was an easy walk down the road and she could pop home for lunch! If she was on the late shift, finishing at 8 p.m., PC White, the village bobby, would time his walk into the village, to pass her on the way, to make sure she was safe and sound.

Hilda Sherlock lived in the Grey House and was the caretaker operator. Beryl says she was a lovely lady and they got on very well. She also worked with Margaret Sherlock, Hilda's daughter-in-law, Idina Cassidy from Brasted Hill Road, Amy Magnus who lived in the High Street and another lady, Mrs Brooker. The supervisor was Miss Stone from The Green in Westerham. Beryl was once invited into her house which was converted from Westerham gaol. The prison keys still hung on the wall. Mrs Towner took the night duty shifts.

The staff would go into an old-fashioned kitchen for their cups of tea. It had a gas fire that was antiquated, but worse still, was an area under the lino that was not solid floor. Beryl refused to put her chair anywhere near it. When the lino was finally pulled up, there was a big gaping hole underneath. An open well had been concealed under that lino, for as long as anyone could remember! When the children finished school for the day, it was great fun for them to stand on the wall outside the exchange and peer in at the ladies working!

However, times were changing and the exchanges were rapidly becoming automated. So, with change coming to Brasted, Beryl quickly transferred to Sevenoaks. It was still an easy journey, as she could cycle there, but eventually that exchange was upgraded too. With all her experience, she was seconded to the local village exchanges, when they were short of staff. She remembers Borough Green, as it took a train and bus ride to get there and back. Her knitting needles clicked together and garments grew fast, during those journeys!

Beryl and Bernie married in St Martins Church in 1957. The church was completely full, with more well-wishers standing outside. John, was a gardener for Lady Strickland-Constable and she provided buckets and buckets of daffodils, to decorate the village hall. Great Uncle Friend Wells was the local road sweeper and drove around in a little green council truck. The family always called him Uncle Friendly, and on their wedding day, he did his bit by transporting all the jellies to the village hall in his truck! Their pile of wedding gifts was truly amazing and each one was a token of the villagers' love and respect for Beryl and her family.

Beryl and Bernie's Wedding Day colour photo

Beryl and Bernie were approached by their wedding photographer, who said he had a roll of colour film in his pocket. If they were willing to pay for it, he would use it, but could not guarantee the results. They were game to try this new film and Beryl still has the

281

photographs, in good quality colour. They were also the last couple to be photographed under the old lych-gate. Soon after their wedding, it was destroyed when a tree fell on it.

After their marriage Beryl and Bernie moved to Forest Row, East Sussex, where they worked together in the same telephone exchange. Bernie worked during the day and Beryl took the night shift. After six months Bernie moved on to East Grinstead.

One by one phone exchanges around the country were being automated. Bernie saw the writing on the wall and went to work for a large Sainsbury's supermarket, in Oxted. The train service was direct to Oxted Station. However, when Beryl had her second child, she stopped working and it seemed a move back to Westerham or Oxted, was a good idea. They put themselves on the local council waiting lists. The Oxted council came to the couple, with an offer of a farm cottage, at Perrysfield Farm. Beryl says that Oxted was like a foreign place to her and Gibbs Brook Lane was long, lonely and countrified. Still, beggars could not be choosers, so they took the cottage. It was a hovel, with weeds up to Beryl's ears, just to get to the front door. Birds had come down the chimney and the cottage needed lots of work. John and his brother helped to make it liveable! There was no electricity, just Calor gas for lighting. A Rayburn stove was fantastic though, for hot water and cooking. A phone was installed as a life-line. Beryl tolerated it for a year, before moving to Hurst Green, near Oxted, where she spent fifty-three years.

When Sainsburys finally planned to shut its doors, Bernie and Beryl ran Henry's Snack Bar, by Oxted station. "It was the hardest work I ever did," said Beryl, "starting at 6 a.m. and working all day." Beatrice, Beryl's mother, would make gingerbread and rock cakes and dad, John delivered them every morning. The lorry drivers, from the Westerham Brewery were regulars and the M25 motorway was just opening. Tea was a bargain ten pence (10p) a cup! "Two dog (sausage) rolls and a cup of tea," was the mantra of the bar.

When the snack bar finally ran its course, Bernie went back to being a postman for a short while. After retirement, he did not enjoy the best of health, but never complained. Bernie died in November, 2016 and his wish was to be cremated without ceremony. Instead, he wanted his family to come together and enjoy a splendid meal, as his memorial. The family went to Pevensey Bay, a place held dear by them all. One day his ashes will be buried with Beryl, but he'll be happy to wait a long time for her.

August 2017

Susan Wood

Susan Elizabeth Wood was born in May 1951 in Pembury Hospital, soon joining her parents in Rectory Lane, Brasted. They were Cecil Arthur Wood, born August 1916 in Biggin Hill, Kent and Freda née Seale, born in August 1922 in The Manor House, Brasted, behind the village green. Freda came from a long line of descendants born in this village. Her mother was Florence (Flo) Seale née Wells. Flo's father had the interesting name of Friend Wells a name passed down through several generations.

The Wells family have had long associations with Brasted, as Friend Wells was the son of William and Fanny Wells, also born here. William was christened in Brasted in 1819 and became a cooper in the village. Friend became a master craftsman bricklayer and worked for Durtnell & Sons, the village builders.

When Cecil Wood left school, his mother took him to Richard Durtnell & Sons, the oldest building company in the country. She put in place a seven year apprenticeship signed in May, 1932. This training had to be paid for and Cecil's mother shouldered the cost. In his first year he earned eight shillings a week. In the second year it went to ten shillings and in the third year it rose to fifteen shillings.

The Wells Family Tree

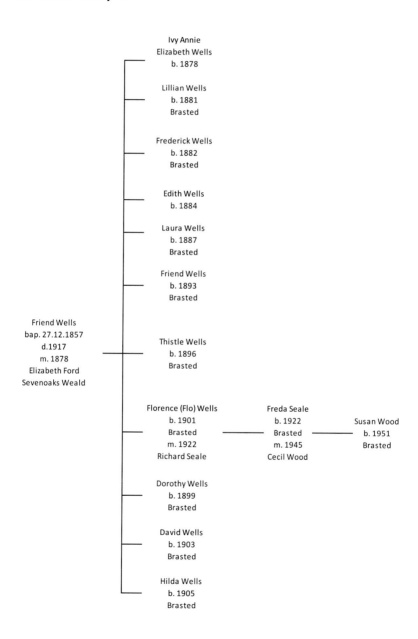

Ivy Annie
Elizabeth Wells
b. 1878

Lillian Wells
b. 1881
Brasted

Frederick Wells
b. 1882
Brasted

Edith Wells
b. 1884

Laura Wells
b. 1887
Brasted

Friend Wells
b. 1893
Brasted

Friend Wells
bap. 27.12.1857
d.1917
m. 1878
Elizabeth Ford
Sevenoaks Weald

Thistle Wells
b. 1896
Brasted

Florence (Flo) Wells
b. 1901
Brasted
m. 1922
Richard Seale

Freda Seale
b. 1922
Brasted
m. 1945
Cecil Wood

Susan Wood
b. 1951
Brasted

Dorothy Wells
b. 1899
Brasted

David Wells
b. 1903
Brasted

Hilda Wells
b. 1905
Brasted

One of Freda's passions when young was to walk to the popular Swan Picture House in Westerham. There she would watch the black and white movies starring her hero Tom Mix, an American actor. He made many western cowboy films during his career which spanned from 1909 to 1935.

Freda left the village school at fourteen and was offered a scholar –ship for further education. Although the education would be

Friend and Elizabeth Wells (centre) and family

Brasted Carnival 1935. In centre, Faith Murkett (groom) and Freda Seale (bride)

paid by a grant, Freda's parents could not afford the uniform or anything else she would have needed. Instead, Freda went to work as a housekeeper and cook. For a while she worked in Mount House, Brasted and later in Hosey Hill, Westerham where she lived in.

When the Second World War started, Freda was asked to join a munitions factory making explosives, shells and bullets for the war effort. The nearest factory was in Westerham, built on the site that was the Swan Picture House. However, this was definitely not how she saw her supporting role and strongly turned down the request. Instead she chose the Wrens and wore her uniform cap with a silver threepenny (3d) coin tied into the bow for good luck. Her posting was to the Fleet Air Arm in Londonderry where she undertook her duties as cook for the sailors and airmen. On one ferry journey over from Stranraer to Larne, the sea was so rough that Freda was tossed up and down in her bed. For days after she suffered the same rolling motion until her body finally agreed it was back on solid ground.

Parts of Londonderry were off limits to British forces even then, and they had to be careful not to enter these areas. Other areas were welcoming and local families asked members of the military to come in and share their Sunday lunch, even though they had barely enough for themselves.

When, choosing meat for her own canteen, she was sometimes offered horse meat, her retort was, "I'm not cooking that, I know what that is!"

It was through Sue's grandfather Richard Seale, who worked for Durtnells, that Freda met her future husband, Cecil Wood, in the village. Cecil was working for Durtnells, when he enlisted in 1939 soon after the war started. He was assigned to the Royal Monmouth

Royal Engineers, as a sapper[20]. This was chosen as the best way of using his building experience. He had various duties some of which involved the Royal Engineers Bomb Disposal Branch, working in London and Essex.

Preparing for a day trip outside Durtnells

D-day was on June 6th 1944 and Cecil was sent to France on the 7th in the second wave of invasion forces. The Engineers worked their way across France and Germany clearing the roads, building bridges and achieving any other engineering solutions that stood in the way of the advancing forces. Near the end of the war he was in Holland when he and his chums were invited to celebrate with a Dutch family. The family had saved a bottle of gin throughout the war and the soldiers virtually emptied it!

---

[20] An engineer is a soldier, now known as a sapper, who maintains railways, roads, water supply, bridges and transport for the armed forces.

Cecil Wood

Freda Seale

One day he called Freda in Northern Ireland and told her to come straight home. He had applied for a special licence to marry and gained permission to take leave - all he needed was his bride. Freda had a satin wedding dress set aside, but this was January 1945 in Brasted and the church had suffered severe bomb damage. As some of the church windows had been blown out, the wedding dress wasn't very practical. Freda chose instead to marry in her Wrens uniform on that chilly morning. Tom Lawrence, the next door neighbour, was the taxi driver for Alderson's taxi company. He drove Freda to the church, but insisted they took the long route just to keep Cecil waiting a little! They both returned to military duties, but Freda was quickly discharged, as married women were not acceptable in the WRENS. For a while, Freda worked as a chambermaid at The White Hart, still a hotel as well as a pub. She lived with her parents Flo and Richard in Rectory Lane, while she waited for Cecil to come home.

Grandfather, Richard Seale was an air raid warden in the Second World War, but in World War One he had earned a certificate for 'gallantry and devotion in the field', for his bravery. He had led a train of donkeys with urgent supplies through the front line action in France, successfully reaching his destination. Recently, Sue donated his award, the Note of Valour and medals to the Queen's Own Royal West Kent Regimental Museum[21], located in Maidstone.

Sue started life in Brasted and at the age of five went to the village school. These were happy years with the good natured headmaster, Mr Blezard, along with her good friends Sue Peake, Joan Pearson, Hazel Rixon, Linda Smith and Brenda Monk. She passed her eleven plus exam and was offered a place at Walthamstow School in Sevenoaks under the direct grant scheme. She remembers trotting off with her satchel to get the bus to school each morning. The first day her mum Freda, went with her, but after that she went alone. As she says, "it was a different world then". Children were not escorted everywhere and they certainly didn't have the luxury of being driven to the school gates.

In the village, the river provided entertainment in many ways. Sue could fish for sticklebacks or climb into the water at 'wide waters' in Church Road. The water washed over watercress beds, which had to be negotiated without slipping over. Other times the river became a menace when heavy rain would lead to flooding. Sue

---

[21] The Royal West Kents were formed in 1881, although under another name they were originally formed in 1756. The regiment was finally amalgamated in 1961. This brought them together with the Royal East Kent Regiment, latterly called the Queen's Own Buffs Royal Kent Regiment. The museum proudly shows the West Kent's history including four Victoria Crosses and many artefacts from its long history. Those treasures are now joined by Richard's medals and the Note of Valour.

remembered one occasion when flooding brought out many sightseers. The wash of their passing vehicles compounded the problems as waves rolled over the door steps. Her grandmother was flooded out and the Baptist minister from the chapel helped her mop out and clean up. Her mum and dad lived two doors away and Sue was sent to a friend's house while all hands helped with the mess. Flooding has always been a problem and still is[22].

Brasted was a thriving community with shops up and down the High Street. They provided local employment and sold everything that residents wanted. Markwicks was a wonderful shop with a post office within it. Mr Giles could often be seen walking through it with sides of bacon. Freda, Sue's mother, looked after the green grocery section and would individually weigh all sales in her cheerful, happy way. In the school holidays, Sue would help refill the shelves. Barry Simmonds was the store manager at that time. Over the years these shops slowly closed as store holders retired and much larger shops were opened elsewhere. Antique shops took their place and now even some of those have gone as parking has become more and more difficult for visitors to the village. The White Hart pub was a cosy place to spend some time. It displayed a board with the handwritten names of many of the RAF Biggin Hill airmen that visited during the war. The board has now gone, replaced by a replica, after the original went to the Shoreham Aircraft Museum. Sadly, it is currently in storage and not displayed at all. The old pub atmosphere has long gone as it focuses on food and has become part

---

[22] Flood control work was later completed in Rectory Lane. It is designed to take the flow of water across the road and back to the river behind Jewson's builder's yard. This cannot solve the whole problem though as the water table is close to the surface and in severe storms the water rises straight out of the ground around Rectory Lane and the village green.

of a chain of pub restaurants. Another loss to the spirit of local community.

A brownie group was held at the village hall. Later Sue went on to guides at Ide Hill. She would hop on the 4 p.m. bus by herself and return home again at 6 p.m. Such freedom was wonderful, but better still were camp days in the local woods. They built fires and lit them themselves with matches. Can you imagine letting a child loose these days with a box of matches? Everything was fine and they had fun cooking their own meals. Sue remembers studying and qualifying for her housekeeping proficiency badge. She had to turn up at someone's house (whoever it was!) and prove her skills to pass the test.

Sue noted that Sundays were always quiet, as the newsagent was the only shop open and that closed at lunchtime. She went to Sunday school at St Martin's Church, which was the only event on offer. It was a boring day, but, "back then we were all allowed to be bored! We had to make our own entertainment." Later she was confirmed in the church by the Reverend Cosgrove. The Sunday school arranged outings and on one occasion, Sue and her mother went to Camber Sands where they had tea and cake. Reverend Cosgrove disappeared off for fish and chips and they all voiced, "Huh, why didn't we get fish and chips?" Somehow, tea and cake seemed a little tame in comparison! On the whole though Sunday school was a fun thing to do.

The Kings Arms pub organised an annual Christmas club where Cecil and Freda would save a regular amount of money through the year. Mrs Wright, the landlady, would pay out the club money a month or so before Christmas. So, with funds in hand the Wood family made a pilgrimage to Croydon to buy their presents. The magical day started with a ride on the 403 bus, which ran through the village and all the way to the shops in Croydon. Sue remembers seeing Father Christmas there and walking through the toy departments in the store. There she had the excitement of choosing her own Christmas present. Back then shopping was not a leisure activity as it is today and the Wood family would only go when they had something special to buy.

Brasted School used the recreation ground for its sports lessons. Sue remembers playing rounders on the field. It had playground equipment for non-school times with a slide, roundabout and rocking horse. There was no safety equipment as we have today and when you came off the end of the slide you could expect grazed knees as a badge of honour! In her teens she would hire a tennis court and play with her friend Jennifer Haynes who lived in Alms Row.

Walthamstow School had a Young Farmer's Club and they kept chickens, pigs and rabbits. Sue hated cleaning out the chickens as they were horribly messy, but she respected the pigs. The club taught the students how to care for animals. Domestic science lessons taught home management and cooking. Sue remembers learning how to make Eggs Benedict with its cheese sauce and bake cakes. Sewing classes taught her how to put a patch on. "Clothes were expensive then," she said. Her favourite lessons were maths, chemistry and physics and they became her A-level exam subjects. She took an S-level chemistry course just for the fun of it. This interest in the sciences and the passing of these exams led ultimately to Sue's lifetime career as a pharmacist.

Sue went on to study pharmacy at Bath University. After graduation she undertook a one year pre-registration course at King's College

Hospital in Denmark Hill. This was a period of employment when Sue would have to prove her knowledge and successful application of her pharmaceutical skills. Of course, she was successful and transferred to Bromley Hospital. Promotion took her to Orpington Hospital and later the closure and demolition of Bromley Hospital led to the centralization of the local hospital pharmaceutical services. This took Sue to the Princess Royal Hospital in Farnborough, Kent. As if that was not enough, combining pharmaceuticals from all three hospitals into a new department was a nightmare. Boxes arrived night and day and at times the department seemed to be drowning in intravenous fluids! Tired and exhausted, the pharmacists were only driven on by adrenaline.

During the university breaks Sue worked as a temporary post lady taking a route along Bradbourne Road in Sevenoaks. It was fun in the sorting office tossing parcels into the correct sacks. After that she said that you certainly had a great appreciation for letter boxes both friendly and unfriendly!!

In the 1970s, chaos was caused when an Esso-owned pipeline was laid across the countryside near the village. It pumped fuel from Fawley Refinery in Hampshire to Gatwick Airport and Purfleet Fuel Terminal in Essex. Today there are still signs pointing to the location of the pipeline in Hogtrough Hill. In 2014 the pipeline was illegally accessed near Chevening and thousands of litres of fuel were stolen over a period of about seven months, before the theft was discovered.

In 1979, the M25 motorway opened, cutting through the village on the site of the disused railway. The Wood family was not too upset about this, except for the loss of walks. Sue remembers them walking up Brasted Hill Road and then along the old railway cutting, towards Westerham. The route was decorated with primroses and bluebells, with butterflies flitting to and fro. Blackberries were abundant in the autumn. There were beautiful dog roses and wild violets before it was all lost, covered by concrete. These days most people miss any pretty plants in the hedgerows as they rush by in a hurry to get somewhere! A kestrel might be hovering in the sky, but they are too busy to notice.

Sue joined her mother in a number of village pursuits, now mostly gone with the passage of time and transience of the villagers. Freda helped run the village library along with Mrs Saxby. When Mrs Saxby sadly died, Joyce Furst née Cole took over helping. The books came from Maidstone on a three-monthly basis, perhaps a couple of hundred at a time. It became harder and harder to remember and order the type of books individual members liked to read. First the books were stored in a cupboard in the main village hall. Later, they went upstairs to a committee room in two cupboards. This service was ultimately cancelled through lack of interest.

Sue and Freda served on the village hall committee along with such members as Rosemary Whittaker-Browne and Helen Muir and once a year they would host buffet parties with hot cottage pie. It was a thank you for all the support the hall received from the village. A lady and her husband would play records and call for country dancing. Good old 'do-si-do' songs with all the fun they generated.

The hall also staged a monthly market for crafts, plants, gifts, food, teas and coffees. The committee worked hard to organise this event. It was an opportunity to sit and natter and stock up on ready-made foods. This closed in the 1990s due to lack of interest and the nearest replacement became the Women's Institute (WI) market in Ide Hill.

The hall committee would invite The Chalkfoot Theatre Company along once a year to entertain in their unique way. They were a small group of actors, perhaps three people who miraculously performed every part of a play, changing in seconds to appear as someone else. The last performance was 'Riddle of the Sands' taken from a 1903 novel written by Erskine Childers. The twists and turns of this espionage plot unfolded with amazing humour. After that the theatre company lost its funding and the ability to travel and perform in local village halls. Another booked entertainment in the hall was a man dressed as a Victorian gentleman. He sat in front of his audience and told ghost stories by candlelight. Wine was on sale to nullify the scariness.

All this fun has gone away and the only current local gathering at the hall is the annual Martinmass supper. In November, volunteers make a buffet and tickets are sold for an evening of food and reconnecting with friends, often rarely seen during the year. The village hall also hosts dog training classes, dance and exercise groups for those that want specific classes.

The 1987 hurricane jolted Sue out of her sleep as the noise of the wind roared around her. It felt like the house was shaking and her bed was next to the chimney! There were two oak trees growing in the field opposite, and one was ripped out by its roots. In the morning, she walked through the village and photographed the damage. There were trees down everywhere especially in Chart Lane, which was blocked for a long time, marooning some of its residents. Phone lines were down and a long queue formed outside the village phone box as people checked on one another and reported the impossibility of getting to work. Later Sue drove to Seal Chart to see the open skyline, probably a view not seen for hundreds of years. Nature being such a wonderful miracle, the same skyline has again disappeared as new trees and undergrowth quickly grew back. Toys Hill became an area of 'scientific interest' as nature was left to recover by itself. Chartwell car park resembled an abandoned game of skittles.

Amongst her hobbies Sue is a keen craftswoman and currently enjoys quilting classes in Seal village. She enjoys embroidery and cross stitch projects too. She certainly has a keen interest in the local flora and fauna. There cannot be anything better than being woken up in the morning by the local blackbird singing about how good life is! Unfortunately, at the other end of the scale there is nothing worse than sitting in bed listening to packs of cyclists flying by shouting at each other!

Sue feeds her birds and a wide variety visit her garden. Collared doves flap in, only a little quieter than the beating wings of the wood pigeons. Goldfinches go from strength to strength as greenfinches have dramatically fallen in numbers due to a parasite that has hit the breed. The territorial robin demands his place amongst the blackbirds, nuthatches, and an occasional treecreeper. The tit family is strong with blue tits, great tits and coal tits. Sometimes long tailed tits turn up, gregarious and noisy, their tails being longer than their little round bodies. In January and February the siskins arrive flashing their green and yellow colouring. The greater spotted woodpeckers tap hard on the surrounding trees and recently Sue had a sparrow hawk that came to sit on her fence. Chaffinches and dunnocks prefer to feed under the bird table and last year a beautiful bullfinch came with its cherry pink breast in full, perfect colour. At night, owls screech and the oak tree opposite the house is owned by a jay.

Several years ago a falling acorn cracked a car windscreen, but this year (2016) the tree developed very few acorns. In the fields opposite her house little egrets sometimes forage for any small creatures they can find. Grey herons wade into the river to search for small fish, amphibians or even small mammals. Quite oblivious to bystanders, they stand stock-still looking for any tiny movements. Sue recently saw a buzzard monitoring a field in Sundridge. As she went by on the bus she mused on how many people actually saw it and how many could recognise it?

Sue's favourite birds are unlikely to visit her bird table as they are birds of prey and all seabirds. Each perfectly formed either for riding air currents or diving into the water. She described a cruise to the Norwegian fjords and watching yellow headed gannets flying over the ship or plunging deep into the sea to re-emerge with fish flapping in their sharp beaks. She saw puffins, fulmars and needed a hard hat as the artic terns swooped from above. She feels that her birds are like a form of perfect meditation, making an enclosed circle between themselves and Sue. She finds them so calming they can take her active brain off any subject and allow her to focus on the birdlife around her.

But wait, what is that huge grey creature on her bird table? Time to do battle with the squirrel, sitting there, "I've a fluffy tail and little paws, how could you not welcome me?" So Sue shakes her fist as usual and wonders if he will ever take any notice of her scaring tactics!

Another happy memory was in the field next to her house. It had sheep grazing and two llamas as their protectors. Llamas suffer no nonsense and see off foxes or other intruders. It was such fun to watch the llamas chase off the invaders. Sadly, a leylandii hedge was planted on the boundary fence and as it grew, this delight was hidden from view. Leylandii is currently the fastest growing conifer in the UK and has become a popular way of growing a hedge quickly, but often to the detriment of all around.

Cars are a problem for the village as they race through, ignoring speed limits. Even vehicles passing her house in Rectory Lane go too fast. Drivers tend to hit their brakes and screech as they are confronted by the flood control humps. Some even take them as a rallying challenge, but often to their detriment, as they noisily scrape metal bodywork into the road surface. Someone recently drove into Sue's parked car knocking off the wing mirror and scraping the side of her car. There was no note of apology or admission and the repair fell to Sue's insurance.

Sue loves to walk the lanes and fields. She commented that it is sad that children nowadays do not have the freedom to roam the countryside or to skin their knees and delight in nature as she did.

December 2016

Rob Peake

Robert Alan Peake was born in November 1959, at 21 St Martin's Meadow, Brasted, the youngest of five children. His parents were Kenneth John Peake, born on 5th July 1924, in Harrow on the Hill and Jean Margaret née Wells, born on 10th May 1928, in Brasted. Jean was part of the greater Wells family that have been in the village for countless generations.

Many are buried in the churchyard, with the oldest registered as John Wells and his wife Ann. Ann died in July 1695, aged forty-three, but John's death is no longer fully legible. It simply reveals that he died on the 10th December 170? (illegible). On the reverse side of the same headstone was Susannah Wells, who died in October 1738, aged fifty-five and below her inscription, John Wells died August 1744, aged seventy-two. It would be likely that the second John was the son of John and Mary. Both couples had children buried in the churchyard. The records show many more burials for the Wells family through the centuries.

Family Tree

The Wells Family Tree - 1

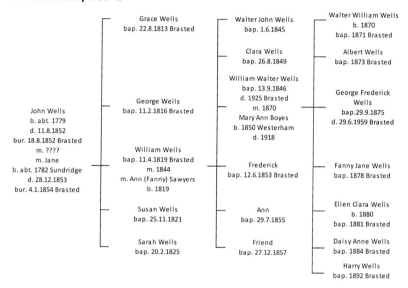

Grace Wells
bap. 22.8.1813 Brasted

Walter John Wells
bap. 1.6.1845

Walter William Wells
b. 1870
bap. 1871 Brasted

Clara Wells
bap. 26.8.1849

Albert Wells
bap. 1873 Brasted

William Walter Wells
bap. 13.9.1846
d. 1925 Brasted
m. 1870
Mary Ann Boyes
b. 1850 Westerham
d. 1918

George Frederick
Wells
bap.29.9.1875
d. 29.6.1959 Brasted

John Wells
b. abt. 1779
d. 11.8.1852
bur. 18.8.1852 Brasted
m. ????
m. Jane
b. abt. 1782 Sundridge
d. 28.12.1853
bur. 4.1.1854 Brasted

George Wells
bap. 11.2.1816 Brasted

William Wells
bap. 11.4.1819 Brasted
m. 1844
m. Ann (Fanny) Sawyers
b. 1819

Frederick
bap. 12.6.1853 Brasted

Fanny Jane Wells
bap. 1878 Brasted

Ellen Clara Wells
b. 1880
bap. 1881 Brasted

Susan Wells
bap. 25.11.1821

Ann
bap. 29.7.1855

Sarah Wells
bap. 20.2.1825

Friend
bap. 27.12.1857

Daisy Anne Wells
bap. 1884 Brasted

Harry Wells
bap. 1892 Brasted

The Wells Family Tree - 2

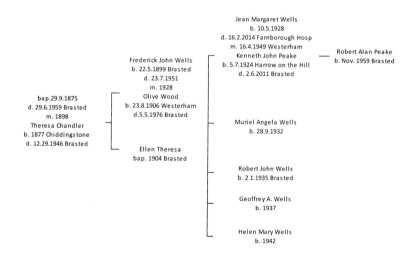

Jean Margaret Wells
b. 10.5.1928
d. 16.2.2014 Farnborough Hosp
m. 16.4.1949 Westerham
Kenneth John Peake
b. 5.7.1924 Harrow on the Hill
d. 2.6.2011 Brasted

Robert Alan Peake
b. Nov. 1959 Brasted

Frederick John Wells
b. 22.5.1899 Brasted
d. 23.7.1951
m. 1928
Olive Wood
b. 23.8.1906 Westerham
d.5.5.1976 Brasted

bap.29.9.1875
d. 29.6.1959 Brasted
m. 1898
Theresa Chandler
b. 1877 Chiddingstone
d. 12.29.1946 Brasted

Muriel Angela Wells
b. 28.9.1932

Ellen Theresa
bap. 1904 Brasted

Robert John Wells
b. 2.1.1935 Brasted

Geoffrey A. Wells
b. 1937

Helen Mary Wells
b. 1942

One of Rob's first memories was the start of the dreaded school days. Like any boy worth his salt, he was not keen at all on the idea of going to school. It didn't help that on his first day, the school served a rather disgusting macaroni cheese which he couldn't bring himself to touch, let alone eat. Told, in no uncertain terms that it was macaroni cheese or nothing, the ravenous young Rob resigned himself to the fact that his initial instincts about school were probably correct!

It wasn't all bad, however, as he did like Mrs Harris, a part-time teacher from Scotland. She was living in Bessels Green and Rob mostly remembers her English lessons. Mr Wilkins the headmaster was kind and Mrs Smith was the playground monitor. The dinner lady was Mrs Dowlen who also lived in St Martin's Meadow and knew Rob well. When his favourite dinners were on the menu she would give him an extra dollop!

Rob's claim to fame at school was winning the 'toffee race' on one particular sports day! It was a relay race, where you had to collect one toffee at a time, return to the start to drop it off and then run back again until all the toffees had been collected. He had lanky legs and so easily beat the other children, but in winning, the only reward he got for his pains was just one toffee – just one!

Jean would meet her children outside the village hall, at the end of the school day. If she shopped on the way home it could take ages. She knew everyone and stopped for a chat with them all. One day they saw a multi-coloured car drive past. The car looked amazing, mostly yellow with bright pink flowers on it. The windows were tinted and all mysteriously dark. Had they but known then, they were looking at the Beatles returning home in their psychedelic Rolls Royce, after filming Strawberry Fields, in Knole Park, Sevenoaks.

The biggest playground any child could desire was the disused railway lines. The tracks had been removed, but Rob and his friends, Brian Bingham and Nicholas Holmden, could build camps and have endless fun running up and down. Rob described them as a younger version of the television programme, 'Last of the Summer Wine', all in their jumpers and wellington boots! The station was derelict and if the boys tried to play in it, old George Bowser would yell, "Get out, it's dangerous," and off they would

Brasted Station and bridge

scuttle. It never mattered what the weather was like. There was a workman's hut with a small fireplace inside. The boys could scout round for odd pieces of coal from Tim Bowser's coal yard and make a fire. Making themselves right at home they even roasted chestnuts for themselves. The railway bridge over Coles Lane was an old metal construction. It had wooden struts laid crosswise, which had once held the tracks in place. Between each strut was a gap, with the road clearly visible below. The friends would dare each other to jump across the gaps. Thankfully nobody fell through, but it was always a risk. Their fun came to an end however, when the bridge was upgraded and the area used for the Sevenoaks to Clacket Lane Services section, of the new M25 motorway.

Behind St Martin's Meadow is a field used as a recreation ground. Mrs Stillwell and her son Bob started the Brasted under fourteen's football team there. At one time the ground was threatened with closure, but the parents petitioned the council and kept it open. Now, the council cut the grass regularly and the local children can have a 'knock about' whenever they like. It is down to one goalpost so football is a little one-sided right now! In the summer Rob and his buddies would play cricket in their field until it simply got too dark to see a ball coming at you from anywhere!

Rob recalls the annual fireworks celebration for which there was always a large gathering of villagers. A collection was made in the village towards the cost of the fireworks. All the families attending would contribute more fireworks, jacket potatoes and hot chocolate. Mike Greenwood and his son, Simon, took on the task of overseeing the display and setting off the fireworks. The girls mostly made the guy each year, as it wasn't much of a boys' task! They were more interested in cutting down trees and building an enormous bonfire. This essential job could take several weeks and the resulting fires were magnificent. Unfortunately, one year a friend of Rob's stood on top of the fire and dropped a match into it. He soon jumped off, as the whole thing went up and goodness, was he in trouble with his parents! They were furious and banned him from going out for three weeks. His mates were charged with rebuilding the whole fire in just one day!

Fires fascinates children and certainly little boys! The lads gathered kindling and made a fire under the railway bridge. For better effect they found lots of greenery that produced so much smoke, it looked like a peasouper smog. Their fun halted abruptly when Mrs Lee yelled, "I know who you are; you're smoking my chickens!" She had her chicken farm close by, so they quickly doused the fire and legged it.

Church was the, 'done thing,' every Sunday until Rob reached a certain age and discovered football instead! Mrs Williamson ran the Sunday school and one particular church outing sticks in Rob's mind. The old charabanc turned up and every one piled in. Off they went, with a box of sandwiches and every expectation of a great day out in Hastings. Unfortunately, the old coach only made it to Lamberhurst traffic lights before dying an unfixable death. A replacement coach took forever to arrive, and their only entertainment was watching the traffic lights go from red to green and back again! When they finally reached Hastings, the group gathered on the beach, walked round the town and of course, played the one-armed bandits, but thanks to the broken down bus, their play time was limited.

Closer to home, the river was a good source of entertainment to everyone who grew up in the village, no matter when they were born. For Rob, he could change into his swimming trunks and splash around up to his waist in water. These days the river is not so deep, as bore holes have been sunk and water is syphoned off for various industries. Rob and his friends could catch sticklebacks and take them home in jam jars. The children made an annual pilgrimage to some pools that formed on the left of the Recreation Ground. Every year the frogs would leave oodles of spawn in them and every year the kids would collect oodles of it and take it home. Rob's father would sigh, "Not more frog spawn again!" Soon there were tiny frogs hopping around everywhere in the garden.

Pooh sticks was another good game they would play from the Rectory Lane river bridge. There could be no cheating, so the kids hunted around for the best stick. They had to be the same size and bits were carefully broken off as necessary. Sets of eager eyes would hang over the opposite wall to see whose stick had won!

On one occasion, Rob borrowed his brother's fishing rod and caught a two and a half pound rainbow trout in the river. It probably came from the Squerryes Estate in Westerham, where they offered fishing licences. With that success, came a lifelong hobby of fishing, often around the banks of Chipstead Lakes, but sea fishing also. There's nothing like a good catch of cod or plaice to share round the family!

Rob had various Saturday jobs before he left school. A village paper round earned him pocket money. On Sundays the papers were so heavy they had to be delivered as two rounds. One Saturday chore, was for Aunt Edna Peake, who lived in Dilgerts Cottage, in the High Street. Rob chopped up wood from City Timbers, into kindling, for her fire and for this she paid him a shilling (1s).

He also worked for Lewis Watts, the butcher, mincing up the beef and making the sausages with the shop assistant, Ted. Whole pigs arrived that had to be carried in on his shoulders. He also had to carry whole sheep and beef that came in quarters, but it was still very heavy. It was back breaking work, but they were happy times. After Rob left school, he continued in the butchers for a while, but left to join the printing department at Marley Tile Company, in Dunton Green. They paid him the princely sum of seventy three pounds (£73) per month and then made him redundant! He did a couple of other jobs, but returned to the print trade, which has been his business ever since.

On the day of the hurricane, in 1987, Rob woke to find his house intact, but trees down everywhere. With no other choice, he started walking to work along the A25. In Riverhead, a man offered him a lift to Dunton Green, which he gratefully accepted. However, once at work, it was all quiet as only two of them made it in that day. So,

Rob left and made his way back home again.

Hurricane damage in Rectory Lane

Rectory Lane was covered in trees and men had arrived with chainsaws to start clearing a way through.

307

Rob joined the gang and spent his time hauling the cut tree limbs away from the road, to open it up again. In The Bull Inn that night, John Wheeler, from Brasted Chart, burst into tears, so shocked at the devastation that the over one hundred miles an hour winds had caused. Chart Lane remained impassable for several weeks, until the army was finally mobilised to help clear the trees.

Hurricane damage on the A25 near The White Hart

The pubs in Brasted were always a source of fun and entertainment. So, Rob started his drinking days in The Bull Inn. Liz and Dave Allen were the landlords then and Rob remembers he paid twenty two pence (22p) for a half pint of Hurlimann's lager; a "decent little brew" from the Shepherd Neame Brewery. Dave collected army memorabilia and held military evenings to buy, swap and simply discuss the merits of various collections.

One day, John Rossey, from the woodyard near Valence School, came running into the pub yelling that a car was on fire in the car park. With typical nonchalance the general reaction was, "Oh, yeah, pull the other one!" Well what a shock to find it was true. Dave jumped clean over the bar and others rushed out to move their own cars away. They all helped to put the fire out and by the time the fire brigade came, it was just a smouldering mess.

Young and old mixed together to chat and play pub games. Rob would make up teams of four, in two pairs, to play dominos. For a while, he wondered why he was apt of lose, before realising the older men were tapping out the number domino they needed with their feet, while their partners opposite discreetly listened. That went on until the younger players sussed out this little ploy! Shove ha'penny had the same pitfalls. Each player had three turns at scoring per round and the number of successes were recorded in chalk. Again, the older players could fix the score. As they recorded their own points, they would lick a finger and rub out one of the opposing players chalk marks! They really had every trick in the book and with a pint as the prize, it was well worth exercising them all. All the pubs had a dartboard and teams to represent them. Rob smiled broadly as he recalled that Bill Barnett would always rap him on the knee with his cane and say, "Alright young 'un?"

Rob has always entered into the spirit of teams and sports. He remembers that Bert Peckham and his wife ran a youth club at the Recreation Ground. They would play records and set up snooker and table tennis games to play. Rob and three others played in the Sevenoaks Table Tennis League through Bert and the club.

Rob became part of the Brasted bat and trap team when he was twenty-one and still loves the game. He started in The White Hart, but as that turned into more of an eating house than a pub, the bat and trap team had to move on. The Bull Inn hosted the team and that went well, until The Bull was sold by the Shepherd Neame Brewery[23]. That caused so much distress in the village, but there was no stopping its closure and the bat and trap team moved on once more, to The Stanhope Arms. There it stayed happily until a landlord decided the team had climbed over his flowerbed and fence, into the churchyard, to collect a lost ball, causing damage to pub property. The team denied it ever happened and after all they should have known! The so-called flowerbed was clearly ivy and weeds and the fence was a stone wall and what's more, they denied the ball went over the fence in the first place! Why this all ended with the team being banned is beyond imagination; but it was. The team changed its name to the Brasted Wanderers and used many pub pitches to continue playing. Ultimately, The Stanhope Arms changed landlords and they were welcomed back to continue playing as The Stanhope Wanderers. This year (2017), they had no luck in the league, but the cup games were a different story. They found themselves in the final playing The Plough, in Basted, Kent. The Stanhope Wanders won 2 – 1 and the trophy plate is coming home.

Pubs held lots of events and everyone put themselves out to participate. One example came to mind when The White Hart held a fancy dress evening. The theme was Frenchmen and tarts. So Rob's 'friends' told him the women would go in French costume and the men would be the tarts. Rob made a huge effort and wore his sister's skirt and pulled on her stockings and shoes. Next, he hit the makeup bag, with gorgeous red lips and splendid eye makeup. So in walks this splendid dame only to be greeted by his buddies dressed as Frenchmen! Still, he did get a pinch on the bum from an admiring gentleman!

---

[23] Editor's note: Ultimately the site became a small housing estate.

Brasted Duck Race and Pancake Race in 1981

Another village entertainment was the annual pram race. It cost five pounds (£5) to enter, which went to chosen charities. With two in a team, they would all scavenge anything they could, to make up a suitable pram or at least something on wheels. On the day, it was into fancy dress and off to the Recreation Ground to start. One year Rob's brother-in-law and partner dressed as Laurel and Hardy and rushed around laughing their heads off! Pyjamas could produce a good effect for dressing up, as indeed, could men in nappies. The first stop was The Stanhope Arms, but there was a gauntlet to be run, at the bridge, in Church Road. One year, a group gathered and hurled eggs and flour and water bombs at the contestants. So looking more like uncooked pastry tarts than in fancy dress, they arrived outside The Stanhope Arms covered in everything. Tables were set up and paper cups of beer were handed over. Once that was downed, it was off to The White Hart and the next beer. Then, on to The Kings Arms, The Bull Inn and finally back to the Recreation Ground. A trophy was awarded to the first three places and medals to everyone else. Sadly, the race had to stop when the police could no longer guarantee slowing the traffic, when the racers had to cross the roads.

The fire at St Martin's Church was a very emotional experience. The first Rob knew of it was hearing loud cracking as it burnt fiercely. He opened the bathroom window and shouted to his father, "Dad, the church is on fire!" Grabbing his camera, he rushed to the scene and was virtually in tears at what greeted him. He watched people carrying out anything they could salvage from the burning building.

The fire at St Martin's Church

Rob took some very dramatic photos, recording the devastation. The chief fire officer was Micky Wortley, from the Westerham Fire Brigade. His mother lived close by in Thorn's Meadow. Afterwards he told Rob it was the biggest fire he had ever seen. With none of the more modern fire-fighting equipment, it could only be contained with hoses and water.

Rob now owns the house he was born in and has lived in Brasted for all but eight years of his life. So when I asked him what had changed about life in Brasted, he was well-qualified to judge.

The shops have gone along with the community spirit of knowing and meeting everyone. Rob would be sent to the Day's farm for milk and eggs. Mrs Lee had her chicken farm and Rob was sent to buy eggs directly from her too! These local enterprises are long gone. A shop called the Brasted Forge, sold paraffin and Rob would be sent to fill a can for the paraffin heaters at home. They would sell bags of nails by weight and packets of seeds for the flower and vegetable gardens. At the grocers, vegetables were bought by weight and tipped straight into a shopping bag! Fresh vegetables and meat were bought daily, as homes did not have the convenience of freezers.

Rob and his mates lived in their wellies, summer or winter, out playing every night. The fields were their playground and the roads so much safer.

With the pubs closing or changing to serve more food, it has stopped another side of the convivial companionship of meeting friends and welcoming strangers, stopping by for a drink. Much of the laughter and banter has disappeared from around the bars! The church does not feature so much in family life and outings no longer take place, whether the bus breaks down or not!

Yes, Brasted is not so much a community now as society has changed and families are more insular and isolated.

September 2017

Julie Taylor

Julie's parents are Neil Taylor and Pamela Viner Hilling who married in Knockholt in 1956. Julie was the youngest of four children being born in October 1972. The family lived at 12 West End.

Julie attended Brasted Primary School which she says she enjoyed - most of the time. The headmaster was Mr Wilkins who later had a road, Wilkins Way in Brasted, named after him. He was a good man and respected by his pupils. They all had to wear uniform with grey jumpers and blue and yellow ties. The school did not have a sports field, just a concrete playground. So once a year a school sports day was held at the recreation ground.

To help give Julie recreational sport, Neil signed her up for Brasted Boy's Football Club. She was the only female player back then and thrived on the challenge, helping the club to win their league. She always played in her red shirt with the number 8. Her mother would wash the shirt rather than risk its loss in the mess of the boys' dirty shirts. For away games Julie changed in her dad's car as there was never a girls changing room! Brasted local Dick Gisby, was one of the two coaches and led the team to promotion to the Tandridge League, where one of the rules was strictly no girls in any team. In disgust Julie left and the team were quickly demoted again. Although asked to rejoin she chose not to play for them again.

Brasted Football Team

From Brasted she went to Hatton Senior School which later became Bradbourne School for Girls, in Sevenoaks. She hated it and was absent for much of the first three years. However when the GCSE exams started to loom up things changed. Sixty percent of the exam result would come from course work and Julie decided she didn't want to leave school without achieving something. She started to attend and actually respected and became quite good friends with the headmistress, Elizabeth Blackburn. With mutual regard Julie was made a prefect in her last year.

There were practical activities at the school which Julie enjoyed and was fully involved with. One of these was an 'Access to the Disabled Club' where a mini bus regularly brought disabled young people to the school to mix with selected pupils. They were encouraged to play golf, netball, basketball and other sports together with the regular pupils. Julie was paired with Wendy a nineteen year old who suffered from a low mental age. Wendy enjoyed her activities and became very fond of Julie. She would make her homemade cards and look forward to their meetings. Then, at home time she would hug Julie and hold on to her tightly, not wanting to leave. Part of this awareness scheme involved Julie and 'Dollop', her best mate, taking a wheelchair into Sevenoaks to experiment with disabled access into shops. Julie had this sewn up of course, as might have been expected. Poor Dollop, otherwise known as Natasha, had to push Julie uphill from the school to the town. The route is quite a steep hill that goes on and then on a bit further! Julie would push Dollop all the way back down again grinning as they zipped down the hill. At that time Julie was identified as having a natural talent for golf and Neil took her to Wilderness Golf Club where she won a couple of competitions. IBM took an interest and offered to sponsor her to attend a golf academy in America, but Julie said, "no!" On reflection and with the passing of time and greater perception of herself, she regrets that decision. Neil was disappointed too.

Hatton School also had a Tuesday Club where chosen students would visit the Emily Jackson Ward at Sevenoaks Hospital. It was a ten week project to chat and entertain older folk. Julie and Dollop took part in this project too. They found

Members of the Hatton School Tuesday Club

themselves paired with a lovely man called Richard who underwhelmed them with tales of meeting the Queen. "Oh, yeah", they thought until he produced photos to show them how true his stories were. Although the club met officially once a week they enjoyed seeing Richard so much, they went in their breaks and lunchtimes every single day. Richard always gave them a box of Milk Tray chocolates and when he died they both attended his funeral.

On days when Julie and Dollop bunked off school they would often head for the Sevenoaks market which was close to Sevenoaks Station. Mondays was the animal market with cows, sheep and other animals all for direct sale or auction. On Wednesdays there were lines and lines of market stalls selling anything from groceries and toys to clothing. So, the two would look around and then drift over to the cafeteria. On Wednesdays, Aunty Pauline would inevitably catch them with their fags hanging out of their mouths. "I'll tell your father," she always threatened, but never did.

When young, Julie was identified as having a form of arthritis in her knees, more commonly known as 'tennis elbow' in the knee. She was in plaster casts for six months at a time, first on one leg and then the other. During this time she was a bridesmaid for her brother Trevor's wedding in 1982, so her dress was made longer to cover the problem. Yes, and she did say, "see I have worn dresses!" At home she shared a room with her sister and she was in the top bunk. Neil would lift her into bed and a night time visit to the loo proved more challenging than can be described here!

In the bedroom her sister Karen had a doll which lived on top of the wardrobe. Whichever way Julie looked at this doll from her bed it gave her an evil eye and stared at her! "I got rid of it, bloody thing gave me nightmares." First she turned it around and it turned back. Then she closed its eyes and someone opened them again. "So, I truly got rid of it." She put it into a black dustbin sack and out it went to the bin. Next thing – it was back. She never really knew how it got back, but there it was. Mother Pam still has the doll and Julie commented, "knowing my luck it will be the only thing I ever inherit."

Her mum and dad bought her a dolls pram when she was six or seven. However, she and her brother Mark took the wheels off and made a super go-cart, perfect for the hills around Brasted!

Growing up in the village offered all sorts of escapades for Julie and her friends and she and Mark could be found with their mates finding mischief wherever possible.

As a small child, fishing in the Darent was a great pastime and Julie could find sticklebacks and crayfish to put in her bucket. Later, it was quite a dare for Julie and her mates to enter the river at Brasted recreation ground and not leave it until they reached The Green at Sundridge. Anyone who got out earlier simply had to go home as a failure.

A neighbour Doug lived at Lindertis House and they had a small swimming pool that the Taylors were encouraged to use. While Neil, Mark and Julie swam, mum Pam was served tea from a china teapot and bone china cup and saucer. Doug's wife was a smartly dressed woman reminiscent of the Victorian era. When she died poor Doug never got over her loss and the loneliness. Sadly, they had never had children of their own. Doug and his buddy Tim Wells would play Julie and Mark at shove ha'penny in The Bull Inn for pints of beer. They always cheated to get their free pints with a nudge here and a wink there, Doug and Tim always enjoyed their pints.

The recreation ground had play equipment. One game Julie and her mates enjoyed was called London which involved using a piece of play equipment called the 'top hat'. It was a hat or bell shape with metal bars forming the structure. It spun around a central pole, but was always slightly off balance giving it a swaying motion. The game involved one person standing on the ground trying to touch those on the 'top hat' hanging and swinging themselves out of the way!

St Martin's Church had two goats for a while to help keep the churchyard grass short and the weeds under control. They were both white, a billy and a nanny. Sadly, the nanny died from eating some yew from the tree. Yew was traditionally planted in enclosed churchyards to make bows when archery was a form of local defence. It also acted as a deterrent to farmers using consecrated land for their animals as it was poisonous to them. After the loss of 'nanny', 'billy' turned grumpy and took it out on all comers. "He was evil and appeared to lay in wait for us," said Julie. One day she and Mark walked into the churchyard and 'billy' took offence. He was untethered, so head down he charged and they quickly ran and shut themselves behind the metal gate of the church entrance. There they waited for six hours before the goat finally disappeared and they could make a bolt for the perimeter gate. During that six hours 'billy' would appear from nowhere every time they stepped out to escape. The goats did a great job of keeping the churchyard tidy, but ultimately 'billy' also met a sad end by eating part of the yew tree.

The kids discovered a tunnel at the church which led from the boiler house to a grate under the altar. One day a service was taking place and singing was filling the church. Julie, Mark and four other friends decided they would crawl through the vault towards the altar. Having entered the tunnel they suddenly found themselves trapped with no way back. That day the service was interrupted when six kids popped out of the grate to everyone's surprise. Some screamed and others just stopped in amazement. Reverend Talbot sort of blessed them as they ran up the aisle and out of the door.

The church was a popular place for entertainment.   Imagine challenging one another to sit in the churchyard on dark, foggy nights to see who could last the longest before being spooked and running off.   How about trying to play,' Chopsticks' on the small organ. Fun until it suddenly started to play by itself!

Sometimes they would all play football at the 'rec' and inevitably the ball would end up on the flat roof of the pavilion. Someone would climb up and along would come the village copper, Mick Toys on his motorbike. He would arrest them for vandalising the pavilion. They would explain themselves and apologize and all was forgotten. Well maybe not quite, as they called him the plastic copper behind his back because of his surname.

Winter in Brasted was colder in the 1970s and 1980s than the milder winters we currently have. Lots of snow would fall and the kids could make sledges out of anything to roar down the hills. On one occasion they came by a car bonnet, the acquisition of which is not for reporting! So off they went to 'Kick Arse Hill' above the Hogtrough Hill and Pilgrims Way crossroads. Five of them linked arms on the bonnet and making it safely down was not an option. Mouthfuls of snow followed and the only thing missing were the carrot noses! On other occasions they unscrewed speed restriction signs and used them as great sledges. They always replaced them, but not always in the right places!

Julie and Mark would disappear off to play with the words of Neil echoing behind them. "Don't go over to the sandpits." "No, dad." Well it was fun over there, they could slide down the banks and play for hours. "Been up the pits, young 'un?" "No dad," Julie said as she took off her shoes and he turned them upside down. The sand poured out onto the door step. With knickers also full of the evidence it was off to the bathroom to deposit it all over the floor.

Opposite the old Bull Inn is a public footpath and once past the gardens of West End it opens into a field. This was known as 'Bull Fields' for the rather obvious reason that bullocks were kept there to be fattened before going off for slaughter. They could be temperamental, but the kids loved to explore the field and were particularly fond of a large fir tree they called the umbrella tree. Its branches were flat and once climbed everyone could have a branch each to lie on. One day the bullocks took particular interest in the proceedings and Julie and Mark were stuck up the tree for several hours while the bullocks looked on and waited!

Another time, the gang of friends went ghost hunting at Combe Bank School. They had heard that a fingerless nun haunted the place, so in all seriousness they went off with one of them having an old tape recorder strung around their neck. As they hunted in the dark they came across a shrine to Jesus Christ and panicked at the sight. They scattered and their ghost hunting days were instantly over except for playing back the recorder. On that they could hear a women's voice and a horse galloping away. Later they heard of a second ghost, a headless woman on horseback. Was it her or not, no one was going back to find out?

After the hurricane of 1987 Julie heard the familiar words, "Come on young 'un, let's go for a walk." Neil led her up Chart Lane which was covered in fallen trees. They clambered up and over and down and under a terrible knot of tangled wood. Julie felt the rising need to dig everyone out. Hero she was not on this occasion as it took the army to finally clear the road sometime later. You have to admire her courageous thoughts though.

At home Mark was allowed to use the petrol mower, but not Julie. With her wonderful determination she changed all that by making a career in gardening. Having set her lifelong career, any mower now lies within her talents.

Julie could not wait to learn to drive so she would offer to clean the family car. This enabled her to sit in the driving seat and practice all the moves she had carefully watched her father making. She watched him change gear using the clutch and gear lever. She watched the accelerator and brake and knew exactly how the ignition key worked. So the moment she was seventeen she took her test and passed. Like most of us this led to the freedom of the road, but only when the car was free!

Julie has an amazing regard for nature and that is where her soul resides. She says her parents gave her an appreciation, respect and love of all creatures. She has always taken in and cared for any sick animal that has crossed her path. Her father would say, "Come on young 'un," and off they would go for walks. On one occasion they found a pigeon with a broken wing. He was lovingly taken home and called Percy Pigeon. Julie would religiously dig up worms and find all the natural foods she could for him. They rarely came home without some needy animal in their pockets.

This summer (2016) she had a mother hedgehog with three babies visiting. She doesn't earn a lot from her gardening career, but out she went and bought cat food to give them. So not that surprisingly a local feral cat turned up as well. Was he turned away? Of course not so out she went for more cat food. He had a damaged head with fur missing and sores, so he had extra food and currently gets through six sachets a day. Now called Fred, he is too cautious to be touched, but Julie is sure the cat will succumb sooner or later.

Some years ago a family rented a nearby house. They decided their only daughter needed a pet and a rabbit was purchased. Well, maybe the child would also like baby rabbits and a male was also purchased. The inevitable happened and soon enough baby rabbits arrived in the dining room of the house! As this fad ebbed away the rabbits were put into an open run in the garden. Brasted is a country village and the rabbits started to disappear and the local fox started to get fatter. A sad tale and soon Julie found the mother and one baby hiding in her small back yard. The mother would rest under her van, so leaving her house was a tricky event as Julie needed to be careful not to hurt her. So, Julie bought a rabbit hutch and Norma and Beatrice took up residence. Later renamed Bert and Norm, they had a wonderful life with daily freedom of the garden and house. Norm's favourite spot was inside on the mat watching the television. They enjoyed eight wonderful years in their new home. None of the other rabbits survived!

Early morning walks with her faithful little companion Saffy dog, are a great source of discovery. One early morning they watched three tiny baby weasels playing in the churchyard. They tumbled over each other nipping and rolling. While the village slept Julie sat down and watched them for a long time. Sometimes there is an early mist and stunning images stand out in the colourless grey tones of the early morning. A heron might be standing in the field or hunting motionless in the river waiting for an inattentive fish. Foxes quietly walk through the grasses and pheasants start by nonchalantly stepping out into their day. Julie has witnessed two calves being born in the fields. Deer are fairly abundant and they can be heard barking, up in the Chart where they live in small groups. Once Julie was working at an uninhabited property in Edenbridge. Two Muntjac deer were quietly sitting on the grass and when the female got up a tiny new baby was underneath her. She walked over to the van and sniffed in the window, but if she thought she was sharing Julie's lunchtime sausage roll she was sadly disappointed. Walks through the churchyard reveal where the deer have dug up wild flowers. Julie replants them as she goes by. In Cudham, she spotted a white squirrel and as she turned away a deer was standing close by taking in the scene.

In Church Road Julie has witnessed several events like a kestrel hovering silently by the lamp post. Suddenly, it dived, a mammal squeaked and off the bird flew with its prey. She once heard a dreadful screaming and discovered a grass snake with a frog in its mouth. She managed to free it, but the snake was not giving up and grabbed it again. At this point she gave up. "It's just nature," she said.

On another occasion she turned up for work in a local garden. At the back two fox cubs had hopelessly entangled themselves in the children's football net. She did no more than rescue them by cutting them out of the mess. The owners came home and were most unimpressed. They demanded a replacement for the goal and Julie said she forked out, "a hundred and forty quid on that little rescue."

Brasted has been regularly losing its pubs for many years, most now converted to houses. However, not so long ago there was an annual pancake race. Four teams, from The Stanhope Arms, The White Hart, The Bull Inn and The Star challenged each other. There were four marshals, two at each end of the green. One would blow a whistle and the first person had to dash to the other end and toss a pancake in a small frying pan. Once the pancake was caught, they could run back to the start to tag the next person and so on. However, if the pancake was missed it had to be picked up in as many pieces as it had fallen into and tossed again. The first team to get all four members back to the start were the winners. For this a trophy frying pan was presented and each year the name of the winning team was inscribed onto it. The pan is currently on display in The Stanhope Arms.

There were also pram races. Teams of two needed a pram or similar and would dress up in fancy dress. Men in nappies were quite a sight! The teams started at the recreation ground and the police would close the road for them. Each team would dash around all the pubs. At each pub they had to drink a pint and get an entry form signed by the publicans. The winners had to reach the last pub and drink their pints before anyone else. The losing team were awarded a wooden spoon, but then, so was the winning team! These games are lost to the village now and nothing has taken their places.

What does Julie miss from the old Brasted she grew up in?
The shops including, one with its little post office, Paddy the hairdresser and Watt's the butchers shop. Julie had a Saturday job there before she left school. Mrs Baker with her little shop where you could buy anything. She would have a little bell on her door which rang as you entered. There was a box full of buttons, so if you lost one you could go through them all until a suitable replacement was found. Then, you could buy the right coloured cotton to sew it back on. Knitting needles, single zips, you name it she had it. Yes, the village is so much poorer for losing the shops and particularly the characters that ran them.

December 2016

Map 1 - Brasted and surrounding towns and villages

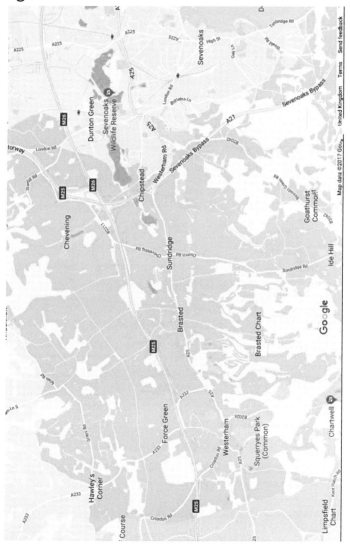

Map 2 - Brasted Village

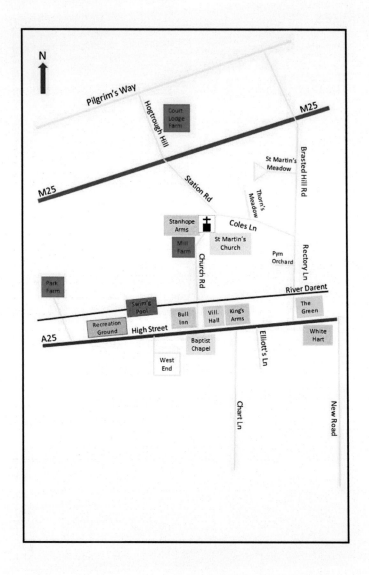

Brasted Village Houses and Shops

The lists below show the village houses and shops along Brasted High Street. Current house names and businesses are shown and where possible details of some of the previous businesses that used to trade along the High Street are also recorded. The most recent businesses are listed first.

The first list commences at The White Hart pub at the eastern end (nearest Sevenoaks) of the village and ends at the Brasted Baptist Chapel at the western end of the High Street. The village houses and shops displayed are on the left hand side of the road walking from east to west.

HIGH STREET BRASTED looking East to West - Left Hand side	
Current House Name or Business	**Prior Businesses and Notes**
The Lodge	
Entrance road to Brasted Place	
The White Hart	
Stables	
Coffee Shop (was Dr Ward's Conservatory)	1. Tart 2. 96 degrees café 3. Delicatessen and greengrocer 4. Dr Ward's surgery

The White House	1. Commercial Horticultural Assn
	    Fed. Of Gdn. And Leisure Manu. Ltd.
	    Int. Trade Assoc. of Pet Equip. Supp.
	2. Dr Kenneth Ward - GP

Rectory Lodge	1. Catch 22 2. Dr Ian Ross's residence

Southdown House	1. Courtyard Antiques and Brasted Clocks 2. Diana Studley Oak Antiques (until she moved to premises at the current Roy Massingham Antiques) 3. Country Gardens - Greengrocer - Alf and Beatty Maybank 4. Shorey's Butchers became Malpass Butchers
Mandy's Antique Shop	
The Red House	1. Vanity Hairdressers
Mulberry Place	
Streatfield House	Formerly owned by Archibald Shorey, Farmer & Butcher
Rough Wood House	
Roy Massingham Antiques (was 2 shops)	1. Diana Studley Oak Antiques (having moved from The Coach House where Markwicks was.) 2. National Westminster Bank 3. Davis's Newsagents 4. Maudsley's Newsagents
Kentish House	Lewis Watts Butchers
Drover's Cottage	1. Albert Joseph Metcalf Atkinson's Tuckshop 2. Betty Brook's Tuckshop 3. Rosie Rice's Tuckshop
Elliotts Lane	· No. 2 - Bill Rich's residence before moving to White Hart Cottages · No. 4 -Stan Seale's residence
Rashleigh	1. The Village Store - Paddy and Beryl O'Donoghue incl. Beryl of Brasted, hairdressers 2. Beryl of Brasted 3. Hebb's the Chemists
Mount Cottage	

Coach House	1. Coach House Interiors 2. MJP Electricals 3. Kimber's Fishmongers
East Cottage	
The Mount House	
The White Cottage	
The Red Cottage	
Chart Lane	
House by Flower and Glory	1. Chartwell Kitchens 2. Wolfe Garage (first in the area) 3. Bond's Garage
Chart Side House	Flats for Locomotor's mechanic and store keeper.
The Village House	
Garden Cottage	
The School House	Brasted Village School
Alms Row Cottages Nos. 1-10 The cottage known as Chimneys is No. 5	
Haynes Cottages Nos. 1 - 4	
Holmesdale House	1. Bed and Breakfast 2. Dr Thomas Weston - GP 3. Dr Symes - GP
Holly Tree House	
Camrie	
Lindertis	
Brasted Baptist Chapel	

The second list below commences at the Bull Inn pub at the western end (nearest Westerham) of the village and ends at Combe Bank Lodge at the eastern end of the High Street. The village houses and shops displayed are on the left hand side of the road walking from west to east.

HIGH STREET BRASTED looking West to East - Left Hand side	
Current House Name or Business	**Prior Businesses and Notes**
The Bull Inn	
Church Road	Leading to: · Rose Cottage · Mill Farm 1. Day Brothers 2. Mr Spink · St Martins Parish Church · The Stanhope Arms · Church End House
Brasted Hall Cottage	Brasted Library
Brasted Hall	
Brasted Hall Lodge	
Wilkins Way	
The Grey House	Brasted Telephone Exchange
Village Hall	Built 1897
Mill House	
Watermill Close	Leading to: 1. Johnsons builders merchants 2. Locomotors 3. The Old Mill
Granary Cottages - Nos. 1-5	1. Mobil Petrol Station 2. Fuggles the Bakers
4 High Street	1. The Window Sanctuary 2. Brown's Accountants 3. The Co-op 4. Hann's stores

Eden House	
The Kings Arms	
Behind Kings Arms E H Smith Architectural Clay	1. Fisk & Dailly - Car Repairs 2. Mr Baker's Workshop - Plumber and Builder
Wisteria House	
Brasted House	
Barrington Antiques	Mickey Miles' Sweetshop
W Jones the Boot maker	This shop later became part of Barrington Antiques
Tilings	1. Daren Bakery 2. A bakery with Mrs Mercier and her daughter Brenda 3. Miss Lelieu's Tea Shop. (Vera was the cook and Marjory front of house)
The Shop	1. Dentist – Charlie Francis 2. Paddy O'Donoghue's Barber Shop 3. GM Baker - Haberdashery and agent for dry cleaning. 4. Chris Friend - Clock and Watch Repairs
The House	
Cromers Cottage	
Kent Cottage	
Number 17 Historic Kent Building	Greengrocers - Mrs Evans and her daughter Alice Henson
Alleyway to	Durtnells Cottages Nos. 1 & 2
Old Forge Cottages 1	
Old Forge Cottages 2	Jack Horscroft Shoe Repairer
Old Forge Cottages 3	
Fig Tree	1. Beryl of Brasted Ladies Hairdressers 2. Paddy O'Donoghue's first Barber Shop - in the front room

The Old Bakery	Cowlard's Bakery. Frank Cowlard baker, May King front of house
Ivy House	1. McMasters Antiques 2. Timothy Wells Transport Café 3. Woodhams Grocers
Bartons Cottages Nos. 1-4	
Bartons Cottages 5	1. The Cleaning Partnership 2. Stott's Sweet & Teashop
Swan House	1. Holloways of Ludlow (light fittings) 2. Miss Swan's Haberdashery & Drapers
The Coach House	1. Vanity London Beauty 2. Diana Studley Oak Antiques (before moving across the road) 3. Barry Simmons - grocer 4. Markwicks & Post Office
Jones the Bootmaker	Moved behind Markwicks as Barrington Antiques expanded
Darenth Cottage	
Dilgerts	
Eversley	
Constables	
Rectory Lane	Leading to: · Darenton · R Durnell & Sons
On village green	
• Manor Cottage	
• The Old Manor House	Bed & Breakfast
Over driveway with village pump on it	
Behind No. 6, The Green, Brasted	1. Buxton Construction Ltd 2. Laura Ashley
The Green Brasted	
• The Forge The Green	1. W W Warner Antiques 2. Blacksmith & Forge (George Harris Farriers)

• Old Forge Flat	
• Swaylands House	Keymer Son and Co Ltd antiques
• Brasted Village Store, 8 The Green	1. Off Licence 2. Mr Turner's Hardware Shop 3. Hardware Shop (Part of the Forge) run by Fred Still, coachbuilder and wheelwright.
Rosena	
The Hollies	
Driveway to Jewsons	1. City Timbers 2 Stratton Campbell
• Brasted Forge Flat	
• Brasted Forge	
• Park Garage	1. Sevenoaks Minis 2. Park Garage 3. George Alderson's Coach Garage
White Hart Cottages Nos. 1 - 6	Bill Rich, Chimney Sweep lived at No. 2 Hodges and King (behind Brasted Forge), 3 Old White Hart Cottages
The Old Forge	1. Entech Ltd. 2. Smith's Garage with workshops
Paddocks	
Paygate	
Driveway to Tanners	Formerly the entrance to Combe Bank Convent
Combe Bank Lodge	Mr Strickland's residence, caretaker of the Darent Valley Swimming Baths

The UK Currency

Many of the values quoted in this book are expressed in terms such as one penny (1d) or one shilling (1s). These are terms used for the currency used in in the UK prior to February 15th 1971 when the UK converted to the decimal currency that is in use today.

The unit of currency in both the pre decimal and post decimal eras is the pound sterling. In the pre decimal currency, the pound comprised twenty shillings (20s) or two hundred and forty pennies (240d), denoted as 's' and 'd' respectively. In the post decimal currency, the pound comprises one hundred pence (100p) each penny denoted as 'p' to differentiate between the old and the new penny.

The table below shows the pre decimal coins and their respective values, names and nicknames.

Pre Decimal Coinage

Pre Decimal Currency Units	No of 'Old Pennies'	Known As	Post Decimal Equivalents
¼d	0.25	A farthing	N/A
½d	0.5	A halfpenny or ha'penny	N/A
1d	1	A penny or a 'copper'	N/A
2d	2	twopence or 'tuppence'	N/A
3d	3	threepence or 'thruppence' or threepenny bit	N/A
6d	6	Sixpence	2.5p
1 shilling	12	A shilling or a 'bob'	5p
2 shillings	24	A florin or two 'bob'	10p
2 shillings and 6 pence	30	Half a crown	12.5p
1 crown	60	A crown	25p
10 shillings	120	Ten 'bob'	50p
£1	240	A pound or a 'quid'	£1

Index

Simon Greenwood, 304
Smith, Amelia Evelyn, 34
Smith, Linda, 290
Smith, Mrs, 302
Smithers, John, 190
Solefields Road, 260
Spinks, Mr, 24
Squerryes Estate, 306
St John's Hill, Sevenoaks, 82
St Martin's, 20, 30, 32, 72, 74,
    79, 80, 84, 87, 101, 103,
    106, 131, 163, 176, 191,
    195, 197, 227, 233, 236,
    255, 261, 265, 267, 292,
    300, 304, 312, 320
St Martin's Church Fire, 193,
    212, 227, 248
St Martin's Meadow, 300,
    302, 304
St Martin's, 209, 210
St Mary's Church,
    Westerham, 33, 254
Stanhope, Lord, 4, 12, 13, 47,
    83, 95, 135, 177, 232, 236,
    250
Stanhope, Philip, 159
Stanley Berwicks Ltd, 127
Staples, Joseph, 177
Star Hill, 130
Station master, 109, 234
Station Road, 17, 18, 19, 106,
    269

Steven, Bob, 96, 248, 252,
    277
Steven, Henry, 189
Steven, Jack, 95
Steven, Mary Gilmoor
    Robertson, 72
Steven, Mrs, 234
Steven, Tommy, 66
Stevens, Jack, 117
Stewart, Keith, 265
Still, Pam, 106
Still, Roy, 106
Stillwell, Mrs, 304
Stone, Miss, 280
Stormont Company
    Engineering, 125
Stott, Mr and Mrs, 275
Stott, Mrs, 208, 260, 263
Stratton Campbell, 276
Strawberry Hollow, 253
Strickland, Mr, 108, 119, 179,
    272
Strickland-Constable, Lady,
    281
Sundridge, 249
Sundridge and Brasted
    Horticultural Society, 19,
    217
Sundridge barrage balloon
    depot, 220
Sundridge Fire Brigade, 196
Sundridge Hospital, 81, 115